tear here

Principles for Creating the Perfect Resume

Set aside at least three hours (that's an average length of time to complete a resume if all goes smoothly). Before you start, tear out this card and tape it to your computer, on the wall next to your desk, or someplace where you'll see it throughout the process. Once you've used the Resume Commandments that follow to craft your perfect resume, turn this card over and use the Top Ten Checklist to make sure you've covered everything.

The Resume Commandments

I. *Thou shalt not write about your past; thou shalt write about your future!* Your resume should paint a picture of you at your next job. Without realizing it, the reader of your resume will be "tricked" into envisioning you working for him or her.

II. *Thou shalt not confess.* In other words, you don't have to "tell all." Stick to what's relevant and marketable.

III. *Thou shalt not write job descriptions; thou shalt write achievement statements.* Talk about your experience in terms of your achievements instead of monotonous job descriptions.

IV. *Thou shalt not write about stuff you don't want to do again.* Promote only the skills you enjoy using.

V. *Thou shalt say less rather than more.* Give your resume more power by distilling your qualifications into a minimum of words.

VI. *Thou shalt not write in paragraphs; thou shalt use bullet points.* Make your resume quick and easy to read by breaking your information into bite-sized pieces.

VII. *Thou shalt not lie.* You can be creative, but always be honest.

alpha
books

The Top Ten Checklist for Creating the Perfect Resume

Here's a handy checklist to make sure you don't forget anything important on your resume. Take your pencil in hand (or get out a box of gold stars) and give yourself credit for each one of the items on this list that you've completed.

1. Your name appears in the top center or on the upper right-hand side (not in the upper left-hand corner) of the page.

2. Your resume starts with a brief and clear Job Objective statement or a strong indication of what position you are seeking.

3. Everything on your resume supports your Job Objective.

4. Achievements, rather than job descriptions, are stressed.

5. Achievement statements start with action verbs and do not contain vague terms such as "responsible for."

6. There are no paragraphs anywhere on the resume. Bulleted statements make achievements quick and easy to read.

7. Statements and sections are prioritized so the most impressive information comes first.

8. Your resume fits on no more than two pages. The exception to this two-page limit applies to resumes (also called curriculum vitae) for the academic and scientific communities.

9. If you have a two-page resume, "Continued" appears on the bottom of page one, and your name and "Page Two" are placed at the top of the second page.

10. There are no misspellings, grammatical errors, or other mistakes.

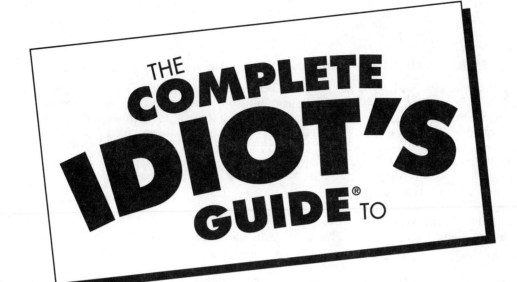

THE
COMPLETE IDIOT'S GUIDE® TO

The Perfect Resume

Second Edition

by Susan Ireland

alpha
books

Macmillan USA, Inc.
201 West 103rd Street
Indianapolis, IN 46290

A Pearson Education Company

Publisher
Marie Butler-Knight

Product Manager
Phil Kitchel

Associate Managing Editor
Cari Luna

Acquisitions Editor
Randy Ladenheim-Gil

Development Editor
Amy Gordon

Production Editor
JoAnna Kremer

Copy Editor
Heather Stith

Illustrator
Jody P. Schaeffer

Cover Designers
Mike Freeland
Kevin Spear

Book Designers
Scott Cook and Amy Adams of DesignLab

Indexer
Nadia Ibrahim

Layout/Proofreading
Darin Crone
Stacey Richwine-DeRome
Terri Edwards
Mary Hunt
Ayanna Lacey
Heather Hiatt Miller

Contents at a Glance

Contents

10 Step Five: Education and Extra Credit 149

11 Step Six: The Big Production 169

xiv

Foreword

Since Susan Ireland first published her highly instructive and highly successful guide to the perfect resume in 1996, a whirlwind force has hit resume preparation—and it's called cyberspace.

Even in the new millennium, the resume remains one of the most important tools in your job search, and in this updated version of her earlier book, Ms. Ireland—an expert resume consultant and writer—gives you the basic, insider information you need to make sure you're the one who gets that job interview by showing you how to create the perfect resume.

Additionally, in this, her latest book on the subject, she emphasizes the importance of your electronic job search—and spells out how to pursue it. No job seeker can afford to be without her straightforward, Internet-correct directions on how to conduct an online job hunt.

Even if you're not a cyber geek, you don't have to worry about the challenging task of searching the Internet for appropriate sites or posting your resume on the World Wide Web because Ms. Ireland tells you exactly what to do. As a job seeker, you probably worry—and rightfully so—about whether your resume, when sent electronically, actually will get there in readable form. And there are other Internet concerns: Do you format it in an attention-getting way, do you have the right keywords to arouse the employer's interest, and do you send it as an attachment to an e-mail?

These are important questions, and if you follow Ms. Ireland's advice—and she doesn't miss a keystroke—you can be confident that your resume, the one you worked so hard on, will get through as a viable record of your skills and experience.

She directly approaches the issue of recruitment Web sites, and what they can do for you. In fact, she calls them "online resume banks," and gives invaluable information about which are the most interest-producing resume databases, which industries actually bank on them, where to find the banks that are best for your job search, how to "deposit" your resume in them, and how to follow up on your online search—all the new resume rules for this high-tech age.

But whether you transmit your finished product by e-mail or snail mail, Ms. Ireland walks you through the entire process of creating the best resume for you. Following is one of the author's many invaluable insights that particularly appeals to me because it dissipates so much of the anxiety that many job seekers bring to the challenging process of writing a job-getting resume:

> *Because your resume is not a confessional, you don't have to tell all. Be selective. Pick through all your information and choose only what's relevant to your job objective.*

That's the kind of advice that gives you a leg up on every other applicant for the job you want because if you follow her directions, you'll have the perfect resume.

—Carol Kleiman

Carol Kleiman is a nationally syndicated Jobs columnist for the *Chicago Tribune*. The author of several career books, her latest is *Getting a Job*.

Introduction

Success in finding your ideal job depends largely upon having a dynamite resume. Drastic changes are taking place in the way resumes are reviewed by managers and human resource professionals. Would you believe that the number of applicants per job has increased to such a point that each resume is given only about eight seconds to grab the reader's attention?

In some organizations, resumes are never read by human eyes. They're put into a resume scanner and electronically entered into a database for automated selection. Some companies want resumes sent to them via e-mail, or they just download them from an online resume bank.

Knowing how to create a resume for this new job market could make or break your job search. But don't panic! Just follow the guidelines in this book, and you'll create a resume that will be considered by a hiring manager of any job you sincerely believe you're qualified for.

This new edition of *The Complete Idiot's Guide to the Perfect Resume* expands upon Internet job-search strategies and electronic resumes so that you'll be ready to hit the ground running in cyberspace. I've also added some valuable tips on solid career planning and effective cover-letter writing.

As a professional resume writer who has helped thousands of job seekers, I've seen how well-written resumes (not boilerplate forms) lead to promising interviews and job offers. I've also seen how a carefully crafted resume can help a job seeker (like you) get through the seemingly impossible task of finding career satisfaction. In other words, a great resume can help you find a position that you enjoy with a paycheck that supports your lifestyle.

As the proud owner of *The Complete Idiot's Guide to the Perfect Resume*, you have me as your personal resume coach. Imagine that I'm sitting right at your elbow as you work at your desk or kitchen table. My job is to guide you through the entire process as you

➤ Develop a winning resume strategy.

➤ Write each line to make the most of your qualifications.

➤ Create a great format for your resume.

➤ Distribute your new resume to employers.

To illustrate my points, I've included lots of resumes (made anonymous) from real job seekers that reflect goals and challenges similar to what you're facing. Their solutions may spark some ideas that you can use in your resume.

The secret to success in using this book is to relax and take one step at a time. You'll be surprised how painless the process of writing a resume is!

Between the Covers

Because helping you craft a top-notch resume is the goal of *The Complete Idiot's Guide to the Perfect Resume*, let's talk about what's inside.

Part 1, "Plan to Succeed," explains how to plan your job search, why you need a good resume, and what that resume can do for you. You'll also find the "Resume Commandments," which are my secrets to creating a compelling resume.

Part 2, "Six Steps to a Perfect Resume," is where you'll find my straightforward, six-step resume-writing process. Before you know it, you'll be finished with your resume.

Part 3, "So, You Need a Special Resume," shows you variations on a typical resume, including achievement resumes, hybrid resumes, and curriculum vitae.

Part 4, "Letters That Work," gives you tips on how to write effective cover letters and thank-you notes that will keep your job search going in the right direction.

Part 5, "The Electronic Job Search," teaches you about resume scanning and using online services for your job search. You'll learn how to create a successful electronic resume that won't get lost in cyberspace!

Advice Along the Way

Whether you read this book from cover to cover, or open it to specific points to get help with your job search, you'll notice the following sidebars throughout:

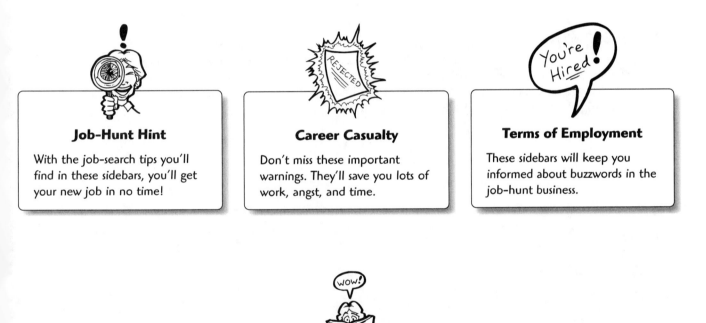

Job-Hunt Hint

With the job-search tips you'll find in these sidebars, you'll get your new job in no time!

Career Casualty

Don't miss these important warnings. They'll save you lots of work, angst, and time.

Terms of Employment

These sidebars will keep you informed about buzzwords in the job-hunt business.

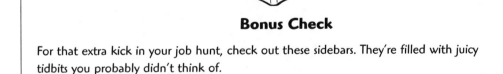

Bonus Check

For that extra kick in your job hunt, check out these sidebars. They're filled with juicy tidbits you probably didn't think of.

Acknowledgments

I'd like to thank Beth Brown, Juliette Ramirez, and Ruth Schwartz (professional resume writers on my team) for the resumes they contributed to this book. Special gratitude goes to Geoffrey Welchman and Lynn Northrup (for their editorial support), Clara Horvath (for her technical consultation), Andreé Abecassis (my agent at Ann Elmo Agency), Randy Ladenheim-Gil (my editor), JoAnna Kremer (my production editor), Amy Gordon (my development editor), and Heather Stith (my copy editor). And many thanks to my friends: Yana Parker, Greg Herman, Vickie Zenoff, Robyn Kliger, Jane Conger, Bruce Black, Anne Sparks, Robin Holt, my clients at Alumnae Resources Career Center in San Francisco, and, of course, Mom.

Dedication

To my Dad, who taught me at an early age the value of building character through work.

Trademarks

All terms mentioned in this book that are known to be or are suspected of being trademarks or service marks have been appropriately capitalized. Alpha Books and Macmillan USA, Inc., cannot attest to the accuracy of this information. Use of a term in this book should not be regarded as affecting the validity of any trademark or service mark.

Part 1

Plan to Succeed

It's been a long, hard day at the office for Ms. Hiring Manager. Her eyes are glazed over from looking at 75 resumes, trying to find the right person for an opening in her department. She's about to put on her coat and head for home when something on her desk catches her eye. It's another resume—yours. "At last!" she announces, after spending less than a minute scanning the page. "Someone who fits the bill!"

That's the kind of immediate recognition you can expect from your resume once you grasp and employ the principles presented in these chapters. After reading this section, you'll be miles ahead of your competition. The principles in Part 1 alone are well worth the price of this book. So turn the page and find out what most job seekers don't know about writing a job-winning resume. Before you know it, your resume will be sitting pretty on your next employer's desk!

Chapter 1

Mapping Your Job Hunt

> ### In This Chapter
>
> ➤ Developing a career plan that takes you where you want to go
>
> ➤ Staying organized and motivated every step of the way
>
> ➤ Finding the jobs and circulating your resume
>
> ➤ Priming yourself for job interviews and salary negotiations

Job hunting is like going on a trip. Depending on how well you plan, it could go as smoothly as a drive in a Jaguar, or it could be like a bumpy ride in an old jalopy.

It makes sense that, as you start out, you have mixed feelings about your journey. You're probably excited about reaching your destination (your new job), but you're also concerned about how long it's going to take to get there and what problems might arise along the way.

In this chapter, I'm going to help you avoid the bumps by drawing a map of your job hunt—one that incorporates the easiest and most direct routes possible.

Order! Order!

Without a plan, your job hunt could be as risky as a jungle safari without a guide. I'm not saying you won't survive it, but I suggest you at least pack a map!

Seriously, most job hunters have an easier time and get better results if they have an overall strategy. A solid job-search strategy incorporates these five steps:

1. Develop a career plan.
2. Investigate the job market.
3. Write your resume.
4. Go on job interviews.
5. Negotiate your salary.

"That sounds so simple," you say. "I'll do one of those steps each day and have a great job in just a week." Whoa there! It would be wiser to take as much time as you need and can afford, especially on the first two steps, so that you end up with a job you love.

For most folks, the steps run in the order I just mentioned and can span anywhere from a few weeks to several months. An old career-development formula says it takes one month of job searching for every $10,000 in annual salary you make. In other words, if you make $80,000, prepare to spend eight months looking for your new job.

Of course, that equation is only a rule of thumb and will vary based on the job market, your drive, your connections, and—you guessed it—your resume. From my experience with hundreds of job seekers, I can assure you that a dynamite resume can cut that time formula in half.

Let's look at each of the five job-search steps and start thinking about your great future.

Bonus Check

To ensure that you get a job you really love, take as much time as you need to

➤ Explore your career-move possibilities.

➤ Understand all that a job entails before you accept it.

➤ Find out about the organization's culture.

➤ Learn what advancement possibilities the job holds.

Get a Life

Whether you're looking for your first job or you're at a crossroads in a 20-year career, it pays to do some long- and short-term planning before looking for a job. Although no one's future is guaranteed, good planning leads to wise choices, which usually lead to satisfying results.

You can get help making your life plans in several ways:

➤ Join a career center (private, nonprofit, state, or college) where you can work one-on-one with a counselor, attend career-related classes, and browse through its resource center.

➤ Hire a private *career counselor* who will sit down with you for one or several sessions to help you assess your values, personality, skills, and interests and to brainstorm about how those can be fulfilled by your career.

➤ Work with a *career coach*, someone who will help you develop a strategy and motivate you to reach your career goals.

If you're a do-it-yourselfer, you can plow through the career-planning stages on your own. Try these strategies:

➤ Take some of the online career-development tests to help you determine what line of work suits you best. On my Web site (http://www.susanireland.com), you'll find links to career-test sites I recommend. They're also listed in Appendix C, "Other Cool Resources."

➤ Conduct some informational interviews with folks who do the kind of work you're considering. These interviews can be fun and will give you a taste of what it would be like to work in that arena.

Bonus Check

Want to change careers but don't know what to change to? Here's a way to get some ideas:

➤ Make a list of keywords that define your areas of interest.

➤ Input those keywords into your Internet search engine, entering between one and three words per search.

➤ Check out the Web sites that come up and see if those sites stimulate any ideas for your career change.

See Chapter 19, "Getting Hooked on the Internet," to learn how to get up and going online.

➤ Volunteer in the field before looking for employment there. Some real experience will tell you if it's what you want.

➤ Follow the tips in Part 5, "The Electronic Job Search," for conducting an online job search.

Whether you want to get help from a pro or figure out your career plans all by yourself, use the following worksheet to articulate your career goals. Yes, go ahead and write in the book!

Career Casualties

Never ask for a job during an informational interview. An informational interview is strictly for gathering information about a profession that interests you, not for gathering a job!

My Career Goals

1. What skills am I proud of (examples: public speaking, interpersonal, writing)?

    _____

    _____

2. What aspects of my personality impact my performance at work (examples: extro-verted, intuitive, responsible)? _____

    _____

3. What values are important to me (examples: integrity, compassion, professionalism)?

    _____

    _____

4. What interests would I love to see incorporated into my career (examples: gourmet cooking, antiques, promoting the arts)? _____

    _____

5. If asked to paint a picture of myself on the job, what would I paint (examples: speaking before audiences, organizing promotional campaigns, traveling around the country)? _____

    _____

6. What personal goals do I wish I could achieve during my lifetime (examples: author a book, run for political office)? _____

    _____

7. What type of lifestyle would I like my income to support five years from now (exam-ples: be married and starting a family, getting my MBA while living a single life in a suburban community)? _____

    _____

    How about 10 years from now (examples: purchasing a home and starting my own business, spending three afternoons a week on the golf course)? _____

    _____

8. When do I want to retire? _____

    _____

9. What career or careers would fulfill the financial and personal goals I've listed (examples: medical technologist, financial administrator)? _____

    _____

10. Would I like to pursue more than one career in my lifetime? If so, what are they (examples: professional athlete and sports broadcaster; elementary school teacher and freelance writer)? _____

    _____

11. What new job or chain of jobs would advance my career (examples: a series of promotions from sales representative to district sales manager in the pharmaceutical industry; a steady job at a bank supplemented by some personal online trading)? _____

_____

_____

The answers to the questions in this worksheet are important in forming a road map for your life journey. You may not be able to answer all of them right now, or your answers may change as your job search and career progresses. That's okay. This worksheet is for brainstorming; you can revise your answers at any point.

Right Resume Timing

Were you surprised to see "Write your resume" third on the job-search strategy list earlier? A lot of people think it should be first. They say, "I have to write my resume, figure out what kind of work I want, and then go get a job." Big mistake!

As you'll read in Chapter 2, "A Resume for All Reasons," your resume is your marketing piece for your job search, not a historical document about your past. Just like any other marketing piece, your resume needs to be created with an objective in mind.

A marketing professional for an event production company would never create a poster for a concert until she knew what type of music was going to be performed, where it was being held, and who the target audience was. It's the same with your job search. Before you can produce your powerful marketing piece, you need to know what job you're going after, what skills are required for the job, and, if possible, who the reader of your resume is. After you have that information, you can put together a resume that'll get your foot in the door.

With that in mind, start out with some career planning to decide what role (for example: outside sales or marketing communications) you want to play for an employer. Second, investigate the job market to learn what positions you want to apply for. Then write your resume to emphasize the qualifications that are relevant to that line of work.

Out of breath already? Don't worry, it's not as arduous as it sounds, especially when you follow the guidelines in this book.

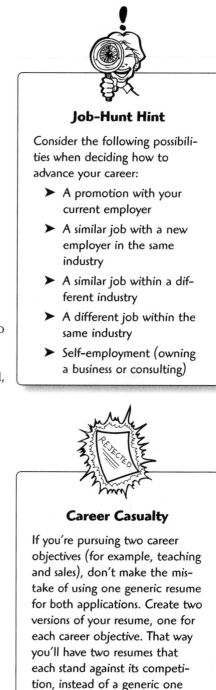

Job-Hunt Hint

Consider the following possibilities when deciding how to advance your career:

➤ A promotion with your current employer

➤ A similar job with a new employer in the same industry

➤ A similar job within a different industry

➤ A different job within the same industry

➤ Self-employment (owning a business or consulting)

Career Casualty

If you're pursuing two career objectives (for example, teaching and sales), don't make the mistake of using one generic resume for both applications. Create two versions of your resume, one for each career objective. That way you'll have two resumes that each stand against its competition, instead of a generic one that looks weak in both fields.

Good Circulation

After you write your resume, you'll want to get it into the hands of potential employers. A good job-search strategy uses more than one means of distribution to ensure success. Read on for some ways you can get your resume into circulation.

Bonus Check

Before sending your resume to an employer on your list, read it through carefully to see whether you can tailor it for that particular job. After all, you want the best marketing piece possible for each application.

A Little Help from Your Friends

Networking among friends, family, business associates, and people with influence in your field is the most valuable means of getting an interview. Be sure to contact everyone you know who might be helpful in this regard, and supply them with your resume and networking cards (you'll learn about networking cards in Chapter 2) so they can pass the news of your job search on to hiring managers.

Job-Hunt Hint

Once you get your resume circulating, be ready to respond to employers and recruiters who offer you job opportunities. Do some research to know what you're worth in today's job market. (See Chapter 19, "Getting Hooked on the Internet" to learn ways to gather data online.

Boss Wanted

You may have a company in mind, one you'd love to have as your next employer. Even without knowing whether there are any job openings, you can submit your resume to human resources, or the manager of the department in which you're interested. Your Job Objective statement (which I cover in Chapter 6, "Step One: Heading Your Way") and resume construction will clearly indicate your relevant skills.

A Pocketful of Jobs

Many career centers, state agencies, and nonprofit organizations have on-site job listings and telephone job hotlines. Some organizations charge a fee for using them; others may ask you to do volunteer work in exchange for the services they provide. To find such organizations, look in the Yellow Pages under employment-related headings such as "Career Centers" and "Employment Agencies," where you should find private, nonprofit, and state-run organizations.

Online Out-Posts

On the Internet, you can *post your resume* in databases for thousands of employers to see. These Web sites also offer job listings by profession and location. For more on this type of resume distribution, turn to Chapter 23, "Banking on Success: Online Resume Banking."

The Recruiting Game

Collaborating with a recruiter (sometimes called a "headhunter") is a free and usually painless way to submit your resume to employers. Most recruiters specialize according to industry (for example, computer or pharmaceuticals) or profession (for example, sales or executive management). When showing your resume to a recruiter, be open to his or her suggestions for adapting it to a particular field or company. The best way to find a recruiter is to get a recommendation from a friend, career counselor, or career center.

Terms of Employment

To **post your resume** means to place an electronic version of your resume on the Internet for employers and recruiters to view.

Fun at the Fair

Attending a job fair can be an efficient way to talk to representatives from several companies in one day. Be sure to bring many resumes, comfortable shoes, and lots of stamina, because you're likely to find yourself in large crowds and long lines. Job fairs are usually advertised in the newspaper and on radio and television.

Classified Information

Although classified ads are considered by many to be the least effective place to land a job, don't exclude them from your job-search strategy. Many prominent companies use the classified ads as a successful recruiting method. A well-written resume accompanied by a cover letter can grab the reader's eye and secure an interview, in spite of the overwhelming amount of competition that newspaper ads generate. Besides, once you have your resume circulating inside a company's human resources department, you may be considered for a range of job opportunities.

Career Casualties

Before approaching a recruiter, make sure you understand his role: A recruiter is not in the business of finding jobs for applicants; he finds applicants to fill jobs for his client, Mr. Employer. So don't ask or expect the recruiter to run around finding you a job. Rest assured, he'll be happy to connect you with an employment opportunity if he knows of one that's a good match.

The Mass Message

To conduct a mass mailing, you need an up-to-date mailing list of potential employers. Several books that catalog employers by industry and location are available in libraries and bookstores. Be sure to check a book's copyright date to know how recent its listings are.

You can also hire an information researcher to create a mailing list to your specifications. Locating an information researcher isn't easy. I suggest asking at a career center or looking online under career-related subjects to see if one is listed. In Appendix C, I recommend a few research services.

Keep Your Chin Up

No matter how carefully you plan, you will encounter challenges during your hunt. I'd be surprised if you haven't already come face to face with a few. Maybe you struggled with trying to choose the best resume book among the many on the bookstore shelf. But see? You made it through that dilemma with flying colors, and you'll make it through the rest. Let's look at some of the hurdles you might run into and ways to cope with or, better yet, jump over them.

Ducks in a Row

We all have our own techniques for getting things done. Some like to use electronic gadgets with lots of bells and whistles, others have elaborate filing systems, and then there are folks who like to tape index-card notes all over their walls. Go with whatever system suits you.

You can use any of these common tools and gizmos to stay on top of contact information, deadlines, appointments—all those slippery details you'll be juggling throughout your job hunt:

➤ Hand-held electronic calendars, like the PalmPilot ™, seem to hold all the names, addresses, dates, times, and comments you can imagine and include cross-referencing capabilities.

➤ Organizational software programs, such as FileMaker ® Pro or ACT! ™ Contact Manager, are database applications that allow you to create columns and rows to suit your needs. Some applications even set off alerts to remind you of an upcoming event.

➤ Time-management systems are very popular. The famous Franklin Planner comes with a management philosophy that millions swear by, along with either a paper or electronic calendar.

➤ Use pen or pencil to take notes and mark important dates in a paper calendar, which you can buy at the local five-and-dime or stationery store.

Being organized doesn't mean spending a zillion dollars on fancy paraphernalia (though of course you can have fun doing that if you want to). As you can see from the preceding list, some excellent tools cost next to nothing. The important thing is to have a system in place so that you can find information quickly, get to appointments on time, and remember to do your follow-up steps.

Out of the Quicksand

Whether you leap or inch your way to your perfect job, there will be setbacks, disappointments, and rejections along the way. The big question is: What are you going to do when you hit a bump and suddenly feel as though you're sinking in quicksand? Here are some ways to prepare for those not-so-joyous occasions:

➤ Join a support group of job seekers. It doesn't matter whether the members are in your profession, just as long as you feel comfortable sharing the joys and woes of your job search with them and listening to theirs.

➤ Hire a career coach or get help from a friend, someone who will meet with you regularly to talk through your job-search strategy and motivate you to stay on track.

➤ Keep a journal of your successes so that you can refer to them when the going gets rough.

➤ Collect inspirational essays and stories that you can draw on when you need to see some light in the middle of the tunnel.

Job-Hunt Hint

Set up a tickler system (an index card, file folder, or database system) that reminds you to do each of your job-search steps and follow-ups.

What motivational techniques have worked for you in the past? Write them down now so you can refer to them at any point during your career development.

My Quicksand Rescue Plan

What four activities could I do to ease the disappointment of a job-search setback?

Job-Hunt Hint

Ask your friends what organizational and motivational techniques work for them. When you hear of ones you like, borrow them!

1. _____
   _____
2. _____
   _____
3. _____
   _____
4. _____

Who are good people for me to talk with when I feel down about my job hunt?

1. _____
2. _____
3. _____
4. _____

What books, movies, stories, music, or humor inspire me?

1. _____
2. _____
3. _____
4. _____

What other things could I do to get out of the quicksand and back on solid ground?

1. _____
2. _____
3. _____
4. _____

Now tuck this worksheet away where you can find it whenever you need a pick-me-up.

Giving Yourself a Pep Talk

The secret to staying on top of your job search is organization and motivation. I already talked about organization, now let's look at what motivates you. Your main motivation is probably one or more of the following:

➤ **Opportunity.** You know that if you complete a task by a certain time, you could capture an opportunity.

Career Casualty

Don't do your job search alone, if at all possible. Team up with another job seeker so you can share ideas and inspiration.

➤ **Deadlines.** You work well under the pressure of a deadline and sometimes perform at your peak during the 11th hour.

➤ **Routine.** You like to establish a routine of completing one small step each day in order to reach your goal with the least amount of stress.

➤ **Reward.** You respond to little (or big) incentives for reaching milestones toward your goal.

➤ **Commitment.** You feel compelled to achieve something that you commit to either in writing, verbally, or through a personal promise.

➤ **Competition.** You love the feel of a neck-and-neck race to the finish line, and you'll work hard to win.

Did I push at least one of your motivational buttons? I hope so! Use any combination of these motivations to inspire yourself to follow through on each of your job-hunt steps. Incorporate them into your plans by telling yourself something like the following:

"I might seize such-and-such opportunity if I finish this task promptly."

"When I wrap up this task by such-and-such day, I'm going to get the satisfaction of checking it off my to-do list."

"I'll break this big step into smaller ones so that my project won't feel so overwhelming."

"As soon as I've completed this tough project, I'm going to take myself out for dinner and a movie."

"I promise (to myself and maybe to a friend) that I won't give up until I've taken a certain step."

"There's another smart and capable job seeker out there who's in search of my ideal job. I have to beat him to the punch and win that position!"

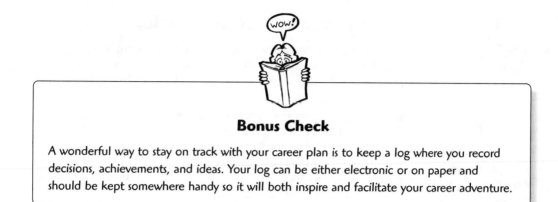

Bonus Check

A wonderful way to stay on track with your career plan is to keep a log where you record decisions, achievements, and ideas. Your log can be either electronic or on paper and should be kept somewhere handy so it will both inspire and facilitate your career adventure.

By pushing your own motivational buttons, you'll get things done!

The Interview Scorecard

With that terrific resume of yours (which you'll have in just a few chapters), you're going to land an interview. In fact, you'll probably interview with *several* employers before finding the job you want.

Interviewing is like any skill: The more you work at it, the better you'll get. So take every opportunity to hone your interviewing skills:

➤ Go on as many interviews as you can, even if they're not for your dream jobs. You'll gain more and more confidence with each meeting.

➤ Attend career fairs where you can practice chatting to recruiters about your qualifications.

➤ Practice interviewing with a career counselor or coach. You may want to find someone who can videotape your practice sessions so that you can review them later.

➤ Make a list of the questions you're afraid to be asked, and then rehearse your answers until you feel comfortable.

➤ Invite (or bribe) a friend to look at your resume and ask you questions about items you've listed.

➤ Read books, listen to audio tapes, and watch videos about interviewing. You'll find them in libraries, bookstores, and catalogs.

Many job seekers don't bother to prepare for their interviews, so chances are, if you do even one of the preceding suggestions, you'll be miles ahead of your competition.

Job-Hunt Hint

Take an early or late lunch and allow some of that time for your job search. That way you can reach your contacts during business hours when they're apt to be at their phones.

Career Casualties

Your attitude, dress, and body language could make or break the interview. Be sure to get good advice on what's cool and what's not (like, don't arrive with twenty bags and briefcases hanging off your arms) before stepping into the manager's office. Appendix C lists books and career professionals who can help you with this stuff.

Big Bucks, Little Bucks

Negotiating your salary doesn't have to be nerve-wracking, especially if you have a good strategy and understand the rules of the game. Following are a few things you can do to prepare for the bargaining game:

➤ Be sure that your resume reflects the level of responsibility and compensation you deserve. (You'll learn how to do that in Part 2, "Six Steps to a Perfect Resume.")

➤ Before going to the negotiations, figure out your desired salary range: how much money you need to make (the lowest amount you'll accept) and how much you'd like to make (the amount you'd be offered in a perfect world).

➤ Understand what comprises the whole compensation package being offered (for example, stock options, bonuses, and healthcare insurance) and how you can negotiate its components to meet your needs.

➤ Do a mock negotiation with a career counselor, friend, or fellow job seeker to polish your bargaining skills.

➤ Read books on salary negotiations, such as *Negotiating Your Salary: How to Make $1,000 a Minute* by Jack Chapman (Ten Speed Press) and my book, *Get a Better Job The Lazy Way* (Macmillan USA).

➤ Hire a negotiating coach to hold your hand through every step. This coaching is especially helpful if you think you don't have good money sense or if you tend to fall apart under pressure.

Because each of your subsequent raises is based on your initial salary, negotiations at the time of your job offer are extremely important. Take the time now to build your knowledge of and confidence in how to talk money so that you'll be a winner in the long run.

Bonus Check

Here's how to evaluate whether it's cost-effective to hire a salary-negotiation coach: Hire him if you think there's room in the negotiations to increase your salary by more than the amount of his fee. In other words, if his flat fee is $450, hire him if there's a good chance you could gain $500 or more with some professional advice.

The Least You Need to Know

➤ Develop a career plan that fulfills your personal, financial, and professional dreams.

➤ Write your resume only after deciding what type of work you want to do next.

➤ Use several approaches to investigate the job market and to distribute your resume.

➤ Set up systems for keeping yourself organized and motivated through thick and thin.

➤ Take time to learn and practice good interviewing and negotiating skills.

Chapter 2

A Resume for All Reasons

In This Chapter

➤ Defining your next career move with a good resume

➤ Getting job interviews with your resume

➤ Using your resume to bring you bigger bucks

➤ Working your network with networking cards

Why do you need a resume? There are lots of reasons, and some of the ones in this chapter may surprise you. For instance, a strong resume can significantly increase your leverage in salary negotiations. Your resume can accelerate your career in several other important ways as well. Once you have a handle on the "why" behind a good resume, you'll be ready to create a resume for all reasons.

Your Personal Road Map

The reason you need a *resume* is that you're probably looking for a job or planning to change positions in the near future. You might be looking for

➤ Your first job out of school.

➤ A move up the career ladder.

➤ A promotion within your company.

➤ A career change.

➤ A job to save you from an imminent or recent layoff.

The very process of writing your resume helps you put your job search in perspective. To sell yourself to an employer, your resume should be focused on a job objective (more about that in Chapter 6, "Step One: Heading Your Way"). That means you have to figure out where you're headed on your career path or at least figure out what your next step is.

If you don't quite have a handle on where you're going, don't panic! Just review Chapter 1, "Mapping Your Job Hunt," to help get a career plan in place.

When you know what your job objective is, you can easily take inventory of your skills and present your favorite and most marketable ones. That makes for a powerful package: a resume that says what you want and why you should have it!

Changing Directions

Resumes are especially important for career changers who may be relying solely on their marketing documents to represent them in new territories. If that's your situation, rest assured that the following resume tricks will help you stand up to your competition and even surpass it.

➤ Use a functional format (see Chapter 5, "Get Functional") for your resume.

➤ Highlight only the qualifications that are relevant to your job objective.

➤ Write about experiences that reflect an understanding of the job you're seeking.

With a resume that uses these principles and others that I'll explain in Part 2, "Six Steps to a Perfect Resume," you're going to look like you should own the company. Okay, maybe not quite own the company, but you're going to look like you belong there.

Interview Influence

An interview may get you sweaty, but it doesn't have to give you an aneurysm. Your resume can take the edge off of your big encounter with Mr. Interviewer in many ways.

Your Brochure

For most people, the resume's most important job is to solicit interviews—it's a brochure to potential employers. Because your resume may stand against hundreds of other resumes in competition for a job, it needs to present you in the best light possible.

Charting Your Course

What you decide to put on your resume will suggest the topics for discussion during the interview. In other words, the resume is your chance to say, "Hey, let's talk about my strengths. Here's what I'm really good at!"

Easy Answers to Tough Questions

A resume also prepares you for job interviews. The process of putting your resume together will help you figure out the answers to sticky interview questions such as the following:

Terms of Employment

The most common meaning of the word **resume** is a short account of one's professional experience and qualifications, typically used by a job applicant. However, resumes are also used for projects that don't involve a job search, such as business plans, school applications, and consulting proposals.

Career Casualty

Don't write a "general" resume that makes you look like a Jack of all trades. The more focused your resume is toward a job objective, the more confident and more valuable you look.

➤ What makes you think you'll do well in this new job?

➤ What achievements are you proud of that relate to this new position?

➤ Why do you think you'd fit into our company culture?

➤ What do you consider to be your biggest strengths and weaknesses?

➤ How has your previous work experience prepared you for this position?

➤ What kinds of challenges have you faced in past positions and how did you handle them?

Don't worry if you don't know the answers to these questions right now. You'll have a handle on them by the time you finish writing your resume, with the help of the exercises in Part 2.

Bonus Check

A side benefit of developing a functional resume (frequently used by career changers) is that you'll be forced to define your transferable skills, which is a must for effective interviewing. See Chapter 5 to learn about functional resumes.

Write Your Own Recommendation

After you've had a successful interview, your interviewer may need to get hiring approval from someone higher up the ladder. If you've armed your interviewer with a dynamite resume to pass on to the higher-ups, the interviewer's positive recommendation has a better chance of being approved.

Let the Bargaining Begin

Believe it or not, salary negotiations start with your resume. Even though you don't include monetary expectations on your resume, the bargaining begins by the way your resume presents you. Here is some information that prospective employers can gather from your resume:

➤ How much experience you have

➤ How old you appear to be

➤ How focused you are in your career objective

An effective resume highlights information that answers these questions to the reader's satisfaction.

Job-Hunt Hint

Write your resume with the idea that it's a marketing piece for your future (instead of a boring description of your past). This marketing approach is the surest way to convince an employer that you're a promising candidate for the job. (There's more on this concept in Chapter 3, "Winning Resume Wisdom.")

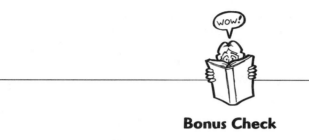

Bonus Check

Be careful how you respond to a job announcement that asks for a salary history. To comply with the ad's request and get past the screening process without giving away your exact salary figures, include a sentence in your cover letter that briefly refers to your salary. See Chapter 17, "The Cover Letter Connection," to learn how to address the salary issue in your letter.

Career Casualty

Before going to your interview, go through your resume line by line and practice elaborating on the topics and achievements you've listed.

Terms of Employment

Your **network** is like a carefully crafted web that has you in the center. Made of invisible threads that extend from you to all the people you know, to the people they know, and so on, your network is a conduit for information and favors. With a strong network, you could receive big payoffs!

Ready, Set, Network!

When you have your resume in hand, you're ready to exploit one of your most powerful job-search tools: your *network*. The importance of networking can't be overestimated.

Case in point: Sarah ran a successful dry cleaning business for six years before she sold it in order to go back into the corporate world as a salesperson. One morning after selling her business, she ran into Rod, one of her former customers. It wasn't long into their chat when Rod suggested that Sarah give him her resume to pass on to his wife, who was a partner at a nearby electronics firm. Within three weeks, Sarah landed a sales job at the wife's company.

As you can see, opportunities pop up in unexpected ways. Be prepared with a resume (or the networking card mentioned in the following section), and use it to stimulate networking. Circulate it among your friends, relatives, and business associates. They may know someone who knows someone who knows of the perfect job for you!

Beat the Business-Card Strategy

How many times have you returned home from a party, professional meeting, or other networking event with a pocket full of business cards only to realize that you had no idea which card went with which person? When that happens to me, I throw away all of them except the one (maybe two) that conjures up an image of the person who gave it to me.

If your business card had been in my pocket, it very well could have been tossed, unless you had put something on it to jog my memory. And that's the idea behind a networking card.

A *networking card* is a hybrid between a resume and a business card. It's an ideal marketing tool when a resume is too long and a business card doesn't say enough. You can design it to fit your special purpose, whether that's to find a particular job or to explore career options.

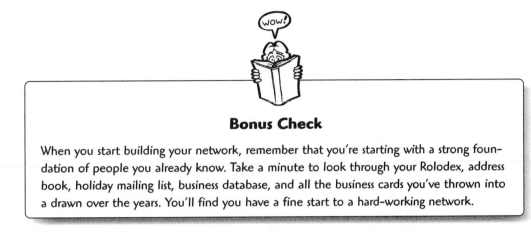

Bonus Check

When you start building your network, remember that you're starting with a strong foundation of people you already know. Take a minute to look through your Rolodex, address book, holiday mailing list, business database, and all the business cards you've thrown into a drawn over the years. You'll find you have a fine start to a hard-working network.

An Intelligent Network

Networking really does work, sometimes in the most unexpected ways. (Remember the networking story about Sarah and her former customer, Rod?) Capitalize on every word-of-mouth opportunity by arming your friends, relatives, and allies with your networking cards so that when someone asks one of them a tricky question like "What exactly does your friend do?" your spokesperson can look at your networking card and respond intelligently. That's right: A networking card is a cheat sheet!

Instant Networking Cards

To make your networking card, follow these steps:

1. Write your resume.

2. Transfer your most marketable information into a 2" × 3½" (the size of a business card) card format. This can be done in MS Word by setting your margins accordingly (top: 1", bottom: 8", right: 1", left: 3½"), in which case you'd print one per page. Or you could produce them in PageMaker or PhotoShop where you can print more than one per page.

3. Design the card's layout using bullet points, indents, bold type, and a few sizes of print so that information is easy to read.

4. Print the information on card stock, and the cards are ready to go!

Job-Hunt Hint

Always have a few networking cards with you in your briefcase, pocket, purse, or glove compartment so that you can pull one out at a moment's notice.

Information that you could steal from your resume and place on your networking card might include a few or all of the following:

➤ Job Objective statement.

➤ Education.

➤ Work history.

➤ Highlights of qualifications.

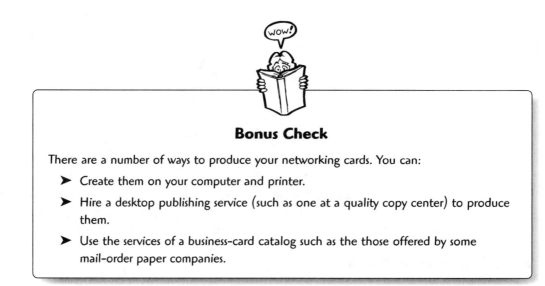

Bonus Check

There are a number of ways to produce your networking cards. You can:

➤ Create them on your computer and printer.

➤ Hire a desktop publishing service (such as one at a quality copy center) to produce them.

➤ Use the services of a business-card catalog such as the those offered by some mail-order paper companies.

Making your networking card can take just minutes when you have a strong resume to draw from. The following examples demonstrate some ways in which a strong resume and a few key points on a networking card can combine to get you the job you want.

Create the Future

Sue wasn't sure exactly what type of marketing position she wanted, so she wrote a resume (following) and networking card (following) that emphasized the skills she wanted to use, rather than a job objective. She got many interviews as a result and landed a job that an employer created just for her.

If you're in the initial part of your job search and haven't figured out exactly which direction you're headed, consider using a networking card to navigate your way, as Sue did.

Sue Hernandez's networking card.

SUE HERNANDEZ

1234 Franklin Way • San Francisco, CA 12345 • **(123) 123-1234**

PROFESSIONAL PROFILE

Nine years in marketing and sales with emphasis on project management of strategic marketing communications campaigns. Expertise in:

➤ **Organization** — successfully manage large and small multiple projects, handling many details simultaneously.

➤ **Interpersonal Communications** — easily develop strong rapport with clients, management, and co-workers.

➤ **Team Leadership** — build cohesive teams, motivate members to produce quality work, and use tenacity to complete the job.

EXPERIENCE

1995-1999   **Marketing Communications Consultant**
HIGH-TECH INTERNATIONAL, Mountain View, CA

- Managed marketing communications projects for the $3 billion Worldwide Customer Support Division.
- Oversaw collateral development, direct marketing campaigns, and testimonial programs.

Accomplishments

➤ Developed creative strategy for dealer end-user literature accompanying the "Certified Workstation Reseller" program rollout.

➤ Produced analysis of the market position of key competitors (DEC, IBM, EDS), used as a guideline for sales brochure for major program launch.

➤ Drove development of *The Competitive Support Field Guide*, a 150-page compendium of 32 competitors, detailing support services and key selling points.

1988-1995   **Account Manager**
INFONET CORPORATION, Redwood Shores, CA

- Drove entire process for creation of sales and collateral materials for this $1 billion software company.
- Managed 20 projects simultaneously, including: brochures, logos, and signage.

Accomplishments

➤ Co-developed strategy and directed production of *Distributed Solutions Guide*, a $250,000 brochure which successfully targeted select Fortune 500 senior managers.

➤ Enhanced Oracle's public image by serving as company liaison to "The Human Race," a non-profit fundraiser. Collaborated with government officials, culturally diverse volunteers, and internal staff to promote the event.

EDUCATION

B.S., Business Administration/Finance, University of Utah, Salt Lake City, 1988

Sue Hernandez's resume.

Job-Hunt Hint

When having conversations with members of your network, ask your friends if they know of anyone else you should talk to about your career move. In that way, you'll continue to build your network.

Underscore to Win

A networking card is not a substitute for a resume; it's a marketing tool in its own right. When asked to submit a resume, send the real thing, not a networking card. And when you send out your resume, you don't need to include a networking card. Harold had many years in fiscal management, both in for-profit and nonprofit organizations. Because he wanted his next job to be in the nonprofit arena, he wrote a resume (following) that highlighted his nonprofit experience. Then he created a networking card (following) that included a Job Objective and Summary of Qualifications, both of which underscored his desire to work for a nonprofit organization.

A networking card serves as a capsule of the very best you have to offer. It says who you are, what you want, and why you should have it. Pretty good for a little card!

HAROLD BUZWELL
123-123-1234 • 12 Sandlewood Street • Greene, NC 12345

OBJECTIVE: Fiscal Manager for a nonprofit organization

SUMMARY OF QUALIFICATIONS

- Over 10 years in nonprofit fiscal management.
- Record of creating systems for maximum efficiency.
- Supervise staff with emphasis on effective training and open communication.

Harold Buzwell's networking card.

HAROLD BUZWELL

123-123-1234 • 12 Sandlewood Street • Greene, NC 12345

OBJECTIVE: A position as Fiscal Manager for a nonprofit organization

SUMMARY OF QUALIFICATIONS

- More than 10 years experience in nonprofit fiscal management.
- Create, implement, and maintain systems for maximum efficiency and accuracy.
- Cooperative spirit that contributes to the organization's goals.
- Ability to supervise staff with an emphasis on effective training and open communication.

PROFESSIONAL EXPERIENCE

1991-pres. *FISCAL MANAGER / FINANCIAL CONSULTANT*
- Provide bookkeeping and accounting services to nonprofit organizations and small businesses. Services include:
  - All phases of bookkeeping through financial statements.
  - Budget preparation/monitoring and cash flow management.
  - Reporting to government and private funding agencies.
  - Evaluation and upgrading of financial systems.
  - Accounting software selection and installation.
  - Development and maintenance of internal controls.
  - Payroll, A/R, A/P, and tax preparation.
- Clients include:
Greene Community Music Center	St. Francis Center
Greene Community Counseling	Health Care Works
Make-A-Theatre	Atlantic East Restaurant

1985-90 *FINANCIAL MANAGER / ADMINISTRATOR*
THE MISSION FOUNDATION, Greene, NC
- Managed all internal financial and administrative functions including:
  - Grants program and loan fund administration.
  - General finance and accounting.
  - Staff supervision.
- Developed policies and procedures that facilitated smooth operations.

1984-85 *FULL CHARGE BOOKKEEPER*
ANSEL POWELL, C.P.A., Greene, NC
- Performed all phases of bookkeeping for a clientele of small businesses.

EDUCATION

B.S., Business Administration, Duke University, 1991
Accounting Program, North Carolina State University

Workshops for Nonprofit Organizations: Budgeting   Accounting Software
Fundraising Software Insurance Requirements

Harold Buzwell's resume.

Mini Leads to Maxi

After composing her resume (following), Marilyn designed a vertical networking card that looks like a mini-resume. Notice how both the graphic layout and contents of her card could lead a potential employer to ask for Marilyn's complete resume. Very clever!

Whether you lay out your information vertically or horizontally, it should resemble a resume enough to stimulate the reader to ask you for the real thing.

Double Your Networking Power

You can exploit your marketing real estate by putting information on both sides of your networking card. That way you can tell the reader more and still have lots of white space around the print. Notice Pamela's double-sided networking card. See how she used an arrow in the lower-right corner of each side to entice the reader to turn the card over? That's good marketing technique!

Marilyn P. Jenkins

123 Francisco Place, Apt. 4
Santa Ana, TX 12345

(123) 123-1234

JOB OBJECTIVE
Assistant to the administrator
of an organization responding to
environmental issues

SUMMARY OF QUALIFICATIONS
- Committed to addressing environmental, political, and urban concerns.
- Enjoy research; able to extract information and analyze results.
- Strength in identifying target audiences and promoting programs.
- Computer literate: PC and Macintosh.

Marilyn Jenkins's networking card.

Marilyn P. Jenkins
123 Francisco Place, Apt. 4, Santa Ana, TX 12345, (123) 123-1234

JOB OBJECTIVE
An assistant to the administrator of an organization responding to environmental issues

SUMMARY OF QUALIFICATIONS
- Committed to addressing environmental, political, and urban concerns.
- Enjoy research; able to extract information and analyze results.
- Strength in identifying target audiences and promoting programs.
- Computer literate in PC and Macintosh.

RELEVANT ACCOMPLISHMENTS

RESEARCH

Forest Island Project:
- Successfully used resources and interviewing techniques to research the health food industry in respect to ecological issues.
- Researched effects of tourism on the environment and benefits of sustainable tourism.

Stanley, Promise and Randall:
- Conducted research; presented successful marketing plan for client's hotel/restaurant.

PROMOTIONS
- Developed national distribution network and coordinated promotion schedule for Old Chicago Foods (health food manufacturer).
- Organized Rita Studio's art exhibitions; handled promotions including local media contacts and mailings.
- Traveled nation-wide to trade shows and prospective market areas for both Old Chicago Foods and Rita Studio.

ENVIRONMENTAL INVOLVEMENT
- Photographed the United Nations Conference on Environment and Development (UNCED) in Santa Ana for the U.S. Citizen Network.
- Currently working on photo documentary defining the political imbalance between business and environmental interests.

RELEVANT WORK HISTORY

Concurrent with Education:

2000	Intern	Forest Island Project (environmental project), Santa Ana, TX
1997-1999	Artist Representative	Rita Studio, Santa Ana, TX
1996	Intern	Stanley, Promise and Randall (direct marketing), Santa Ana, TX

Previous Experience:

1992-96	Sales Representative	Old Chicago Foods, Santa Ana, TX

EDUCATION
B.A., Business and Humanities, Texas University, Houston, 2000

Marilyn Jenkins's resume.

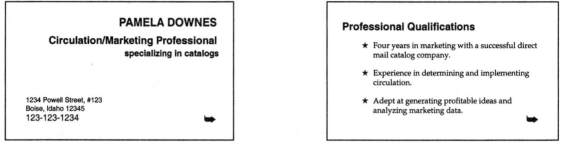

Pamela Downes' networking card.

Bonus Check

If you want a fancy-schmancy networking card, work with a professional desktop publisher to design a two-sided card that folds the way a greeting card does.

The Least You Need to Know

➤ Writing a resume is like drawing your personal map; a resume states clearly what your next career move will be.

➤ Creating a strong resume helps you articulate your skills and attributes, which is a must for a successful interview.

➤ A good resume opens the door for a job interview.

➤ A strong, well-thought-out resume starts you off on the right foot when negotiating your salary.

➤ You can distill the qualifications on your resume to produce a 2"× 3½" networking card.

Chapter 3

Winning Resume Wisdom

In This Chapter

➤ Designing a resume that creates the future you want

➤ Using past successes for future rewards

➤ Keeping secrets from the employer

➤ Making your resume quick and inviting to read

➤ To lie or not to lie

Writing the perfect resume takes a little time and concentration, but when you finish it, you'll feel like a million bucks—or as if you could *make* a million bucks!

Trust me, time spent working on a resume is time well spent. I've seen lots of people walk away with finished resumes, saying they never knew they could look so good on paper; they never thought their work history could appear so impressive; or they never thought they could look qualified for something they'd never done in the past.

A few principles lie behind the kind of job-winning resume I'm talking about. This chapter discusses key concepts that will not only provide you with resume wisdom; they'll also solve every resume problem you'll encounter.

The Commandments

Before you boot up your computer (or get your ballpoint pen and paper if you're sitting at your kitchen table), I want to impart a few tricks that even most professional resume writers don't know. (Your competition surely doesn't!) These concepts can make the difference between a boring resume that just sits on a manager's desk (or, even worse, gets thrown away) and one that demands, "Read me, read me! Call me, call me!" These resume tips are so important I've dubbed them The Resume Commandments.

Job-Hunt Hint

Of all the Resume Commandments, the first is so powerful that it can answer every question you have about resume writing. So memorize it, repeat it like a mantra, and watch its magic unfold as you go through each step of creating your resume in Part 2, "Six Steps to a Perfect Resume."

✳ The Resume Commandments

I. Thou shalt not write about your past; thou shalt write about your future!

II. Thou shalt not confess.

III. Thou shalt not write job descriptions; thou shalt write achievement statements.

IV. Thou shalt not write about stuff you don't want to do again.

V. Thou shalt say less rather than more.

VI. Thou shalt not write in paragraphs; thou shalt use bullet points.

VII. Thou shalt not lie.

Now let's look at each of these commandments to understand why they are so important.

Thou Shalt Not Write About Your Past

Because your resume is a marketing piece for your next job, it concerns your future, not your past. If you're writing a chronological resume (explained in Chapter 4, "Chronologically Speaking"), don't write your resume as if it were a historical document. Even though the body of your chronological format is structured around your work history (your past), the achievement statements should support your job objective statement (your future).

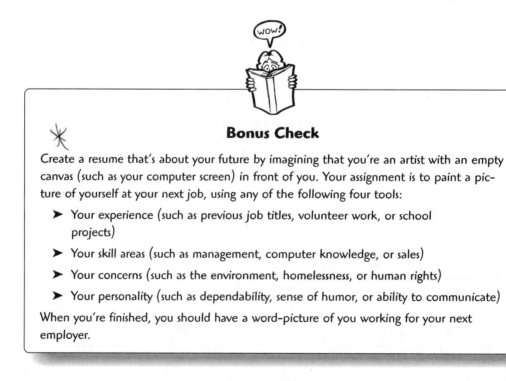

Bonus Check

Create a resume that's about your future by imagining that you're an artist with an empty canvas (such as your computer screen) in front of you. Your assignment is to paint a picture of yourself at your next job, using any of the following four tools:

➤ Your experience (such as previous job titles, volunteer work, or school projects)

➤ Your skill areas (such as management, computer knowledge, or sales)

➤ Your concerns (such as the environment, homelessness, or human rights)

➤ Your personality (such as dependability, sense of humor, or ability to communicate)

When you're finished, you should have a word-picture of you working for your next employer.

"My resume is about my future?" you ask. "But it talks about my work history and what I did at my previous jobs. Doesn't that mean it's about my past?"

That's exactly what most people think, but the secret to getting a new and exciting job is to build your resume around the job you're striving for, not the ones you've previously held. So before you even start writing your resume, you need to plan what kind of work you want to do next.

What will the employer think of your future-oriented resume? At first glance, she may assume she's reading about your past, but as she gets drawn into it, she'll find herself imagining that you're working for her. And that's what will make her want to call you for an interview.

Thou Shalt Not Confess

"Forgive me, Father, it's been a year since I last updated my resume," you cry. Have no fear, my friend; I'm here to fill you in on all the tips, including this one: Don't let one trace of that confessional tone leak onto your resume!

Why? Because your resume is not a confessional—you don't have to tell all. Don't waste space or distract the reader by putting anything on your resume that doesn't support your job objective or cast you in the best light possible with regard to experience, ability, age, and personality. (In Part 2, I'll talk about how to work with these issues specifically.)

Be selective. Pick through all your information and choose only what's relevant to your job objective. The following resumes show you how to apply this commandment.

Job-Hunt Hint

Think of your resume as an advertisement about a new product: you! And like an advertisement, your resume needs to be customized for its particular audience.

Shooting Yourself in the Foot

Teresa Smith was having trouble finding a position as a marketing director. She needed a job desperately and decided to go for a position as an administrative assistant. If she listed her MBA degree under her Education heading, she knew she would look overqualified for a clerical job. Take a look at her resume. Notice that she decided not to include her degree in order to improve her chances of getting an interview.

If you're applying for a job for which you might appear overqualified, consider leaving the heavy-weight qualifications off of your resume. Remember, your resume is not a confessional; you aren't obligated to disclose all.

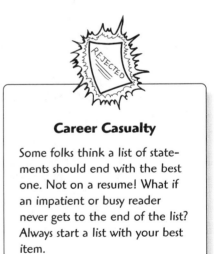

Career Casualty

Some folks think a list of statements should end with the best one. Not on a resume! What if an impatient or busy reader never gets to the end of the list? Always start a list with your best item.

Get Your Priorities Straight

Trudy Caldwell had been a secretary and receptionist for a number of years and wanted to move into the field of human resources. In preparing for her career change, she had gone back to college and earned a degree in human resources while continuing her occupation as a secretary.

Teresa Smith
0001 Serendipity Lane
Pierre, SD 12345
(123) 123-1234

JOB OBJECTIVE

Administrative Assistant

HIGHLIGHTS OF QUALIFICATIONS

- Seven years combined administrative and research experience.
- Adept at handling sensitive business issues with discretion and professionalism.
- Cited as one of the top administrative assistants at Kramer Associates, Inc.

PROFESSIONAL EXPERIENCE

1995-pres. Kramer Associates, Inc, Pierre, SD
ADMINISTRATIVE ASSISTANT

- Charged with organizing and generating correspondence for major clients involved in confidential government activities.
- Re-designed the office computer system, enabling 125% more work to be processed.
- Commended for creating weekly "Casual Day," which brought a friendlier and more cooperative atmosphere to the workplace.
- Prepared legal and business documents using word processing and spreadsheet applications.

1993-1995 **University of South Dakota,** Pierre, SD
RESEARCH ASSISTANT

- Conducted bibliographic research that contributed to paper delivered at the National Psychology Symposium in Washington, D.C.
- Word-processed voluminous notes and provided accurate transcriptions of university and professional lectures.
- Translated German scientific text and compiled readers for undergraduate and graduate classes.

EDUCATION

B.A., Business Administration & German
University of South Dakota, Pierre, SD, 1993

Teresa Smith's resume.

Notice how Trudy prioritized information on her resume (following) to make the most marketable items pop out at the reader. Because her degree was more marketable than her work history, she decided to show it off by positioning her Education section near the top of her resume. This organization helps the reader of this resume quickly see that she's a new graduate in human resources who worked her way through school. Trudy then de-emphasized her former job titles by placing Work History at the bottom of the page and listing the job titles after the company names.

When a busy manager receives your resume, she'll skim it very quickly to see whether she's interested in reading it word-for-word. For that reason, it's vital that you place your material according to how relevant it is to your job objective. Prioritizing correctly will make your resume declare, "I'm the one you're looking for!" (You'll read more about this concept in Part 2.)

Terms of Employment

A section entitled **Work History** may include paid and unpaid work because work is work, whether it's done for free or for hire. A section called **Employment History,** on the other hand, must include only paid work.

By prioritizing the sections of your resume, you can highlight aspects that are most relevant to your job objective. For instance, you might wish to move your volunteer experience near the top of your resume if it's particularly meaningful to the job you're applying for.

Drop Irrelevant Info

For the last two years, Christopher Bond spent most of his time managing a family crisis, a situation he decided was not appropriate to put on his resume. During that time span, he did some freelance catalog production for a former colleague.

Notice how Christopher constructed the *Work History* section on his resume without mentioning his personal situation, even though it consumed about 80 percent of his time and energy.

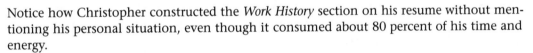

Bonus Check

Rely on the "Thou shalt not confess" commandment if you have something you'd rather not talk about such as one of the following:

➤ A family death

➤ Illness, injury, or disability

➤ A failed business venture

➤ Rehabilitation from substance abuse

Rather than list such off-limits topics, mention other, more positive things so that an interviewer won't even think to ask about your awkward issue.

Trudy Caldwell

123 Fremont Avenue • San Francisco, CA 12345 • (123) 123-2345

Human Resources Professional

SUMMARY OF QUALIFICATIONS

- More than five years experience in business office work with recent assignments in personnel administration.
- Competent project manager with an eye for added results.
- Eager to pursue a career in human resources.

EDUCATION

M.S., Human Resources, University of California, San Francisco, CA, 1998

RELEVANT ACCOMPLISHMENTS

PERSONNEL ADMINISTRATION

- Processed a minimum of 100 applications per week, using a database to file and sort data accessed by 12 managers. (Barstow & Bigelow, Inc.)
- Conducted orientations for new hires: explained company policies and gave employee tours of company. (Goodman Lumber)
- Coordinated payroll data by compiling information from time card machine and tallying employee vacation calendars. (Barstow & Bigelow, Inc.)

PROJECT MANAGEMENT

- Completely redesigned the mail system to expedite sorting and delivery. (Williams Sonoma Co.)
- Managed a 4,000-piece direct mail effort that met seasonal marketing deadlines despite heavy in-house workloads. (Barstow & Bigelow, Inc.)
- Initiated a company-wide recycling program that resulted in excellent publicity for the firm. (Goodman Lumber)

WORK HISTORY

1997-present	Executive Assistant, Barstow & Bigelow, Inc., San Francisco, CA
1994-1997	Administrative Assistant, Williams Sonoma Co., San Francisco, CA
1988-1994	Receptionist, Goodman Lumber, Daly City, CA

Trudy Caldwell's resume.

Christopher Bond

001 Piedmont Avenue
Atlanta, GA 12345
123-123-1234
chrisbond@thenet.net

Catalog Production Coordinator

SUMMARY OF QUALIFICATIONS

- Seven years as a print production professional, working in corporate and independent settings.
- Degree in journalism with additional training at daily news publication.
- Noted for accelerating production through strong managerial skills.

PROFESSIONAL EXPERIENCE

1999-pres.   **Thomas Govington** (independent artist), Atlanta, GA
BROCHURE PRODUCTION SPECIALIST
- Designed and coordinated production of a four-color brochure that portrayed the artist's talent in three media: paint on canvas, ceramics, and bronze.

1994-99   **Johnson Paper, Incorporated,** Atlanta, GA
CATALOG PRODUCTION COORDINATOR
- Managed full production of a 400-page catalog distributed to more than 4000 retailers and 80 distributors.
- Coordinated deadlines among six departments that sprinted from creative to shipping in less than two months per run.
- Supervised 35 artists and technicians; handled relations with more than 15 vendors.
- Represented the Production Department at management meetings.
- Instructed local college interns in print production techniques and systems.

1991-93   **Emory University Press,** Atlanta, GA
PRINT PRODUCTION INTERN
- Gained hands-on experience in every aspect of print production, working under the press's most senior printer.
- Frequently assisted in technically demanding assignments for major clients.

EDUCATION AND AFFILIATIONS

B.A., Journalism, Emory University, Atlanta, GA, 1985
Junior year abroad in Madrid for work-study program at prominent newspaper

American Printers Association
International Paper and Print Production Institute

Christopher Bond's resume.

Career Casualty

Don't be afraid to leave things off your resume if you're worried those items might make you look like the wrong candidate for the job. It's acceptable to delete information that isn't relevant to your job objective, as long as you don't create gaps in your work history.

Like Christopher, you may have a situation in your work history that you don't want to mention on your resume. As long as you don't create a void in your work history, it's perfectly fine not to bring up the sticky matter on your resume. To find creative ways to deal with tricky issues in your work history, turn to Chapter 8, "Step Three: Been There, Done That."

Understate Too Much Experience

When applying for a specific position, use the job posting as a checklist for what should appear on your resume. Without copying the ad's exact wording, try to match each of the qualifications the employer is seeking in his candidate.

Sara Cartwright had 15 years of experience as an auditor and accountant. Because jobs were scarce in her field, she was compelled to take a lower position than she would have liked. In creating her resume, she thought that if she put "15 years as an accounting professional" in her Summary of Qualifications section, she might seem too high-powered because the job announcement asked for five to seven years of experience.

As you can see from her resume (following), Sara decided to write "More than seven years as an accounting professional." Sara's revised statement is true (because 15 years is certainly more than seven years) and makes her look more suitable for the job she's seeking.

You may choose to generalize your qualifications on your resume in order to downplay them. This is perfectly acceptable as long as your statements are honest.

The second commandment is going to come in handy in Part 2 when you figure out the following:

➤ How far back to go in your work history

➤ What to say about gaps in your employment

➤ Whether to present your volunteer work

➤ How to list sensitive issues

Your resume should serve as a teaser. It should contain statements that say enough to spark the manager's interest without giving away all the details, especially when those details are about a sensitive issue that would be better addressed in the job interview, if at all.

Until then, let this commandment give you peace of mind, knowing that you don't have to write a complete autobiography.

Thou Shalt Not Write Job Descriptions

If you were an employer, what three questions would you ask a job candidate? You would probably ask

➤ Do you have any experience?

➤ Are you good at what you do?

➤ Do you like this kind of work?

SARA CARTWRIGHT, CPA
001 Turandot Street • Oakland, CA 12345
(510) 123-1234 • scartwright@thenet.net

OBJECTIVE

A position in Audit Management

SUMMARY OF QUALIFICATIONS

- More than seven years as an accounting professional with particular strength in conducting audits.
- Skilled at gaining cooperation from internal and external professionals.
- Experienced consultant to executive management on sensitive financial issues.

PROFESSIONAL EXPERIENCE

1999-pres.   Auditing Operations Manager, Anderson Electronics, San Leandro, CA
- Realized $40,000 in six months for the company by discovering several major unnoticed past due collections.
- Audited expense reports to verify compliance with company and governmental policies.
- Implemented CEO- and CFO-directed projects to restructure accounting procedures.

1993-99   Senior Auditor, Internal Accounting, Dartmouth Enterprises, Oakland, CA
- Conducted quarterly and annual audits for headquarters and 15 branch offices.
- Guided management through setup of accounting departments in four new business units located in separate Western states.
- Facilitated external audits that showed 100% compliance with professional standards.
- Authored analysis sections of SEC annual 10K and quarterly 10Q corporate reports.
- Designated Senior Auditor after four months with company as Internal Auditor.

1985-93   Accountant, Brokaw, Farnsworth & Associates, CPAs, San Francisco, CA
- Provided auditing services to corporate clients engaged in international manufacturing.
- Served as financial consultant to one of the nation's largest banking institutions.
- Prepared federal and state tax forms for a wide range of corporate structures.

EDUCATION AND CERTIFICATION

B.S., Accounting, California State University, Hayward, CA
CPA since 1992

Sara Cartwright's resume.

Don't be shy—answer "Yes" to all of these questions before the employer asks by writing about achievements instead of job duties on your resume. Achievement statements are the most powerful way to say "I'm good at what I do!"

Make sure your achievements are stated appropriately for the type of work you're interested in. For example, a salesperson's achievement statements will probably be much more dramatic (for example: Exceeded sales quotas by 300%) than the ones that appear on an accountant or technician's resume (for example: Used spreadsheet applications to analyze reports for upper management).

Examine the next two resumes for Diane Short. The first is a job-description resume (blah!); the second is an achievement-oriented resume (yes!). See how much more enticing the second one is? Diane's achievement statements provide the following information:

➤ She has particular experiences.

➤ She's good at what she does.

➤ She believes in and likes her work.

She's given the employer three good reasons to call her for an interview.

I'll expand on this commandment in Part 2 when you write your achievement statements. At this point, I want you to understand the concept of using your resume to brag a little (or a lot) about your successes.

Thou Shalt Not Write About Stuff You Don't Want to Do

Writing your resume is like writing your next job description, because everything you put in your resume suggests what you're eager to do in your new job. Never write about duties that you don't want to do again, no matter how good you are at them!

Bonus Check

If your resume generates job interviews for work you're not interested in, something is wrong with your resume! Before sending your resume to another employer, revise it according to the following points to ensure that it markets you for the type of work you want to pursue.

➤ Use a resume format that highlights the appropriate skills and experience.

➤ Don't mention responsibilities you don't want to hold on your next job.

(Job-Description Resume)

DIANE SHORT
Marketing Communications Director

0002 Walnut Avenue, #2, Berkeley, CA 12345, d_short@thenet.net (123) 123-1234

SUMMARY OF QUALIFICATIONS

- More than 10 years in marketing with recent experience as Director, Marketing Communications for the largest manufacturer in its classification.
- Creative thinker whose ideas have directly increased profitability.
- Manage multiple projects at once, with strict adherence to time and budget constraints.

PROFESSIONAL EXPERIENCE

1995-pres. MACY's, San Francisco
Director, Marketing Communications, 1999-present
Director, Public Relations & Licensing, 1996-1999
Marketing Consultant, 1995-1996

- Created sales collateral and ran creative aspects for advertising campaign.
- Developed and managed a national publicity program.
- Authored and designed press kits.
- Developed GWPs (gift with purchase).
- Collaborated with University of San Francisco Medical Center to design a promotion.
- Currently developing a merchandise strategy for a TV program.
- Analyzed competition, oversaw product development, approved prototypes, and managed business relations with licensees.
- Designed merchandise packaging and displays; negotiated with licensees to use visuals.

1991-1995 Delaney Advertising, Inc., New York City
Director, Marketing Communications Services
- Directed the New York office.
- Supervised staff and managed photographic production and budgets.

1987-1991 Gap, Inc., San Francisco
Media Coordinator
- Developed and implemented advertising campaigns. Managed creative development and execution. Monitored media budget.

EDUCATION

B.A., Communication Studies, with a minor in Business Administration
San Francisco State University, San Francisco, CA

Multimedia Program, University of California, San Francisco, currently enrolled

This version of Diane Short's resume has boring job descriptions.

(Achievement-Oriented Resume)

DIANE SHORT
Marketing Communications Director

enue, #2, Berkeley, CA 12345, d_short@thenet.net (123) 123-1234

...RY OF QUALIFICATIONS

- More than 10 years in marketing with recent experience as Director, Marketing Communications for the largest manufacturer in its classification.
- Creative thinker whose ideas have directly increased profitability.
- Manage multiple projects at once, with strict adherence to time and budget constraints.

PROFESSIONAL EXPERIENCE

1995-pres. MACY'S, San Francisco **Director, Marketing Communications,** 1999-present
Director, Public Relations & Licensing, 1996-1999
Marketing Consultant, 1995-1996

- Created sales collateral (including videos) and ran the creative efforts for national advertising campaign that established Macy's as the manufacturer of quality products.
- Developed and managed a national publicity program that increased retail sales more than 5% and dramatically enhanced brand recognition.
- Authored and designed the first press kit that clearly defined the company's image and product range.
- Enhanced product value and increased sales by developing GWPs (gift with purchase).
- To position company as an advocate for women's health, collaborated with University of San Francisco Medical Center to design a promotion that shared proceeds.
- Currently developing a merchandise strategy for an hour-long Cable television program to air Christmas of next year.
- Analyzed competition, oversaw product development, approved prototypes, and managed business relations with national and international licensees.
- Designed merchandise packaging and displays, and successfully negotiated with licensees and retailers to utilize these visuals to maintain consistent image.

1991-1995 DELANEY ADVERTISING, INC., New York City, **Director, Marketing Communications**

- Directed the New York office for this national full-service advertising company.
- Supervised staff and managed high-volume photographic production and budgets.

1987-1991 GAP, INC., San Francisco, **Media Coordinator**

- Developed and implemented advertising campaigns. Managed all phases of creative development and execution. Monitored media budget.

EDUCATION

B.A., Communication Studies, with a minor in Business Administration
San Francisco State University, San Francisco, CA

Multimedia Program, University of California, San Francisco, currently enrolled

This achievement-oriented version of Diane Short's resume is much better.

For example, when George was applying for a database programming position at a high-tech firm, he specifically did not want to supervise any staff. Even though in his previous job he had been in charge of a department and had been commended for his ability to build team spirit under adverse conditions, he was determined not to acquire that kind of responsibility in his next job. In his resume, he spoke about his many programming projects, but never once mentioned that he had managed anyone. Consequently, he attracted a programming job he loves with no supervisory responsibilities.

I'll remind you about this commandment as you go through the steps in Part 2. For now, just keep in mind that you are in the seat of power: you get to create your future by choosing what to put in and leave out of your resume!

Job-Hunt Hint

On scratch paper, make two lists: one of the tasks you love to perform and one of the things you hate to do. As you write your resume, be sure to include the tasks you love and avoid mentioning the ones you dislike.

Thou Shalt Say Less Rather Than More

Ah, the oxymoron that works so well in marketing: Less is more. Let's consider why it has withstood the test of time.

When it comes to things we all value, time sits near the top of the list, along with wealth and health. We say things like, "Time is money" and "It's not worth my time." Because time is at a premium in today's hectic world, it stands to reason that a promotional piece that takes less time to read is more likely to succeed than a lengthy one. Therefore, less text is more effective at grabbing the reader's attention.

Following the "less is more" theory has another advantage. By distilling all of your skills and experience into a minimum of words on one or two sheets of paper, you automatically put down only the very best stuff. So less is more in the sense that even though you provide less information, it's all high-quality information, which makes the resume more impressive.

Career Casualty

Use wisdom when writing about topics that could be misunderstood (like the *New York Times* article you authored that promoted the resume reader's competitor as #1 in the field). By being discreet and concise on your resume (maybe say only that you wrote a *New York Times* article that explored industry trends) you increase your chances of getting an interview where you can talk about the experience in person.

The Eight-Second Test

In today's job market, your resume has only about eight seconds to catch an employer's attention. In eight seconds an employer scans your resume and decides whether she will invest more time to consider you as a job candidate. The secret to passing the eight-second test is to make your resume look inviting and quick to read. That's why I recommend having a one-page resume if possible. Having a one-pager says, "I'm organized, and I'm not a motor-mouth."

Goody Two-Pages

For those who have a beefy career history or lengthy list of must-read accomplishments, one page may not be enough. If you're one of those people, go for it—just don't exceed two pages unless you're sure the reader is expecting more. For instance, if you're applying for an academic or scientific position, you'd probably have a seven- or eight-pager called a *curriculum vitae*. (See Chapter 15: "When You Really Are a Brain Surgeon: The Curriculum Vitae.")

If your resume is just a little more than a page, do your best to get it down to one page by using your editing and computer graphics skills. Then ask yourself, "Does it look easy to read?" If the print is too small or dense, you're better off with a two-page resume that's easy to read.

Career Casualty

On your paper resume, don't substitute an asterisk (*) for a bullet point (➤). An asterisk tells the reader to look below for a footnote. That's not what you mean! In Part 5, "The Electronic Job Search," I'll talk about how to use asterisks in an electronic resume.

Terms of Employment

A **bullet point** is a graphic symbol (➤) used to highlight a statement.

Terms of Employment

Nondisclosure (not mentioning something) is not the same as **lying** (telling something that isn't true). Nondisclosure is acceptable on a resume. Lying *is* not!

Thou Shalt Not Write in Paragraphs

Many resumes have long paragraphs filled with juicy information. The problem is that a busy manager is unlikely to read a resume made up of long paragraphs. A paragraph demands too much time to read.

Do the reader (and yourself) a favor by using *bullet points* to break your material into bite-sized pieces. A bullet at the beginning of a statement effectively says, "Here's an independent thought that's quick and easy to read," whereas a paragraph implies that one has to read the whole thing to get the full meaning.

For the best effect, start each achievement statement on a new line so that all the bullet points line up on the left, like the following:

➤ Made classroom presentations to students K–8, demonstrating the importance of art to man's physical and mental survival.

➤ Tutored high school students of Project Read, integrating reading and writing to offer new perspectives and respect for their own life stories.

➤ Conducted cultural field trips to sites including businesses, performing arts centers, and museums.

In case you're not convinced that bullet statements are a good idea, take a look at the following two versions of Marty Ramirez's resume. You'll see the same resume in two graphic layouts: the first uses paragraphs; the second uses bullet points to break up the blocks of print. Which do you think looks quicker to read?

Thou Shalt Not Lie

I'm starting to sound like your mother, aren't I? I have to say it anyway: Never tell a lie on your resume.

If you're wondering what kinds of lies I'm talking about, here are some that frequently appear on resumes and are apt to catch an employer's attention:

➤ Stating experience at a particular place of employment where you never worked

➤ Misrepresenting the level of responsibility you held (for example, listing "Art Director" when you were really a graphic designer)

➤ Listing a school that you didn't attend

➤ Claiming to have a degree that you didn't obtain

➤ Taking credit for someone else's achievement

➤ Overstating skill levels in a technical field

(Resume with paragraph formatting)

Marty Ramirez

123 Antelope Avenue
Boston, MA 12345
(123) 123-1234

OBJECTIVE

Field Representative for Local 510

DEMONSTRATED EFFECTIVENESS

Effectively negotiated and arbitrated grievances and contracts. Served on three contract negotiating committees, each strengthening the union shop. Co-developed first steward training classes for Local 510. Enforced collective bargaining agreements, health and safety standards, and grievance procedures as Rotating Floor Steward or Permanent Shop Steward since 1981. Chaired strike committees in 1994 and 1997, developing picketing plans, choosing picket captains, and informing membership of legal behavior on the picket line. Co-developed and led Local 510 affirmative action workshops, using bilingual and bicultural skills to stress commonalities among people. Conducted training and strategy sessions for U.N.H. labor and academic professionals, resulting in Partnership Programs.

WORK HISTORY

1978-present **Journeyman Installer**
SIGN, DISPLAY, AND ALLIED CRAFTS, LOCAL 510, I.B.P.A.T.

1995 **Primary Campaign Manager**
WILSON RILES, JR., MAYORAL CANDIDATE, BOSTON, MA

1992-95 **Teacher, World Cultures/Spanish/Bilingual**
OAKLAND UNIFIED SCHOOL DISTRICT

EDUCATION

B.A., Comparative Culture, University of New Hampshire, 1978
Graduate Studies, Latin American Culture, Harvard University

MEMBERSHIPS

West County Central Labor Council
Local 510 Political Action Committee
Boston Direct Action Committee
Former Member, A.P.R.I & C.B. T.U.

This version of Marty Ramirez's resume uses paragraphs.

(Resume with bullet-point statements)

Marty Ramirez
123 Antelope Avenue, Boston, MA 12345, (123) 123-1234

OBJECTIVE

Field Representative for Local 510

DEMONSTRATED EFFECTIVENESS

- Effectively negotiated and arbitrated grievances and contracts.
  - Served on three contract negotiating committees, each strengthening the union shop.
  - Co-developed first steward training classes for Local 510.
  - Enforced collective bargaining agreements, health and safety standards, and grievance procedures as Rotating Floor Steward or Permanent Shop Steward since 1981.
- Chaired strike committees in 1994 and 1997, developing picketing plans, choosing picket captains, and informing membership of legal behavior on the picket line.
- Co-developed and led Local 510 affirmative action workshops, using bilingual and bicultural skills to stress commonalities among people.
- Conducted training and strategy sessions for U.N.H. labor and academic professionals, resulting in Partnership Programs.

WORK HISTORY

1978-present **Journeyman Installer**
Sign, Display, and Allied Crafts, Local 510, I.B.P.A.T.

1995 **Primary Campaign Manager**
Wilson Riles, Jr., mayoral candidate, Boston, MA

1992-95 **Teacher, World Cultures/Spanish/Bilingual**
Boston Unified School District

EDUCATION

B.A., Comparative Culture, University of New Hampshire, 1978
Graduate Studies, Latin American Culture, Harvard University

MEMBERSHIPS

West County Central Labor Council
Local 510 Political Action Committee
Boston Direct Action Committee
Former Member, A.P.R.I & C.B. T.U.

Bullet points make this version of Marty Ramirez's resume easier to read.

Lying on your resume can cause more damage to your career than you may realize. Here are two good reasons to create a resume that contains only the truth:

➤ A lie on your resume can undermine your self-confidence during a job interview. If you're anything like me, just knowing that the interviewer might ask a question about your fib will make you nervous. To make matters worse, noticeable anxiety will most likely make a bad impression on your potential employer.

➤ After you're hired, a falsehood on your resume can be grounds for termination. If your resume is examined as part of your promotion review, you could lose your job if someone discovers a lie.

➤ A lie on your resume may indicate that you don't believe you're qualified for the job. Maybe you need to rethink your job objective or perhaps you need counseling to build your self-esteem.

As you can see, it's in your short- and long-term interest not to lie on your resume.

The Least You Need to Know

➤ Write about your future on your resume, not about your past.

➤ You don't have to tell everything in your resume. Stick to what's relevant and marketable.

➤ Use your resume to talk about your achievements, not monotonous job descriptions.

➤ Don't write about anything that you don't want to do again.

➤ Grab the reader's attention by being concise and using bullet-point statements.

➤ Be creative but honest in your resume.

43

Chronologically Speaking

Chapter 4

In This Chapter

➤ Why choose a chronological format

➤ When a conservative approach is the way to go

➤ How a chronological resume highlights the strengths of a work history

➤ How to accelerate a vertical or horizontal career move by using a chronological resume

---

Have you ever heard the real-estate adage: "location, location, location"? In resume writing, the adage would be "format, format, format." The format of your resume is so crucial that it can make or break your request for a job interview. The right format will tell the reader right away that you're a top-notch candidate for the job.

The two basic resume formats are chronological and functional. This chapter covers the guidelines, templates, and samples for the chronological resume. Chapter 5, "Get Functional," describes the ins and outs of the functional resume. In a very short time, you'll have made one of the most important decisions in the resume-writing process: choosing the best format.

Highlighting Your History

The chronological resume is the most traditional resume format. It's been around for years and has done well for millions of job seekers.

What It Is

The following template for the chronological resume outlines the content of a resume in this format. Notice that this format highlights a job seeker's dates of employment, places of employment, and job titles (the chronology of the person's work history) by using them as headings. Achievements are then listed under these headings.

(Chronological Resume Template)

Name
Street
City, State Zip
Phone, Fax, E-mail

JOB OBJECTIVE

The job you want next

SUMMARY OF QUALIFICATIONS

- How much experience you have in the field of your job objective, in a related field, or using the skills required for your new position.
- An overall career accomplishment that shows you'd be good at this job.
- What someone would say about you as a recommendation.

PROFESSIONAL EXPERIENCE

19xx-pres.   **Company Name, City, State**
Job Title
- An accomplishment you are proud of that shows you're good at this profession.
- A problem you solved and the results.
- A time when you positively affected the organization, the bottom line, your boss, your co-workers, your clients.
- Awards, commendations, publications, etc., you achieved that relate to your job objective.

19xx-xx   **Company Name, City, State**
Job Title
- A project you are proud of that supports your job objective.
- Another accomplishment that shows you're good at this line of work.
- Quantifiable results that point out your skill.

19xx-xx   **Company Name, City, State**
Job Title
- An accomplishment you are proud of that shows you will be valued by your next employer.
- An occasion when someone "sat up and took notice" of your skill.

EDUCATION

Degree, Major (if relevant), 19xx (optional)
University, City, State

A chronological template.

When to Use It

Many employers (especially those in conservative fields such as law and finance) like chronological resumes for the following reasons:

➤ They're used to reading chronological resumes and therefore feel comfortable with an applicant who uses this conventional approach.

➤ They can see a job seeker's work history in a flash because it's highlighted in the body of the resume.

If you are applying for a job in a conservative industry or company, use the chronological format. You should also use this format if you want to emphasize your work history for any of the following reasons:

➤ You want to make a *horizontal career move* within your current field.

➤ You'd like to make a *vertical career move* within your current field.

➤ Your most recent (or current) position is one you are proud of.

➤ You have no major gaps in your work history.

Now let's look at some sample resumes from real job seekers that demonstrate situations in which the chronological resume is the best choice.

The Horizontal Slide

Andrew Gregory had been in audit management for a number of years and wanted to remain in that line of work. His chronological resume (following) clearly showed that he had a stable history as an audit professional with experience in management. Without reading the small text of the bullet-point statements, the employer could see from the headings of his chronological resume that Andrew was a likely candidate for the job.

If you're making a horizontal career move and have no gaps in your work history, the chronological format is an excellent way to market yourself.

Career Casualty

The templates in this book are not boilerplates! The bullet-point statements are ideas that I might suggest if I were with you as you create your resume. Because not all of these statements will apply to your situation, use only the ones that give you the opportunity to support your job objective. If these prodders aren't enough, check out the brainstorming exercises in Chapter 8, "Step Three: Been There, Done That."

Terms of Employment

Chronological implies that events (such as the jobs in your Work History section) will be listed in the order in which they happened. However, in most chronological resumes, the events are listed in reverse chronology (most recent listed first).

Andrew Gregory, C.P.A.

0001 Trenton Place • Newark, NJ 12345 • (123) 123-1234

in Audit Management

SUMMARY OF QUALIFICATIONS

- More than five years as an internal and external auditor with a strong financial and operational background in industries including manufacturing.
- Confident professional who facilitates cooperation among parties.
- Knowledge of data processing and spreadsheet applications.
- Personal activity in futures and options trading.

PROFESSIONAL EXPERIENCE

1999-2000 **Senior Auditor**
HOME AND MORTGAGE, INC., Newark, NJ
- Saved company $4,000 - $12,000 a month by analyzing project needs and recommending improved utilization of contractual and full-time staff.
- Audited management and employee expense reports to verify compliance with company policies and procedures.
- Originally contracted to perform field operation audits that led to CEO- and CFO-directed projects.

1996-1999 **Manager, Internal Audits**
NORTH AMERICAN BUILDING SUPPLY, Morristown, NJ
- Attained functional level of audit manager, reporting to Senior Corporate Controller.
- Conducted extensive due diligence and auditing of more than 15 prospective company and customer contract acquisitions (up to $20 million).
- Made numerous productive recommendations to senior management, based on operational benefits and numerical findings.
- Coordinated participation of external auditors to complete timely audits according to professional standards.
- Co-wrote the management discussion and analysis sections of the SEC annual 10K and quarterly 10Q corporate reports.

1993-1996 **Senior Accountant**
SMITHERS & WONG (Formerly Smithers and Troutt), Florham Park, NJ

EDUCATION

B.S., Accounting, Magna Cum Laude, New Jersey State University, Morristown, 1992
Recipient of First New Jersey Accounting Scholarship Award

Andrew Gregory's resume.

Vertical Climb

In the next resume, Stacy Vernon's job titles alone told the story of her gradual climb from administrative assistant to events coordinator/executive assistant. Her chronological format easily demonstrated that moving up the ladder one more rung to event planner was a logical step.

If you're seeking a vertical career move, promote yourself with a chronological resume. It's the surest way to highlight the thread of success that runs through your career.

A Strong Start

Although Roger First was a volunteer project coordinator in an educational setting for six years, his recent paid experience was the most impressive to a potential boss. Roger's chronological format highlighted his recent position by listing that job first in his work history. You can include volunteer experience in the body of a chronological resume if you entitle the section Relevant Experience instead of Employment Experience or Professional Experience.

If your most recent positions are highly relevant to your job objective, the chronological resume is definitely the format for you. Also, if your recent position or positions are more impressive than the others in your work history, give them greater resume real estate by listing more bullet-point statements under those job headings. The other job titles can follow with just a few or no statements under them.

Job–Hunt Hint

If your work history supports your job objective and you fit the other requirements listed in this chapter, the chronological resume is the safest way to market yourself.

Terms of Employment

Horizontal career move means that someone is taking a new job that is of equal status to the one he now holds within a given field. **Vertical career move** means a person is transitioning to a higher level within the same profession or industry.

Bonus Check

You can examine many more chronological resumes by browsing through Part 2, "Six Steps to a Perfect Resume," and Appendix B, "Portfolio of Sample Resumes."

Stacy E. Vernon

001 Stonestown Road • Fremont, LA 12345 • (123) 123-1234 • eventshappend@thenet.net

JOB OBJECTIVE: Position in Event Planning

SUMMARY OF QUALIFICATIONS

- Over 12 years' experience planning business and social events including conferences, celebrations, parties, dinners, and luncheons.
- Skilled at leading and working within a team to produce events that promote the organization's image, mission, and objective.

PROFESSIONAL EXPERIENCE

1998-present **Events Coordinator/Executive Assistant to General Manager**
TRAFALGAR & SONS, INC., Fremont, LA

- Coordinated the company's 20th Anniversary Celebration at the Fremont Museum of Modern Art for more than 200 top investors. This black-tie event included dinner and dancing to Martin Andrews' Orchestra.
- Planned and produced an executive business retreat at a California winery.
- Orchestrated a 150-person private party in Manhattan. Arranged invitations, entertainment, accommodations, and transportation.
- Set up numerous live national and international video-conferences requiring special equipment, rooms, meals, and information packets.

1995-1998 **Administrative Assistant to President and to Vice President, Consumer Products**
WESTINGHOUSE, INC., South Fremont, LA

- Served on the UNICEF Campaign event planning committee that promoted and produced the 1800-person kickoff rally and closing party with celebrity speakers, entertainment, food, and contests.
- Organized 9 Board and 45 officers' luncheons per year; planned menus and floor plans.
- Served as liaison to Board members, stockholders, staff, and general public on behalf of President and Vice President.

1988-1995 **Administrative Assistant to CEO and to Executive Vice President**
THOMAS FOODS CORPORATION, West Bend, LA

- Planned annual Christmas parties at major West Bend hotels for 200 employees and guests. Collaborated with hotel caterers on all aspects.
- Commended for producing the company's first outdoor employee events on very limited budgets, which boosted morale during merger.

EDUCATION

B.S., Business Administration, Louisiana State University, New Orleans, LA
Independent Study: Cooking, Southern Cuisine School, New Orleans

Stacy Vernon's resume.

Roger E. First

001 Franklin Street • Cleveland, OH 12345 • (123) 123-1234 • rfirst@thenet.net

Educational Program Coordinator

SUMMARY OF QUALIFICATIONS

- More than seven years experience coordinating projects in academic environments.

- Excellent at generating new ideas and improving upon existing systems to further the administration of an organization.

- Success at motivating staff through clear communication and outstanding organizational skills.

RELEVANT EXPERIENCE

1999-pres. **Children's Day School,** Cleveland, OH
Project Coordinator

- Currently creating a promotional multimedia presentation that reflects the high standard of this private preschool-elementary school with a socioeconomically diverse student body.

- Promoted school allegiance and parent participation by:
  - Actively networking among parents, faculty, and students.
  - Organizing at least eight special events per year.
  - Re-evaluating current goals, strategies, and financial management to support extra-curricular activities.
- Chaired the Academic Endowment Fund and Annual Giving Fund Committees.

1993-99 **St. Mary's Elementary School,** Lakewood, OH
Volunteer Project Coordinator

- Played key role in restructuring volunteer activities. Collaborated with administration to prioritize need for volunteers, re-evaluate programs, and make improvements to optimize volunteer participation in light of today's family structure.

- Successfully initiated enhancements to academic programs by surveying needs and facilitating discussion between administration and parents.

- Started Creative Arts Projects which, for the first time, enabled students to gain recognition for their creativity while generating over 17% of annual funds raised.

- Directly supervised 10 parents and indirectly managed 40 volunteers, who organized educational, extracurricular, and fundraising activities.

—Continued—

51

Roger E. First
Page Two

1988-93   **Project Consultant and Reconstruction Coordinator,** Cleveland Heights, OH
- Supervised the reconstruction/remodeling of several residential properties that were resold at sizable profits.

1987-88   **Time-Warner, Inc., Educational Division,** New York, NY
Research Associate
- Conducted research of subject matter to be used for educational films distributed to high schools nationwide.

- Compiled photographs for *Now Is Our Time*, a hardback book to accompany films.

EDUCATION
B.A., Sociology & Urban Studies, 1990, Boston University, Boston, MA

Roger First's resume.

Getting Labeled

One quick glance at the next chronological resume told a hiring manager that Gina had a strong foothold in retail business. Her work history headings screamed sales, and her bullet statements pointed to visual merchandising. Gina's chronological resume made the employer's decision to call her for an interview a no-brainer!

If, like Gina, the job titles in your work history reflect what you want to do in your next job, the chronological resume is a great way to get labeled as a qualified candidate. A quick scan of your job titles and related bullet points (which are highlighted in the chronological format) will reveal that you want to continue in the same line of work.

Bonus Check

To develop a dynamite resume strategy, team up with a friend, fellow job hunter, counselor, or professional resume writer. You need to talk to someone who can ask you questions about your work history and be objective.

Background Check

Jonathan Turner's resume (following) presented his strong background in executive management, leaving no question that he was qualified to take his expertise to a similar position in an Italian firm. Although the small print rang of wonderful achievements, it was the work-history headings that immediately informed the employer that Jonathan was well worth considering for the job.

When your job titles support your job objective especially well, use the chronological resume. You may also want to highlight the titles by putting them in bold print.

Career Casualty

There is a mistaken impression among job seekers that the chronological format is old-fashioned and should not be used. Don't fall for this faulty thinking! The chronological format is still the most widely accepted type of resume and should be used if its criteria fits your career goals.

Conservative Line

Because the railroad industry is rather conservative, Roger Smythe chose the chronological format for his resume (following). Although he had never held a management position (as he was requesting in his job-objective statement), the subheadings under his Professional Experience section clearly reflect that he's an intelligent man with a love of the rail industry. The employer saw that Roger's seven-year career in the field was a suitable foundation for a promotion into management.

Gina R. Schultz

001 Sacramento Street   •   St. Louis, MO 12345   •   (123) 123-1234   •   ginas@thenet.net

JOB OBJECTIVE

Position in Visual Merchandising

SUMMARY OF QUALIFICATIONS

- Experienced in merchandising for two of the nation's most successful retailers, as a sales associate for over 10 years.
- "Your sense of design is so good, you should be doing my job." — Visual Merchandiser for Macy's nationwide.
- Knowledge of:

Fashion accessories	Sportswear
Housewares	Tabletop products
Gift items	Decorative pieces

RELEVANT PROFESSIONAL EXPERIENCE

1997 to 2000   **MACY'S, St. Louis**   **Sales Associate**

- Executed special holiday window and floor displays, using plan-a-grams and personal creativity.
- Maintained displays and floor stock, frequently changing presentations to accommodate inventory and seasonal trends.
- Demonstrated product enthusiasm that generated extremely high sales and numerous customer commendations. Achieved three regional customer service awards.
- Monitored inventory and delivery systems to ensure timely in-store placement of products.

1988 to 1996   **EMPORIUM, St. Louis**   **Sales Associate**

- Merchandised clothing and accessories, following schematics and block plans for a department that generated 35% of store's sales.
- Tracked sales trends and collaborated with department manager to determine effectiveness of POPs and displays.
- Provided excellent service to a wide range of customers. Won several "Employee of the Month" awards.
- Conducted classroom and on-the-job training for new employees.

EDUCATION

Merchandising & Design Program, Washington University, St. Louis, MO

Gina Schultz's resume.

JONATHAN S. TURNER

001 Terrano Street   •   Salvatore, 1234   •   Milan, Italy   •   (01) 123-1234   •   jonturner@thenet.net

OBJECTIVE

Executive management position in Finance and Accounting for an Italian firm

SUMMARY OF QUALIFICATIONS

- More than 10 years as an accounting/audit professional with more than five years in management.
- Extensive experience in international accounting and finance.
- Fluent in Italian; conversant in Italian and U.S. accounting and reporting requirements.
- Successful at designing, implementing, and completing projects to the satisfaction of senior management in a goal-oriented and deadline-driven profession.

PROFESSIONAL EXPERIENCE

1996-2000   **Controller,** FINANCIAL MANAGEMENT, INC., San Francisco, CA
A high-growth company, which in the last two years has expanded from U.S. $3 billion to over U.S. $9 billion in retail, closed-end, and institutional funds under management.

- Oversaw all accounting and reporting for five subsidiaries: an investment management company, a transfer agency, a broker dealer, an insurance company, and a holding company.
- Significantly increased efficiency of accounting and reporting by computerizing manual processes and instituting accounting controls.
- Achieved high integrity in financial reporting with a four-day deadline for submission of final consolidated reporting packages to the parent company.
- Maintained a perfect record of zero proposed audit adjustments through four annual audits. Served as liaison to external auditors.
- Trained and directly supervised five accounting professionals, and indirectly oversaw additional support staff of six.
- Designed and implemented accounting procedures for new products such as Contingent Deferred Sales Charges and Variable Annuity Funds.
- Supervised preparation of quarterly and annual regulatory reports including:
  - Focus reports for the National Association of Securities Dealers and the Securities and Exchange Commission.
  - Investment Management Regulatory Organization reports for the regulatory authorities.
- Controlled and supervised the department's development of computer systems, as the general ledger systems administrator.

— Continued —

55

JONATHAN S. TURNER
Page 2

1994-95   **Director, Financial Markets Accounting,** EURO SECURITIES, LTD., Rome, Italy
One of the largest merchant banks in Italy, which began closing operations in 1994.

- Reviewed monthly accounts and reconciliations for Corporate, Property, and Leasing divisions and Off-shore subsidiaries.

- Managed U.S. and Italian regulatory reporting to the U.S. Securities and Exchange Commission and the Reserve Bank of Italy.

- Prepared the annual financial statements and assisted in preparing tax returns for the Italian parent company, the main operating company, and eight subsidiaries.

1988-94   **Supervising Senior,** KPMG ITALY, LTD., Milan, Italy, 1992-94
Audit Manager, KPMG & ASSOCIATES, San Francisco, CA, 1988-1992
A professional audit firm with locations worldwide.

- Promoted from Audit Assistant to Audit Manager in three years' time.

- Managed multi-audit engagements for publicly and privately owned companies including financial services, oil and gas, real estate, and government agencies.

- Prepared financial statements, incorporating the requirements of U.S. Generally Accepted Accounting Principles and Italian Accounting Standards.

- Delivered presentations to audit staff as a trainer in the firm's national and local training programs. Topics included: technical accounting, auditing, and management training.

- Interviewed and assessed potential new-hires. Conducted annual performance evaluations for professional staff.

EDUCATION AND AFFILIATIONS

American Institute of Certified Public Accountants, Member since 1992
California State Board of Accountancy, Member since 1992

University of California at Santa Cruz, Santa Cruz, California
Bachelor of Science in Economics & Finance, 1988

Italian Securities Institute, Milan, Italy
Money Market and Fixed Investment Securities and Financial Futures, 1995

Proficient in Lotus for Windows, Excel for Windows, and Sunsystems General Ledger Accounting packages

— Currently hold Permanent Resident Visa for Italy —

Jonathan Turner's resume.

ROGER F. SMYTHE

123 Alvarez Street, #2 • San Diego, CA 12345 • (123) 123-1234

JOB OBJECTIVE

A management position within the railroad
with a focus on network design or strategic

SUMMARY OF QUALIFICATIONS

- A thorough understanding of the railroad industry, with a strong interest in the analysis of trends and the integration of marketing and operations to meet future demands.
- A quick study: able to easily gain new skills, ask the right questions, and apply knowledge to work effectively, both independently and in teams.
- Skilled in building relationships and communicating clearly with individuals at all organizational levels.

PROFESSIONAL EXPERIENCE

1995-pres. **CENTRAL PACIFIC RAILROAD,** San Diego, CA   *Maintainer*

- Performed installation and maintenance of centralized traffic control systems, within a safety-sensitive and deadline-driven environment.
- Planned and executed daily construction programs during foreman's absences, providing leadership to team members to ensure quality and timeliness.
- Designed, coordinated, and facilitated the department's regional commercial driver training program, resulting in logistical flexibility and improved productivity.

1993-95 **NEVADA RAILROAD,** Wells, NV   *Trackworker*

- Performed quality control on production tie gang, serving as leadman on backwork crew and on spot maintenance projects.
- Quickly earned the respect of supervisors and crew members alike, based on versatility, technical expertise, an in-depth understanding of work processes, and a commitment to quality and safety.

1992-93 **UNIVERSITY OF ALASKA,** Anchorage, AK   *Research Fellow*

- Specialized in the history of industrialization, with a focus on systems theory, research, and analysis of business, labor, and technology.

1990-92 **RAILROAD MUSEUM, INC.,** Jarbridge, NV   *Conservator*

- Supervised track department: Planned and implemented maintenance activities and construction projects; collaborated with departmental superintendents to create and administer budgets.

EDUCATION

B.A, American History, University of California, Santa Barbara, CA, 1992
Coursework included Economics, Business, and Civil Engineering studies.

Roger Smythe's resume.

If you have experience in an industry and you want to make a big leap ahead within that industry, take advantage of the chronological resume. By accenting your industry experience through your work history, you can demonstrate that you're ready for a step up into the position you seek.

Get It Together

Now that you've seen several sample chronological resumes, can you picture your own resume in that format? Do you fit the guidelines mentioned earlier in this chapter? If so, you're ready to move on to Chapter 6, "Step One: Heading Your Way," where you'll start to put your words into print. If you're uncertain as to whether the chronological resume is the best format for you, turn to the next chapter, where you can check out the functional resume.

Job-Hunt Hint

Here's a way to emphasize that you have experience in the industry you're applying to: Put your company names in bold or all caps and place them before your job titles in your work history.

The Least You Need to Know

➤ The chronological resume is the most traditional resume format.

➤ Use the chronological format if you are making either a vertical or horizontal career move.

➤ Because the chronological format highlights your work history, use it if your history is stable and your job titles are relevant to your job objective.

➤ Choose between the chronological and functional formats based on your situation, not on hearsay about what's trendy.

Get Functional

In This Chapter

➤ How resume writing has adapted to new job trends

➤ When to use a functional resume

➤ What magic is behind a skills–based resume

➤ How to make sore points in your history look healthy

First impressions are crucial and lasting whether you're introducing yourself to your new mother-in-law or your boss-to-be. I'll let you figure out how to win over your mother-in-law, and I'll stick to what I know best: helping you make a stunning impression with your potential employer. In this chapter, you'll discover how to rope in a new boss with a functional resume, before she reads even one word of the small print.

The Times Are a Changin'

Work trends have changed dramatically in the last 50 years. It used to be that someone got a job shortly after graduating and kept it for the rest of his life. If things went well, he might move up the ladder within the company, but he usually felt sentenced to the same boss for 20 years to life. Loyalty to the company equaled stability, something greatly valued by employers (and by mothers-in-law too, for that matter). An applicant who had job-hopped—not to mention changed careers—was considered unstable and therefore a risk for a would-be employer.

But since the early '80s, the rate of job and career change has increased to such a point that it's now typical for a professional to shift careers three or four times during his adult life and to move to a new job once every three years. In this new climate, job-hopping is now called *diversity*, and many employers consider diversity an asset as long as the job seeker's rate of change is in line with the average for the industry.

How did this employment trend affect resume writing? It brought about the need for a new format: the *functional resume*. As an alternative to the chronological format, the functional format works wonders for adventurous professionals such as the following:

➤ Career changers

➤ Parents reentering the workforce

➤ People who took time off to travel or pursue a personal project

➤ Heavy-duty volunteers

➤ Students fresh out of school

➤ Survivors of recent or not-so-recent bouts of unemployment

➤ Entrepreneurs making the transition back into the corporate world

➤ Folks who've had the same responsibilities for years and years at multiple job sites

Do you fit into any of these categories? If so, read on to find out how you can present yourself in a functional resume that will float your potential employer's boat.

What's Your Function?

The functional format presents your accomplishments under skill headings (instead of under job-title headings, as in the chronological format), giving you the freedom to prioritize your accomplishments by significance rather than by chronology.

Thus, the functional resume format enables you to show off your skills to a potential employer. By placing your achievement statements front and center, you put your best foot forward. This format enables you to define yourself by your skills instead of your work history.

As you can see from the following template, Work History is a very concise section at the bottom of the resume, and achievement statements are placed in the body of the resume according to skill headings.

(Functional Resume Template)

Name
Street
City, State Zip
Phone, Fax, E-mail

JOB OBJECTIVE

The job you want next

SUMMARY OF QUALIFICATIONS

- How much experience you have in the field of your job objective, in a related field, or using the skills required for your new position.
- An overall career accomplishment that shows you'd be good at this job.
- What someone would say about you as a recommendation.

RELEVANT EXPERIENCE

MAJOR SKILL

- An accomplishment you are proud of that shows you have this skill.
- A problem you solved using this skill, and the results.
- A time when you used your skill to positively affect the organization, the bottom line, your boss, your clients.
- Awards, commendations, publications, etc., you achieved that relate to your job objective.

MAJOR SKILL

- A project you are proud of that supports your job objective.
- Another accomplishment that shows you're good at this line of work.
- Quantifiable results that point out your skill.
- An occasion when someone "sat up and took notice" of your skill.

WORK HISTORY

19xx-present	Job Title	COMPANY NAME and city
19xx-xx	Job Title	COMPANY NAME and city
19xx-xx	Job Title	COMPANY NAME and city
19xx-xx	Job Title	COMPANY NAME and city

EDUCATION

Degree, Major (if relevant), 19xx (optional)
University, City, State

Template for functional resume.

Career Casualty

A lot of job seekers think the functional format is the resume of the new millennium. Not so! Most employers still prefer the chronological resume. However, if the chronological format doesn't work for your situation, the functional resume can be a very effective alternative.

Likely Candidates

In short, use the functional format if you meet one of the following criteria:

➤ You are changing careers.

➤ You are reentering the job market.

➤ You need to emphasize skills or experience from an early part of your work history.

➤ Your volunteer experience is relevant and needs to be high-lighted.

➤ Your most recent position is not impressive.

➤ You have one or more awkward gaps in your employment history.

Take a look at the following sample resumes from real job seekers to see how the functional format worked with their experience. Maybe you'll find that you have similar reasons for using a functional resume.

The Career Changer's Dream

Thomas Horton wanted to change careers from law to nonprofit management, so he used the functional format for his resume (following). This format emphasized his transferable skills (management, development, and motivation) in the body of his resume so that the employer would see him as a manager with a legal background rather than a lawyer trying to get into management.

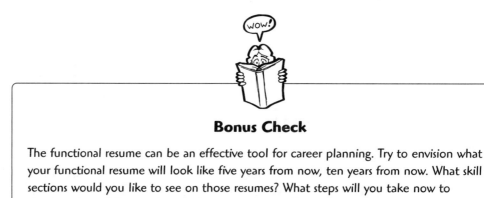

Bonus Check

The functional resume can be an effective tool for career planning. Try to envision what your functional resume will look like five years from now, ten years from now. What skill sections would you like to see on those resumes? What steps will you take now to develop those skills in order to advance your career?

If you're a career changer with a work history that may lead a potential employer to pigeonhole you into your previous line of work, use the functional format. The functional resume allows you to define yourself according to your skills instead of your former job titles.

THOMAS HORTON
001 Danville Road, Cleveland, OH 12345
(123) 123-3456 thomash@thenet.net

OBJECTIVE

Executive Director of a nonprofit organization

HIGHLIGHTS

- Over five years' management experience emphasizing a collaborative yet decisive style.
- Adept at building productive relationships to further the organization's goals.
- Persuasive skills, both written and verbal.

PROFESSIONAL EXPERIENCE (at Caldwell, Stevenson & Horton)

MANAGEMENT

- Achieved a revenue growth from $600K to $1.5M per year within my area of management, while keeping overhead low.
- Planned and adhered to a budget of up to $750K.
- Supervised a staff of 15, involving training, work flow, quality control, conflict resolution, and review processes.
- Directed the acquisition, installation, and maintenance of a 40-workstation system.

DEVELOPMENT/MOTIVATION

- Built a large loyal client base through personal attention, quality service, and consistent follow through.
- Assisted clients in identifying their interests, and motivated them to act accordingly.
- Wrote persuasive letters and documents, frequently influencing decision makers.
- Involved personnel in goal sharing, resulting in dramatically increased productivity.

WORK HISTORY

1997-2000	Law Offices of Caldwell, Stevenson & Horton, Cleveland	Partner
1995-1997	Prudential Insurance Company, Cleveland	Claims Examiner

EDUCATION

J.D., Boalt College of Law, Berkeley, CA, 1993
B.A., Finance & Administration, Georgetown University, Washington, DC, 1987

AFFILIATIONS

Board of Directors, Cleveland Symphony
Advisory Council to the Cleveland AIDS Project

Thomas Horton's resume.

Job-Hunt Hint

To shorten a resume that has a lengthy work history filled with repetitious experiences, switch from a chronological to a functional format. The employer will appreciate your ability to organize material efficiently.

Career Casualty

Don't let anyone tell you that you didn't do anything for the last so-many years because you were a full-time parent. You worked hard and developed many useful skills. So use a functional resume that includes parenting in your Work History section to fill an employment gap with dignity.

Skills Up Front and Center

Beverly Jensen was an accomplished language instructor with years of experience teaching at the college level. (Her resume follows.) The functional resume worked well for her because it presented the skills she'd used in her many teaching positions in concise statements under skill headings. In a chronological format, she would have been forced to repeat these statements for each position she held.

If you've held many positions that carried similar responsibilities (for instance, as a teacher or therapist), and you need an efficient way of presenting your experience, the functional resume may be the way to go. By grouping statements under the functional resume's skill headings, you eliminate redundant statements in each job listing throughout your work history.

Reentry with Force

After being a full-time mom for three years, Chris Montoya felt she was ready to go back into the workforce. She had filled her three unemployed years with volunteer work (in addition to parenting) and wanted to continue in a nonprofit environment, this time for pay. The following functional resume shows how she presented her relevant achievements in the body of the resume and referred to her volunteerism and parenting in her Work History section.

If you were unemployed while being a full-time parent, you can list "Full-time Parent" as a job title under Work History in your functional resume to avoid a gap in dates. After all, parenting is a full-time job, even though you didn't draw a salary from it.

Long, Long Ago

Donald Toni wanted to combine the sales skills he'd developed at the beginning of his career with the administrative skills he'd used in his recent set of jobs. By using a functional resume (following), he was able to highlight his early career achievements by placing them under the prominent Sales skill heading. Notice that his two skill headings (Administration and Sales) added up to his Job Objective (Sales Service Administrator). Pretty cool, huh?

If you have valuable experience that would get buried at the bottom of a chronological resume, create a functional resume so that you can prioritize that experience near the top of your skills sections.

BEVERLY JENSEN
001 Pine Street San Francisco, CA 12345
(123) 123-1234

OBJECTIVE

English as a Second Language Instructor

HIGHLIGHTS OF QUALIFICATIONS

- LIFE California Community College Instructor Credential in Basic Education.
- TESL Certificate with coursework in reading, writing, listening, and speaking.
- Proficient in French, Spanish, and German.
- More than 10 years experience as an ESL teacher at the community college level.

PROFESSIONAL AND RELATED EXPERIENCE

CLASSROOM TEACHING

- Taught English language skills (listening, speaking, reading, writing) at all levels to non-native speakers:
  - Community college and university students
  - French residents in France
- Approached classroom teaching as a facilitator of student learning, providing a wide range of learning activities in a warm, supportive environment.
- Integrated computer training (IBM and Macintosh) with English language instruction in the computer lab.
- Instructed adult students in basic education skills required for vocational training.
- Implemented an individual reading program for students, third grade through high school.

CURRICULA DEVELOPMENT AND COURSE EVALUATION

- Designed and implemented an ESP class in business English and marketing at Aspect ILS (International Language School).
  - Evaluated student needs through informal testing, discussion, and observation.
  - Formulated lessons to meet specific learning objectives.
- Developed three mini-courses for ESL students at Aspect ILS on ethnic art of San Francisco, and the culture of English language communication through music.
- Improved existing Basic Education Curricula at San Francisco State University.
- As member of Excelsior Reading Clinic instructional team, participated in on-going course evaluation and curricula development of reading program.

(Continued)

MULTI-CULTURAL / MULTI-ETHNIC COMMUNICATIONS

- As an ESL teacher:
  - Lived in France for three years, teaching adolescents, university students, and adults.
  - Taught an extremely diverse student population in the San Francisco area for more than 10 years.
- As a Peace Corps Volunteer in Ghana for two years:
  - Taught physical education classes in French.
  - Participated in cross-cultural studies with four African teachers and seven other volunteers.
- Worked as an au pair for one year in Germany.

WORK HISTORY

Teacher, ESL, 1987-present
> City College of San Francisco, San Francisco, CA 1987-94, 1996-present
> John F. Kennedy University, Orinda, CA 1993-95, 98-present
> Aspect International Language School, San Francisco, CA 1997-present
> ACHNA-American Language Program, Paris & Nancy, France, 1990-93

Teacher, Basic Education, 1986
> San Francisco Community College, San Francisco, CA

Reading Resource Teacher, 1986-89
> Excelsior Reading Clinic, San Francisco, CA

EDUCATION

TESL Certificate, University of California, Berkeley, 1990
MA, Secondary Education, San Francisco State University, 1987
BA, French, University of California, Berkeley, 1982
Education Abroad Program, Madrid, Spain, Summer '77

CREDENTIALS

Lifetime California Community College Instructor Credential: Basic Education
Lifetime California Teaching Credentials: Standard Secondary, Reading Specialist

PROFESSIONAL AFFILIATIONS

Teachers of English to Speakers of Other Languages (TESOL)
California Teachers of English to Speakers of Other Languages (CATESOL)
Northern California Council of Returned Peace Corps Volunteers (NORCAL)

Beverly Jensen's resume.

Chris Montoya
001 Newcombe Street, Apt. 6 • Las Vegas, NV 12345 • (123) 123-2345 • cmont@thenet.net

JOB OBJECTIVE: Position in Development

SUMMARY OF QUALIFICATIONS
- More than four years developing strategies and proposals for generating revenue.
- Comfortable initiating and building rapport with affluent individuals.
- Excellent research and writing capabilities. Articulate ideas clearly and concisely.

RELEVANT EXPERIENCE
DEVELOPMENT
- As liaison to individual donors, cultivated ongoing relationships and encouraged donor involvement in fundraising activities. (Environmental Resource Center)
- Collaborated in grant proposal formulation by compiling and summarizing supporting data. (Environmental Resource Center)
- As campaign fundraiser, produced promotional events at celebrity homes that raised funds and generated public support. (Nevada Gubernatorial campaign)

COMMUNICATION
- Used listening and verbal skills to resolve countless technical, political, and interpersonal problems among individuals from diverse backgrounds. (Seacoast Investments, Inc.)
- Persuaded decision makers within the government and business sectors through proposals, reports, and correspondence. (Seacoast Investments, Inc.)
- Increased revenue more than 10% by drafting mutually beneficial contracts that frequently led to renewals. (Seacoast Investments, Inc.)
- Handled media relations, providing an accurate and concise portrayal of the organization's positions on current issues. (Environmental Resource Center)

WORK HISTORY
1998-present	Las Vegas Symphony, Las Vegas, NV Volunteer, Assistant to Development Database Manager
1997-1999	Full-time Parent
1994-1997	Seacoast Investments, Inc., Las Vegas, NV Portfolio Manager
1992-1994	Environmental Resource Center, Las Vegas, NV Regional Development Associate

PROFESSIONAL DEVELOPMENT AND EDUCATION
Center for the Support of Nonprofit Organizations, Las Vegas, NV
Successful Fundraising Strategies
Writing Successful Grant Proposals

B.A., cum laude, English Literature, University of Pennsylvania, Philadelphia, PA, 1991

Chris Montoya's resume.

Donald H. Toni

001 Bernardino Avenue • Seattle, WA 12345 • (123) 123-1234

OBJECTIVE: Sales Service Administrator

SUMMARY OF QUALIFICATIONS

- More than 12 years of administrative experience at the executive level.
- Keen understanding of business concepts in working with budgets and financial presentations.
- Able to manage a vast array of responsibilities including corporate meeting planning.
- Communicate clearly and persuasively; effective in contract negotiations.

PROFESSIONAL ACCOMPLISHMENTS

Administration
- Coordinated events for Arundel Corporation with up to $50K budgets. Negotiated contracts for catering, equipment, entertainment, and accommodations.
- Arranged Arundel's luncheon for more than 200 journalists and politicians to introduce Seattle stadium plan. Produced six-page accompanying booklet.
- Managed KQDD's annual awards program, determining awards and selection process.
- Improved speed and accuracy of president's sales reports, budget development and reconciliation, and expense tracking by computerizing Wide Road Sporting's accounting.
- Supervised work of eight administrative and customer service staff at Clydesdale Travel.

Sales
- As sales agent, successfully persuaded airline representatives to clear space on overbooked flights and make special arrangements for clients.
- Managed Arundel's sales forecasting and development of sales-support collateral.
- Handled customer relations and business correspondence for KQDD's General Manager.

WORK HISTORY

1996-pres.	**Arundel Corporation**, Seattle, WA, *Assistant to the President & CEO*
1994-96	**Wide Road Sporting Goods**, Seattle, WA, *Executive Office Assistant*
1993-94	**Hyatt Regency, American Airlines**, Seattle, WA, *Contractual Sales Administrator*
1989-92	**KQDD-TV**, Seattle, WA, *Assistant to the General Manager*
1987-89	**Clydesdale Travel**, Seattle, WA, *Sales Agent*

EDUCATION

B.S., Business Administration, Duke University, Durham, NC, 1986

Donald Toni's resume.

Bonus Check

There are two ways to emphasize experience from the early part of your work history:

➤ Use the functional format and prioritize achievements from the early jobs under the skill headings.

➤ Use a chronological format and list your jobs in actual chronology (instead of the typical reverse chronology), bringing the earlier jobs to the top of the list.

Best Foot Forward

Rex Robinson's career in financial services was running full-speed ahead until he landed his current job. After giving it a good try, he had to admit that it just wasn't working out, so he decided to look for another position in the same field.

Job–Hunt Hint

The functional resume can be a great relief if you feel embarrassed about your current or last position, because you can tuck that job title away in the Work History section at the bottom of the resume and emphasize the jobs you're proud of.

His functional resume allowed him to list his current position in the Work History section without saying anything more about it. He then spotlighted his best jobs by writing achievement statements under relevant skill headings in the body of his resume. In this clever way, his resume made him look like a star performer without drawing attention to his less desirable position.

If you're currently stuck in a job you hate and don't want to highlight it on your resume, don't use the chronological format. Instead, create a functional resume where you can quietly mention your current job title and company in the Work History, while highlighting achievements from other positions under skill headings in the body of the resume.

Into the Real World

Sean Rosen's functional resume (following) is a great example of how a student can present his limited experience to an employer. By creating relevant skill headings, Sean announced what he could do as a graphic designer (his job-objective). By stating "concurrent with education" in his Work History heading, he explained that he's an industrious fellow who worked his way through school. And the potential employer could pick up on this information before reading any of the small print!

If you're a student, don't worry that your resume is going to be a blank page—the functional format enables you to draw on your school activities, internships, volunteerism, and other unpaid experience.

REX T. ROBINSON

001 Tremont Street • Casper, WY 12345 • **(123) 123-1234**

OBJECTIVE: A Senior Management position in a credit union with responsibilities in branch administration and lending

HIGHLIGHTS OF QUALIFICATIONS

- 15 years experience in financial environments, including mortgage and consumer lending.
- Successfully turned around two credit union operations and three bank branches.
- Continuously achieved designated profitability and market share growth goals.
- "A strong community leader and team member" — Former Mayor of Casper.

PROFESSIONAL ACHIEVEMENTS

MANAGEMENT
- Managed Maplewood Savings' new branch in Casper, turning a deficit of $93,000 to a profit of $450,000 and increasing loan base by $8.3M and deposits by $4.6M.
- Administered all aspects of daily operations at Union Credit.
- Projected Maplewood's budgets for staffing, loan demands, and deposit growth.
- Developed a reporting system to keep Union's senior management abreast of achievements.
- Motivated staff at each institution to extend their best effort in meeting customers' expectations.

LENDING
- Managed loan portfolios of up to $55M at First Interstate.
- Hired, trained, and supervised staff of up to 25 in credit analysis, presentations, lending regulations, and product development and marketing at Maplewood Savings.
- Utilized lending expertise in real estate (secondary market sales/servicing), consumer lending, and VISA credit and debit cards to achieve Union's profitability and market share growth.

WORK HISTORY

1999-Present	**Senior Branch Manager**	Maritime Credit Union, Casper, WY
1994-99	**Vice President/Manager**	Maplewood Savings, Casper, WY
1990-94	**Senior Development Lender**	Union Credit, Casper, WY
1989-90	**Business Development Lender**	First Interstate Bank, Orinda, CA
1987-89	**Commercial Loan Officer**	Bank of America, Oakland, CA
1985-87	**Commercial Loan Officer**	Wells Fargo Bank, Lafayette, CA

SPECIALIZED TRAINING AND EDUCATION

Certificates:	Maplewood Savings: • Management Training Program • Consumer Lending
AIB Training:	• Beginning & Advanced Financial Statement Analysis • Tax Return Analysis
Seminars:	• Negotiating Skills • Communication • Bank Management • Quality Control
B.A./A.B.	University of California, Los Angeles, CA, 1985

Rex Robinson's resume.

Sean M. Rosen

001 Fillmore Street • San Francisco, CA 12345 • (123) 123-2345

Objective	Graphic Designer
Summary	• Experienced with design concepts for packaging, advertising, and corporate communications.
	• Photographer with skills in evaluating prints for reproduction.
	• Familiar with print preparation and production.
	• Understanding of video shooting and editing for television.

• Experienced in: Photoshop   FreeHand   Illustrator
                   Quark Xpress   PageMaker   FileMaker Pro
                   Persuasion   MS Word

Experience

GRAPHIC DESIGN
• Created consumer packaging using PMS and four-color processing; prepared designs for photo shoots.
• Produced ad campaign strategies for a variety of products and services.
    - Designed thumbnails, roughs, and final comps for print advertising.
    - Wrote copy for television and print media.
• Communicated corporate identity through design of logo and collateral.
• Created mechanicals; proofed blue lines and color keys.
• Used a wide range of typography to appeal to specific audiences.

PHOTOGRAPHY
• Photographed fashion and food compositions in studio settings.
• Developed portfolio of color landscape prints from across the U.S.
• Exhibited photos in two Bay Area locations.
• Won award in black and white community photo contest.
• Black and white darkroom and other technical experience.

**Relevant
Work History**
(Concurrent with
Education)

1997-present **Freelance Computer Graphic Designer/Writer**
            San Francisco, CA
1995-97   **Marketing & Graphics Assistant**
            Smith & Co., San Francisco, CA

Education

B.F.A., Graphic Design & Marketing, anticipated Spring 2001
San Francisco Art Institute, San Francisco, CA

Marketing Program, summer 1997
Emory University, Atlanta, GA

— Portfolio Available —

Sean Rosen's resume.

Bonus Check

More new graduates use functional resumes than chronological resumes. That's because functional resumes increase the perceived value of unpaid experiences by spotlighting them in the body of the resume.

Career Casualty

A gap in work history is a red flag for employers, and could get your resume tossed. Fill all gaps in employment in your Work History section. (Turn to Chapter 8, "Step Three: Been There, Done That," for lots of ideas on how to do that.)

Fill in the Gap

Frank Jacoby had a very complicated work history with lots of job-hopping and gaps in employment. To smooth things over, he used a functional format that concentrated on the skills he brought to the table rather than his work history. He then grouped his positions near the end of his page, placed the dates to the far right so they wouldn't be easily noticed, and filled in his gaps with short-term projects and schoolwork. In the end, his functional resume made him look appropriate for a position where short project assignments were common.

This clever technique for listing short-term employment could come in handy for you if you have a tricky work history like Frank's.

Decisions, Decisions!

At this point, you need to decide which resume format you're going to use. If you know which format is best for your situation, you're ready to charge ahead. If you're teetering on the fence between the chronological and functional resumes, try creating your resume in both formats. Then see which one you think works best for you.

When you've made your choice, you're ready to follow the directions in Part 2, "Six Steps to a Perfect Resume," for creating the perfect resume, applying the six steps to the type of resume that you selected.

Bonus Check

For variations on the chronological and functional resumes, try one of the hybrid formats mentioned in Part 3, "So You Need a Special Resume."

Frank Jacoby

001 Alamo Avenue • Salt Lake City, UT 12345 • (123) 123-1234 • fj@thenet.net

JOB OBJECTIVE: A position in Video Production with focus on Editing, Research, and Writing

SUMMARY OF QUALIFICATIONS

- More than 15 years as an editor in documentary film and television, including four years with CBS's *60 Minutes*.
- Ability to create interesting visuals to demonstrate concepts.
- Experienced researcher and interviewer for production projects.
- Continuing professional development in video and multimedia technology.

PROFESSIONAL EXPERIENCE

EDITING

- As Editor for *60 Minutes*, worked with producers and writers to meet deadlines for weekly shows. Emmy Award-winning segments: "Wall Street" and "Farewell to China."
- Edited PBS documentaries on controversial topics such as the accident at Love Canal and the arms race.
- Completed editing projects for corporate clients including Kellogg, Xerox, and Mazda.

RESEARCH AND WRITING

- For several documentary assignments, located archival footage, conducted historical research, interviewed subjects, and wrote evaluations.
- As Coordinating Editor for the "60 Minutes Retrospective," an hour-long special, retrieved 35-50 hours of footage and coordinated distribution to editing teams.
- Performed library research, compiled relevant information, and wrote summaries as a paralegal in a corporate law firm.

WORK HISTORY

Paralegal	Parsons, Fitch, Jones & Birmingham, Salt Lake City, 1995-present
Student	Film Arts Foundation, Salt Lake City, 1993-1995
Editor	Cable TV-27, Consumer Reports Documentary, New York City, 1992-1993
Editor	CBS, *60 Minutes*, New York City, 1988-1992
Asst. Editor	Bill Moyers' Journal, New York City, 1986-1988
Sound Editor	ABC, *20/20*, New York City, 1984-1986
Editor	German Television, Mediafilm, New York City, 1983-1984
Asst. Editor	WGBH Documentary, Boston, 1983
Sound Editor	Telefly (TV commercials), Boston, 1982-1983

EDUCATION

B.F.A., New York University, Institute of Film and Television, New York City
Continuing Professional Development:
Non-Linear Editing/AVID, Video Coalition, Salt Lake City
Video Editing and Interactive Multimedia, Film Arts Foundation, Salt Lake City

—Resume reel available—

Frank Jacoby's resume.

The Least You Need to Know

➤ A functional resume frames your experience according to skills rather than job titles.

➤ The functional format is more widely accepted than it used to be, because job and career changes are more common.

➤ A functional resume allows you to prioritize your achievements according to impact rather than chronology.

➤ Use a functional resume if you are changing careers or reentering the work force after a time of unemployment.

➤ Consider choosing the functional resume if you are a new graduate and have little paid experience in the field of your objective.

Part 2

Six Steps to a Perfect Resume

Picture Christopher Columbus standing at the bow of his ship looking out at the horizon, about to embark upon his famous voyage of 1492. Not knowing how vast the Atlantic Ocean was or exactly what he was getting into, he probably had a major anxiety attack, which is a normal response to a seemingly impossible task. To keep his sanity, he must have taken this monumental trip one knot at a time until he finally spotted land some 34 days after setting sail.

Like Columbus, you're probably feeling a little overwhelmed as you set out to put your life on paper. Most job seekers feel this way. To keep your stress level down and help you reach your destination (getting a perfect job) as quickly as possible, I've divided the process into manageable pieces, which I talk about in this part of the book.

Turn the page and read about the first of six steps for writing your resume. Set aside about three hours (that's an average length of time to write a resume if all goes smoothly). Follow each step, and, like Columbus, you'll reach land. If you get stuck on one step, don't worry about it—just go on to the next step and come back to the hard one later. (Hopefully it won't take you 34 days!)

Chapter 6

Step One: Heading Your Way

In This Chapter

➤ Designing a heading that makes your name stand out

➤ Including the right contact information

➤ Writing a concise Job Objective statement to get the job you want

➤ Substituting a professional title for the Job Objective statement

---

When you introduce yourself at a social, business, or networking event, your name is frequently a springboard for conversation. It's the thing you most want people to remember, because it's what they'll use to find you again. For that reason, clever folks say their name clearly and, if possible, make it stand out. (I often say, "Susan Ireland, like the country.")

The same principle applies to your resume: You want your name to stand out, and you want to tell the reader what kind of job you're looking for. Whether you're writing a chronological or functional resume, the guidelines in this chapter for creating the Heading and Job Objective sections apply.

Look Who's Talking

The Heading section of a resume appears at the top of the page, as highlighted in the following template. The heading includes your name and contact information.

(Resume Heading)

Name
Street
City, State Zip
Phone, Fax, E-mail

JOB OBJECTIVE

The job you want next

SUMMARY OF QUALIFICATIONS

- How much experience you have in the field of your job objective, in a related field, or using the skills required for your new position.
- An overall career accomplishment that shows you'd be good at this job.
- What someone would say about you as a recommendation.

PROFESSIONAL EXPERIENCE

19xx-pres. **Company Name, City, State**
Job Title
- An accomplishment you are proud of that shows you're good at this profession.
- A problem you solved and the results.
- A time when you positively affected the organization, the bottom line, your boss, your co-workers, your clients.
- Awards, commendations, publications, etc., you achieved that relate to your job objective.

19xx-xx **Company Name, City, State**
Job Title
- A project you are proud of that supports your job objective.
- Another accomplishment that shows you're good at this line of work.
- Quantifiable results that point out your skill.

19xx-xx **Company Name, City, State**
Job Title
- An accomplishment you are proud of that shows you will be valued by your next employer.
- An occasion when someone "sat up and took notice" of your skill.

EDUCATION

Degree, Major (if relevant), 19xx (optional)
University, City, State

The Heading section of the resume.

You've been putting your name at the tops of papers since you learned how to write in first grade. It's so automatic you probably just plop it there without thinking. Before you do that on your resume, read on for some tips on how to make your name and other contact information stand out.

What's in a Name?

You may have a non-gender-specific first name (such as Chris, Pat, or Robin) and want to know if there are some tricks to hint at whether you're male or female. There are, but before you let your secret out, be sure that you want the employer to know. The following two scenarios may help you decide whether you want to keep your gender a mystery.

Giving a Clear Signal

In some cases, it's to the job seeker's advantage for the employer to know the applicant's sex. For instance, Robin Harris (a man) knew that even though sex discrimination is illegal in the job-placement process, the company for whom he wanted to work gave its most productive sales territories to men. Therefore, he wanted the employer to know right off that he was a man, because that would put him ahead of all the women candidates in the stack of resumes.

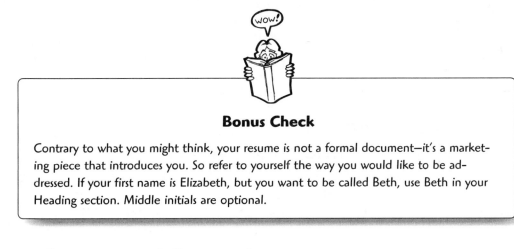

Bonus Check

Contrary to what you might think, your resume is not a formal document—it's a marketing piece that introduces you. So refer to yourself the way you would like to be addressed. If your first name is Elizabeth, but you want to be called Beth, use Beth in your Heading section. Middle initials are optional.

Here are a few ways you can clarify your gender on paper:

➤ Use a gender-specific nickname instead of your given name (for example, Rob Harris instead of Robin Harris).

➤ Include a middle name if it's clearly male or female (for example, Robin Frank Harris).

➤ Start your name with Mr. or Ms. (for example, Mr. Robin Harris).

If you're considering this last option, think twice. This technique is seldom used and looks somewhat awkward. However, if you're applying within the United States and have an unusual or non-American name that probably won't be recognized as male or female no matter what you do to it, the Mr. or Ms. technique would work.

Keep 'Em Guessing

Now let's look at a situation where it might not be to the job hunter's advantage for his or her gender to be known. Terry Hoover (a woman) was after the same job that Robin (in the last scenario) wanted. In order to be considered for the job, she chose not to add anything to her name—she simply put Terry Hoover on her resume, knowing the employer would have to guess whether she was a man or a woman until Terry met the employer in person. At that point, she'd be at the interview and able to sell herself as a fully qualified candidate.

Showing Off Credentials

If you have a degree or credential that indicates your profession, you could put the initials of your degree or credential next to your name in the Heading section. For example, Francine Wilks was going for a position as a CPA in an accounting firm where her credential was extremely important to the job. She showed it off nicely by placing it in her heading.

Warren Samuels wanted the reader of his resume to immediately see that he's a physician. He got the message across quickly by placing his degree next to his name in the Heading section of his resume.

Job seekers respond differently to seeing their credential or degree letters next to their names. Some folks like the look of it; others aren't at all comfortable having them there. It's entirely up to you; do what feels appropriate for your field and personality.

Home Sweet Home

Putting your street address in your heading is preferable to listing a P.O. box number, because a home address conjures up a more stable image. If, however, you have a specific reason not to give out your street address, it's acceptable to use a post-office address.

Career Casualty

If you have a second resume page, you must put a mini-heading at the top of that page, composed of your name and the page number. Otherwise the second page might get lost if the two are separated. Your name on page two should match the print of your name on page one, and may be the same point size or a little smaller.

Job-Hunt Hint

Place your name in the top middle or the upper-right corner of the page. Why? After your resume is read, it will probably go into a filing cabinet with the left-hand side of the paper placed against the spine of a folder. Your name will be noticed easily if it's in the top middle or in the upper-right corner of the page.

Francine Wilks, CPA

123 Linden Place • Tempe, AZ 12345 • (123) 123-1234

Francine Wilks's Heading section.

Following are some examples of addresses in headings. Patricia Ferrari used her home address in her Heading section. Juanita Cuellar didn't feel comfortable giving out her street address, so she chose to use her P.O. box number in her Heading. Both Headings are permissible, but Patricia's address made her look a little more stable than Juanita.

Bonus Check

Make the font size of the letters of your credential one or two point sizes smaller if you place them immediately after your name. In this way, they maintain importance without graphically overpowering your name.

Warren Samuels, M.D.

123 Franklin Avenue, #2, St. Paul, MN 12345   **(123) 123-1234**

Warren Samuels's Heading section.

Patricia Ferrari

123 Rippling Rock Avenue
Memphis, TN 12345
(123) 123-1234

Patricia Ferrari's Heading section.

Juanita Cuellar
P.O. Box 123 , Charlotte, NC 12345-1123
(123) 123-1234

Juanita Cuellar's Heading section.

Job-Hunt Hint

Consider incorporating a horizontal line or shaded bar into the design of your heading to set it apart from the rest of the resume. Browse through the sample resumes in the other chapters and Appendix B, "Portfolio of Sample Resumes," to get ideas, or come up with your own creative approach. All of the resumes in this book were created in MS Word, using techniques you can learn from the program's Help menu.

Career Casualty

Don't go overboard by listing every contact number you have (home, office, cell, and pager). Give only the one or two needed to reach you or to leave a message.

I Got Your Number

Your phone number is critical in your resume heading because your first contact from an employer will probably be by phone. Depending on your situation, you may want to list one or two phone numbers. By putting a phone number on your resume, you automatically give your potential employer permission to do the following:

➤ Call that number

➤ Leave a message about your job search

➤ Expect you to speak freely if you pick up the phone

Be sure you're okay with all three of these assumptions for each phone number in your heading. Following are a few cases in point.

Gretchin Hendley didn't want any job-search phone calls at her place of work, so in her heading, she listed only her home number where she had an answering machine that she could check from work. Larry Picasso, on the other hand, was being laid off, and everyone in his department was aware that he was looking for a new job. Therefore, it made perfect sense for him to list his office phone number in his heading, because he could receive messages and speak freely about his job search during business hours.

If you list only one phone number in your heading (as Gretchin did in the previous example), it will be assumed that it's your home or personal line. If you give more than one phone number, you need to indicate the difference between them (as Larry did in the second example).

That's the Fax

The fax rule of thumb: Don't list a fax number in your heading unless you're sending your resume to a recruiter. Recruiters frequently fax job postings and related information to job candidates, so they appreciate having the fax numbers readily available. Melissa Groden was sending her resume to a recruiter, so she included her fax number in the heading of her resume (following).

Gretchin Hendley
123 Greenboro Lane • Harristown, VA 12345 • (123) 123-1234

Gretchin Hendley's Heading section.

Larry Picasso
1234 Fountine Blvd. • Denver, CO 12345
Office: (123) 123-1234 • Home: (123) 123-1235

Larry Picasso's Heading section.

Melissa Groden

123 Beachwood Street, #2, New Orleans, LA 12345
Phone: 123-123-1234, Fax: 123-123-4321

Melissa Groden's Heading section.

Employers, on the other hand, hardly ever fax a response to a job applicant, so putting a fax number on a resume you're sending directly to a company is a waste of valuable space.

E-Mail Giveaway

Listing your e-mail address (if you have one) in the Heading section is beneficial, providing that it can do two things:

➤ Expedite the employer's response

➤ Demonstrate that you're online savvy (a plus when applying for certain positions)

If either of these points applies to you, by all means put your e-mail address in your heading.

Because Alice Friend was applying to a high-tech firm, she put her e-mail address on her resume, proving she's comfortable online.

Job-Hunt Hint

If you list your fax number, introduce it with *Fax:* so that your potential employer can distinguish it from your phone number.

Bonus Check

Yahoo! and other online services offer free e-mail accounts with local access around the world. If you don't already have a personal e-mail account, consider getting one of these freebies for your job search.

Alice Friend
1234 Fruit Tree Blvd.
Omaha, NE 12345
(123) 123-1234
alice_friend@ibm.net

Job Objective: Software Engineer

Alice Friend's Heading section.

Deborah Lord
1234 Moody Beach Lane
Mobile, AL 12345
(123) 123-1234
DDLord@eco.net

Job Objective: Volunteer Coordinator

Deborah Lord's Heading section.

Career Casualty

Avoid listing your work e-mail address on your resume, because doing so would send your prospective employer the message that you use company resources for personal pursuits—in this case, your job hunt. Instead, fork out the dough for a personal e-mail account (if you don't already have one) and put that address in the Heading section.

Deborah Lord's research found that the small nonprofit where she was applying was planning to establish a presence on the Internet. Therefore, she put her e-mail address on her resume to suggest that she could help them out with that process.

Hot URLs

URLs (Web site addresses) are not commonly found in headings for two reasons:

1. Most people don't have a personal Web site (and most people don't need one for their job search).
2. Personal Web sites often contain private information and other stuff a potential employer shouldn't see.

However, if you're in Web site development, multimedia, or any field where your image might be enhanced because you have a spiffy personal Web site, put your URL in your heading along with your other contact information.

Dawson Peroni, for instance, was applying for assignments as a Web game developer. Because his personal Web site had links to some of his projects, he included his URL in his resume's heading.

Dawson Peroni

1234 Highland Ave.
Santa Fe, NM 12345

(123) 123-1234
d_peroni@cool.net
http://www.dawsonp.com

Job Objective: Web-game developer

Dawson Peroni's Heading section.

Be Careful What You Ask For

Now that you've created a Heading section that tells the employer who your are, it's time to write a Job Objective statement that says what you want.

Whether you're a world traveler or a job seeker, it's important to know where you're going in order to get there. (At least Columbus thought he knew where he was going when he set sail.) And when asking for help in getting there, you need to tell the guide where you're headed.

On your resume, this destination is shown through the *Job Objective* that appears just below your Heading. The highlighted section of the following resume template shows where your Job Objective should be placed. (To learn about alternatives to having a Job Objective section on your resume, see "Breaking the Rules" later in this chapter.)

Career Casualty

Don't clutter up your heading with unnecessary stuff. When writing your e-mail or Web address in your heading, there's no need to prefix the addresses with *E-mail:* or *Web address:* because most readers know that an e-mail address contains an @ sign and URLs have *http://www* in them.

The Weight of a Job Objective

By starting your resume with a statement of your Job Objective, you immediately tell your potential employer:

➤ What position you're looking for.

➤ Who needs to get your resume. A human resources clerk will probably be the first person to see your resume. Your Job Objective statement will indicate to that clerk which hiring person should receive your resume.

➤ How to interpret your resume. Your Job Objective statement tells the reader, "Everything that follows is relevant to this position." That's an important point to make, because this is a marketing piece, not your life history!

In short, a Job Objective statement makes it easier for a potential employer to understand what you have to say in your resume.

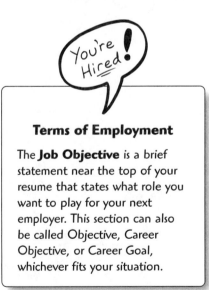

Terms of Employment

The **Job Objective** is a brief statement near the top of your resume that states what role you want to play for your next employer. This section can also be called Objective, Career Objective, or Career Goal, whichever fits your situation.

(Job-Objective Section)

Name
Street
City, State Zip
Phone, Fax, E-mail

JOB OBJECTIVE

The job you want next

SUMMARY OF QUALIFICATIONS

- How much experience you have in the field of your job objective, in a related field, or using the skills required for your new position.

- An overall career accomplishment that shows you'd be good at this job.

- What someone would say about you as a recommendation.

PROFESSIONAL EXPERIENCE

19xx-pres.   **Company Name, City, State**
Job Title

- An accomplishment you are proud of that shows you're good at this profession.

- A problem you solved and the results.

- A time when you positively affected the organization, the bottom line, your boss, your co-workers, your clients.

- Awards, commendations, publications, etc., you achieved that relate to your job objective.

19xx-xx   **Company Name, City, State**
Job Title

- A project you are proud of that supports your job objective.

- Another accomplishment that shows you're good at this line of work.

- Quantifiable results that point out your skill.

19xx-xx   **Company Name, City, State**
Job Title

- An accomplishment you are proud of that shows you will be valued by your next employer.

- An occasion when someone "sat up and took notice" of your skill.

EDUCATION

Degree, Major (if relevant), 19xx (optional)
University, City, State

The Job Objective section of the resume.

Wording with an Objective

I've said it before, and I'll say it again: Less is more! You need to say everything as concisely as possible, starting with your Job Objective statement.

Putting your Job Objective statement near the top of your resume is the clearest way to tell the reader what you want for your immediate future.

Some resumes have flowery opening statements with job objectives buried deep inside them. They use phrases like "challenging position," "room for advancement," and "opportunity to grow." Give the reader of your resume a break—cut out all the fluff because it doesn't say much anyway. Stick to what's important:

➤ The job title you'd like next, if you know it (for example, Manager or Sales Representative).

➤ The area of work you want to be in (for example, Marketing or Sales). On rare occasions, this might include an area of specialization (for example, "with an emphasis on new business development" or "focusing on graphic design").

Take a look at the following examples:

Not so good: A challenging position that will utilize my skills and experience as Director of Marketing

Yawn! Everyone wants to be challenged, and of course you'll be using your skills and experience.

Much better: Director of Marketing

Not so good: An administrative position in a growth-oriented company where I can use my background in finance to promote the firm

This statement sounds like you're judging the company's ability to provide for your future.

Much better: Administrative position with a focus on finance

Not so good: A position as Associate Field Producer in TV Programming that offers room for advancement and high rewards

Bad idea! It sounds like you want the job of the person reading the resume!

Much better: Associate Field Producer, TV Programming

Want to see this concept at work? Review the concise Job Objective statements in the following resumes.

Job-Hunt Hint

If you're a professional consultant with a Web site about your services, be sure to include your site's URL in your resume heading.

Career Casualty

A resume without a Job Objective effectively says, "This is what I've done. Could you figure out what I should do next?" That's a weak approach! A Job Objective gives your resume focus and strength and makes a powerful first move toward title and salary negotiations.

Career Casualty

Don't include "entry-level" in your Job Objective statement. Why tell the reader you want the lowest job? Leave it out, and you may be given a position that's a little higher up the food chain.

Job-Hunt Hint

Keep your objective statement simple and, if necessary, use graphic goodies such as indents, bold, bullets, dashes, and columns to make it readable in just a few seconds.

Straight as an Arrow

Jack Kraus knew exactly what position he was going after at the university, so he listed the precise title that was in the job posting he was responding to in his Job Objective. His concise statement had no frills—it went straight to the point and didn't waste the reader's time.

If you know the exact title of the job you're applying for, by all means use that as your Job Objective. Doing this leaves no doubt as to what position you want. If you later apply for a job with a slightly different job title, you can always change your Job Objective to match.

Spreading Your Umbrella

Like an umbrella, David Goldstein's Job Objective covered a number of things: his prospective job title and his three areas of expertise. By creating a column with eye-catching bullet points, he suggested to the employer several ways he could fit into the organization. Smart guy!

The Job Objective approach that David used is a good one for professionals such as

➤ Consultants who offer several services.

➤ Generalists who want to show off their special skills.

➤ Administrators who need to say they can wear several hats.

➤ Technical folks who have expertise in a number of areas.

Do you fall into one of these categories? If so, you might benefit from the umbrella technique David used.

Bonus Check

Challenge yourself to write your Job Objective in 10 words or less. (Of course, the employer won't count, so it's OK to exceed 10 words if you have to.) Give yourself a bonus check if you can narrow it down to just a few words.

Jack Kraus

123 Godfrey Avenue, #2, Philadelphia, PA 12345   **(123) 123-1234**

JOB OBJECTIVE

Student Affairs Officer II, Housing & Dining Services: Residential Programs

SUMMARY OF QUALIFICATIONS

- 19 years as a professional educator with strengths in program development and administration.
- Enthusiastic team leader and outstanding communicator, both one-to-one and before groups.
- Creative in solving problems and maximizing resources. Computer literate.

EDUCATION

M.A., Educational Administration,Temple University, Philadelphia, PA, 1990

B.A., History, St. John's College, Santa Fe, NM 1980

RELEVANT ACCOMPLISHMENTS

PROGRAM ADMINISTRATION

Philadelphia Unified School District
- Developed new educational programs including:
    - Tutoring program for ESL students that achieved highest recommendations.
    - "Future System" curricula, a hands-on approach that included a computer lab.
    - $12,000 ham radio station project for high-achieving students.

- As Teacher-in-Charge, supervised 45 teachers in principal's absence and assisted in administrative decision-making and program development.

- Chaired ESL Advisory Committee comprised of parents, administrators, and teachers, that served as a forum for student issues.

TEACHING

Church Street School
- Currently teach basic college courses (English, history, and writing) to students, ages 18-50 and from diverse educational and cultural backgrounds.

- Tutor and advise students regarding study skills and career development.

Philadelphia Unified School District
- Instructed adults in basic education skills, GED preparation, and ESL, in addition to holding a full-time elementary teaching position.

TXN Newsroom Guest Speaker
- Delivered presentations to school groups and cable companies on new technologies in the classroom.

WORK HISTORY

1998-present	Instructor	Church Street School, Philadelphia, CA
1996-1998	Guest Speaker	TXN Newsroom, Philadelphia, PA
1980-1998	Educator	Philadelphia Unified School District, Philadelphia, PA

Jack Kraus's resume.

David Goldstein

001 Lincoln Avenue • West Hollywood, CA 12345 • **(123) 123-1234**

OBJECTIVE: Sales Trainer in the areas of: Interpersonal Communication
Sales Techniques
Product Knowledge

SUMMARY OF QUALIFICATIONS
- 15 years as a successful sales professional.
- Experienced at teaching others how to improve interpersonal communication.
- Skilled at training sales associates in proven sales techniques.
- Ability to develop presentation and training materials.

PROFESSIONAL ACCOMPLISHMENTS
TRAINING

Jewel Junction
- Trained 24+ franchisees regarding: Product knowledge Projected trends
                                       Merchandising   Proven selling techniques
- Trained City Center sales staff including 23 associates and one assistant manager.
- Led staff meetings to introduce lines and instill respect and enthusiasm for products.
- Served on the product development committee charged with determining seasonal merchandise and promotions.
- Diffused numerous conflicts among sales staff through group and individual counseling.
- Designed employee incentive program that rewarded improved performance.

Clearwater, Inc.
- Trained sales staff in numerous department stores nationwide for short-term promotional sales of Clearwater accessories.

SALES

- Consistently ranked among the highest in sales at Jewel Junction, using strong presentation skills to sell luxury items in a slow economy.
- Commended for achieving above average sales and for developing strong rapport with customers at Grove Jewelry Distributors.
- Exceeded sales record 20% in a ten-state, 20-store region of Clearwater, Inc.

WORK HISTORY
1997-present	Merchandising Manager, Jewel Junction, Inglewood, CA
1995-1996	Customer Service/Sales Associate, Grove Jewelry Distributors, Long Beach, CA
1992-1994	Sales Associate, Beemans (department store), Miami Beach, FL
1991	Promotional Representative, Clearwater, Inc., Santa Monica, CA
1985-1990	Sales Representative, Frost's Fifth Avenue, Hollywood, CA

EDUCATION
Liberal Arts, Quincy College, Key West, FL
Professional development courses: Interpersonal Communications
Sales Training
Product Knowledge and Presentation

David Goldstein's resume.

Breaking the Rules

Now that you've learned the rule of having a Job Objective statement, I'm going to tell you about a technique that breaks, or at least bends, that rule.

If you're continuing in a profession in which you have substantial experience, consider putting your professional title next to your name or near the top of your resume. This can be a stronger approach than using a Job Objective statement. A title effectively says, "This is what my profession is." A Job Objective statement says, "This is what I want to be." If you have enough experience to give yourself a title, it can be a more forceful introduction.

Using your professional title instead of a Job Objective statement can do the following:

➤ Give you an edge on your competition by presenting you as an established professional in your field.

➤ Set a strong foundation for title and salary negotiations.

Look at the resumes that follow. Do you see how the professional-title technique makes each job seeker look accomplished in his or her career?

Terms of Employment

Your **professional title** could be an official job title you've held or simply the professional role you're qualified to fill. For instance, a resume writer (such as myself) could use any of the following professional titles at the top of her resume:

Resume Writer

Resume Consultant

Career Counselor

Career Development Professional

She would choose her professional title based on what type of work she was looking for.

Titles That Talk Big

Robert McFarland had been a construction-dispute consultant for a number of years and was using his resume to move to another consulting firm. By placing his *professional title* immediately under his heading, he established himself as someone grounded in his field. This assertive approach not only won him an interview, but it also paid off big when he negotiated his salary.

Do you have a professional title that would tell the employer which role you want to play in his organization? If so, consider using it on your resume instead of a Job Objective statement.

Heading Within a Heading

In her resume heading, Katrina Lambros inserted her professional title right under her name. Notice how confident Katrina looked with her title up top and stunning achievement statements in the body of her resume. Her whole presentation made her look like the type of salesperson the employer wanted on his team!

Whether your professional title is incorporated into your heading or positioned immediately under your heading, it's bound to stand out and impress a potential employer.

Robert McFarland

123 Middlesex Street • Wethersfield, CT 12345 • (123) 123-1234

Construction Dispute Consultant

HIGHLIGHTS OF QUALIFICATIONS

- 16 years as construction consultant and owner of mid-sized construction firm.
- Extensive experience in woodframe construction.
- Skilled at resolving contract disputes.

RELEVANT EXPERIENCE

CONSTRUCTION BUSINESS MANAGEMENT

- Built a prominent construction business that grew from 0 to 250 employees and from annual gross of $25K to $9M in six years.
- Managed approximately 300 construction projects including:
  New commercial buildings
  Commercial tenant improvement
  New and remodel residential work
  Structural rehabs
- Oversaw 500,000 sq. ft. per year wood framing operation.

PROBLEM RESOLUTION

- Successfully negotiated numerous contract and labor disputes, initiating compromises that led to resolutions of up to $125K.
- Collaborated with architects and owners to create most cost-effective designs on projects up to $2.5M in value, frequently requiring resolution of competing interests.
- Continually generated technical and interpersonal solutions that met tight budget and time constraints.

PRESENTATIONS

- Wrote hundreds of analyses for construction projects, focusing on financial, safety, and time issues.
- As guest lecturer at local community college, spoke on resource efficient construction.

WORK HISTORY

1997-present	Construction Consultant /Contractor, Cosgrove Contractors, Hartford, CT
1987-1997	President/Operations Manager, Golly Co., West Hartford, CT
1981-1987	General Contractor, Ruby Builders Construction, Hartford, CT

EDUCATION

B.A., Religious Studies, Springfield College, Springfield, MA

Robert McFarland's resume.

Katrina Lambros
International Sales Representative / Sales Manager

001 Glyndon Avenue • Pikesville, Maryland 12345 • (123) 123-1234

SUMMARY OF QUALIFICATIONS

- 12 years successful direct sales and sales management career in corporate culture.
- Courageous selling style that results in: Win-win gains for client and company
  Achievement of unlikely sales
  Reversal of lost sales
- Skilled at closing sales through ingenious and spontaneous "packaging" of products.

PROFESSIONAL ACCOMPLISHMENTS (at VM Tech)

Personal Quota Attainment
- Consistently attained top national rankings out of 110 managers:
  - 125-150% of quota, five out of six years   - #2 Sales Manager
  - #1 Female Sales Manager   - #3 Sales Manager
- Won annual awards including "Top Systems Sales Performer."
- Ranked #1 out of 475 sales representatives.
- Exceeded annual quota 125% the first year, with no previous sales experience.

Selected Achievements
- As an outsider in an established market, closed a $150,000 sale of a newly launched product.
- Increased business substantially with a major client and exceeded average monthly sales quotas by 43%.
- As District Manager, increased sales force productivity by 25%.
- Introduced training to develop each salesperson's abilities in proven sales techniques.

Promotions
- One of eight women nation-wide promoted to District Manager.
- Promoted to Sales Manager out of field of 17 candidates.
- Advanced to Manager, Key Accounts due to mastery of technical system selling.
- Out of 723 Sales Representatives, chosen as coach for training center.

WORK HISTORY

2000	RENWICK INC., Baltimore, MD	Organizational Consultant
1999	PHONE SERVICE SYSTEMS, Washington, DC	Sales & Marketing Consultant
1987-1998	VM TECH, Bethesda, MD	District Manager (1996-1998)
		Sales Manager (1990-1996)
		Manager, Key Accounts (1988-1989)
		Sales Representative (1987)

EDUCATION
B.S., Psychology, 1986, Catholic University of America, Washington, DC

Katrina Lambros's resume.

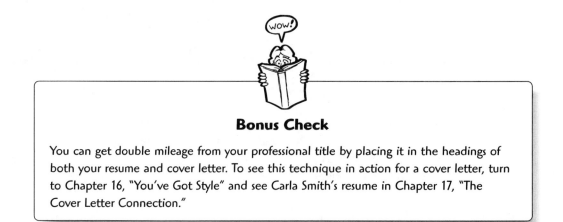

Bonus Check

You can get double mileage from your professional title by placing it in the headings of both your resume and cover letter. To see this technique in action for a cover letter, turn to Chapter 16, "You've Got Style" and see Carla Smith's resume in Chapter 17, "The Cover Letter Connection."

Go for It

Ready to commit your thoughts to paper? Good. Use this worksheet to write your contact information for the Heading section of your resume. Then insert a concise Job Objective statement or professional title, using the creative approaches discussed in this chapter.

Resume Heading and Job Objective Sections

Name: _____

Address:_____

City, state, and zip: _____

Phone number(s): _____

Fax number (only if applying to a recruiter): _____

E-mail address (optional): _____

URL (optional): _____

Job Objective statement:

Professional title (if not using Job Objective): _____

Having done that, you can pat yourself on the back for completing the first step in writing your resume.

The Least You Need to Know

➤ When designing your resume Heading section, place your name in the center or on the right-hand side of the page.

➤ Create a stable image by providing a street address instead of a P.O. box number.

➤ List only those phone numbers where employers can leave messages and where you can speak freely.

➤ Include your e-mail address if you think it will impress your potential employer or be relevant to the job.

➤ Keep your Job Objective concise and to the point.

➤ Instead of using a Job Objective statement, you can use a professional title.

Chapter 7

Step Two: Knock 'Em Off Their Feet

In This Chapter

➤ Starting off your resume with a strong kick with your Summary of Qualifications

➤ Avoiding resume clichés that put the employer to sleep

➤ Facilitating a smooth career change with effective phrases

➤ Creating a mini-resume with your Heading, Job Objective, and Summary of Qualifications

---

Experienced players in the marketing game know it's important to create a splash right away in a promotional piece. The way to do that on your resume is to give top billing to qualifications that will knock the employer off her feet. In this chapter, you'll learn how to choose and compose opening statements that will draw in employers and make them start itching to call you.

Right from the Start

Kick off your resume with a *Summary of Qualifications* section. This section is a list of the top three or four reasons you're qualified for the job you're seeking. The following resume template shows where the Summary of Qualifications section appears on the resume.

(Summary of Qualifications Section)

Name
Street
City, State Zip
Phone, Fax, E-mail

JOB OBJECTIVE

The job you want next

SUMMARY OF QUALIFICATIONS

- How much experience you have in the field of your job objective, in a related field, or using the skills required for your new position.
- An overall career accomplishment that shows you'd be good at this job.
- What someone would say about you as a recommendation.

PROFESSIONAL EXPERIENCE

19xx-pres. **Company Name, City, State**
Job Title
- An accomplishment you are proud of that shows you're good at this profession.
- A problem you solved and the results.
- A time when you positively affected the organization, the bottom line, your boss, your co-workers, your clients.
- Awards, commendations, publications, etc., you achieved that relate to your job objective.

19xx-xx **Company Name, City, State**
Job Title
- A project you are proud of that supports your job objective.
- Another accomplishment that shows you're good at this line of work.
- Quantifiable results that point out your skill.

19xx-xx **Company Name, City, State**
Job Title
- An accomplishment you are proud of that shows you will be valued by your next employer.
- An occasion when someone "sat up and took notice" of your skill.

EDUCATION

Degree, Major (if relevant), 19xx (optional)
University, City, State

The Summary of Qualifications section of the resume.

For example, the opening section of Christopher Columbus's resume might have read as follows:

Summary of Qualifications

➤ First European to make verified contact with Americans since the Vikings five centuries before.

➤ Christened six Caribbean islands (whose names now signify choice vacation spots).

➤ Noted captain and navigator of four Atlantic crossings who set contemporary world sailing records.

Wouldn't you want this guy to captain your next transoceanic sailing trip?

You may not be able to tout mind-blowing achievements like Columbus, but you can look pretty terrific with three or four smashing statements that set you apart from the crowd. Talk about anything that makes you stand out in your field. That something could be any of the following:

➤ Your experience

➤ Your credentials

➤ Your expertise

➤ Your personal values

➤ Your work ethics

➤ Your background

➤ Your personality

In the Summary of Qualifications, you're free to make claims, drop names, and do your best to entice the employer to call you for an interview. Remember, all claims must be substantiated later when you write the body of your resume, so be honest while giving yourself full credit.

Say It with Style

Whatever you do in your Summary of Qualifications, don't use hackneyed phrases such as "Excellent written and oral communication skills," "Outstanding organizational abilities," "Goal-oriented individual," or other overused, vague lines.

Columbus's resume would have gotten lost in the pack if it had read as follows:

Summary of Qualifications

➤ Exceptional organizational and people skills

➤ Goal-oriented, self-motivated individual

➤ Excellent written and communication skills

Terms of Employment

The **Summary of Qualifications** section is a brief set of points that say you're qualified for your Job Objective. This section can also be called:

Highlights of Qualifications

Qualifications

Highlights

Summary

Profile

There's room to be creative in naming this section, so go for it!

Career Casualty

Don't make the employer read the entire resume to realize that you're the perfect candidate for the job. Hit a home run with stunning statements in the first few lines.

Don't get me wrong—the meanings behind most of those phrases are wonderful and may be perfectly true for you. But because these clichés appear on almost everyone's resume, they don't have punch and, frankly, are not taken seriously.

Bonus Check

Writing your Summary of Qualifications section is a great way to prepare for in-person introductions at networking events. In such quick conversations, you'll want to say the most impressive things about yourself in less than a minute. Although you don't want to recite your Summary of Qualifications verbatim, you can talk naturally about the ideas you've developed for that section.

Job-Hunt Hint

Throughout the resume, write in the first person without using pronouns. In other words, phrase your statements as though you were talking about yourself without saying *I*. For example, write "Understand the art of conflict resolution" instead of "I understand the art of conflict resolution."

Before you put a sentence in your Summary of Qualifications, ask yourself: Is it a grabber? Is it news to the reader? If it's what everyone else says, it's not news, and it won't grab the reader. It has to be said in a way that's remarkable and memorable.

Always make your point as concretely as possible. Use facts to create credibility and to instill a sense that you are unlike any other candidate applying for the job. Ask yourself the following questions:

➤ What specifically have I done that demonstrates that I have the desired quality?

➤ How do my skills translate into success at my next job?

Here are some examples of what I mean:

➤ Fred was applying for a pizza-delivery position. Because this type of employment has a high turnover rate, he felt his reliability was a marketable asset. So instead of writing "Excellent record of attendance," he wrote, "Never missed a day of work in 11 months."

➤ When Sandy was going for a customer service position, she knew the potential employer was looking for someone with excellent communication skills. She wrote, "Deemed Customer Service Rep of the Month for resolving problems diplomatically."

➤ Instead of "Goal-oriented professional," Frank wrote, "Exceeded quotas for four consecutive years," on his resume for a sales position.

For more ideas on Summary of Qualifications statements, browse through the following two resumes.

Keeping Up with the Fast Trackers

Jamie Choi designed a Summary of Qualifications section in his resume (see the following) that told his potential employer that he's experienced in his field and valued by those who work with him. Notice his clever technique of getting someone else to say he was a good employee-relations specialist: He quoted one of his former clients. His summary statements alone made the employer want to read his entire resume.

Look through your evaluation forms and letters of recommendation from former employers to see if you have a quotable quote for your resume.

On the Lines of a Career Changer

The Summary of Qualifications is one of the most important sections on a career changer's resume because it becomes a bridge between the job seeker's past and future. In his resume, Charles Humphries used just three statements to provide the following information:

➤ He had experience in the field he was moving into (even though he'd never held the job title he was going after).

➤ He had the required skills and motivation for the position.

➤ He had a technical background, which was something his competition might not have.

His Summary of Qualifications section packaged Charles as a low-risk, high-value candidate.

Job-Hunt Hint

Although the Summary of Qualifications appears at the top of the page, you may find it easier to compose after you've written the rest of your resume.

Terms of Employment

Over and **more than** are two terms that are often confused. On your resume, use **more than** to mean "in excess of." For instance, use "more than 10 years of experience" instead of "over 10 years of experience."

Bonus Check

Your Summary of Qualifications statements should so strongly paint the picture of you at your next job that there appears to be little or no transition into your new job, even if you're making a big career change.

Jamie Choi

123 Montecito Street, #1 • Santa Cruz, CA 12345 • (123) 123-1234

OBJECTIVE: Employee Relations Specialist

SUMMARY OF QUALIFICATIONS

- More than ten years as an expert in:
             Wholeness in the Workplace
             The Psychology of Work

- Skilled at assisting people from all levels of employment and cultural backgrounds.

- "You've changed my understanding of work. I now find it a dynamic and energizing principle." — Manufacturing Manager

TRAINING AND DEVELOPMENT ACCOMPLISHMENTS

1998-pres. Chrysalis, Santa Cruz, CA   **Instructor**, Wholeness in the Workplace
- Taught professionals, managers, office workers, and tradespeople from multicultural backgrounds. Topics include:

    Dealing with Stress   Concentration
    Responsibility and Commitment Organizational Skills
    Dynamics of Teamwork   Dealing with Difficult People

- Turned around a failing institutional library and, with no previous professional librarian experience, produced an efficient system within four weeks.
  - Trained volunteers.
  - Organized holdings and standardized procedures.

- Managed building renovation project, training and supervising a crew of student volunteers with no experience in construction. Finished project within time constraints.

1990-1997 MacMillan Institute, Albuquerque, NM **Trainer/Manager**
- Trained professionals, artists, tradespeople, and students in productive work habits that increased proficiency, work satisfaction, and income.

- Created a "work laboratory" that provided hands-on experience in development of:
    Teamwork   Self-Esteem
    Conflict Management Skills   Client Relations
    Dynamic Work Style   Time Management Skills

1988-1990 Center for Humanistic Studies, Santa Fe, NM **Full-time Student,** Human Development

1983-1985 Los Alamos Properties, Los Alamos, NM **Co-manager**
- Trained and supervised renovation staff working on residential projects.

EDUCATION

    M.A. equivalent, Training and Development: University of California, Santa Cruz, CA
                        Mandala Institute, Monterey, CA
                        Jungian Studies Center, Carmel, CA
                        Center for Humanistic Studies, Santa Fe, NM

Jamie Choi's resume.

Charles E. Humphries

123 Baytown Avenue • Jacinto, TX 12345 • (123) 123-1234 • c_humphries@thenet.net

JOB OBJECTIVE: Technical Sales Account Manager

SUMMARY OF QUALIFICATIONS

- 13 years as an engineer collaborating on key marketing/sales strategies for one of the nation's largest corporations.
- Enjoy making sales presentations that motivate audiences to "buy into" new products.
- Technical versatility: construction, computer systems, telecommunications, and safety.

PROFESSIONAL ACCOMPLISHMENTS

SALES / MARKETING

- Increased premium product sales 15% ($4.1 million) by designing a $2.7 million advertising and point-of-sale strategy. Led team of sales experts, merchandising specialists, market researchers, P.O.S. vendors, and product engineers.
- Made winning "sales" presentation regarding a $37 million retail automation project. Built consensus among company divisions with competing interests by facilitating needs assessment, goal setting, and cooperative strategy planning.
- Increased revenue $12 million annually by convincing 8,300 retailers to use electronic funds transfer system.
- Led several testimonial and training presentations that "sold" new technologies to audiences with resistance to change.

TECHNICAL PROJECT MANAGEMENT

- Led the technical development of customer activated credit/debit card payment system implemented at AP stations nationwide. Increased corporate annual sales $154 million.
- Led development of a computerized maintenance dispatch system for 8,250 retail outlets and 60 bulk facilities that eliminated down-time, increasing sales $8.4 million per year.
- Directed the $49 million construction of 40 service stations, designing architectural plans that met environmental regulations and local government demands.

WORK HISTORY

1987-present   American Petroleum Inc., Houston, TX

   Environmental Safety Fire and Health Specialist, 1999-present
   Trading Analyst, 1997-1999
   Project Manager, Market Place Development, 1996-1997
   Project Manager, Electronics Systems - Service Stations, 1993-1996
   Analyst for Product Order and Delivery, 1992-1993
   Project Manager, Service Station Construction, 1989-1992
   Staff Engineer, 1987-1989

EDUCATION

   B.E., Chemical Engineering, Massachusetts Institute of Technology, Cambridge, MA, 1987
   Professional Development: American Demographics Annual Marketing Conference
                               Sales and negotiations seminars

Charles Humphries's resume.

Go Figure

Now it's time to write your Summary of Qualifications statements. To help you come up with three or four strong statements, answer the following questions. If one doesn't apply to your situation, skip it and move on to the next.

Summary of Qualifications Worksheet

1. How much experience do you have in this profession, in this field, or using the required skills? _____

   Example: Someone staying in the field of financial management might write, "I've worked as a financial manager for a mid-sized company for the last 14 years."

   Summary statement: Fourteen years as the financial manager of a company with current sales of $75 million.

   Example: A job seeker making the transition from teaching to corporate training might write, "I spent the last seven years teaching things to all kinds of kids."

   Summary statement: Seven years of professional experience using strong communication skills to enhance learning of children from diverse backgrounds.

2. Imagine that your best friend is talking to the hiring person about the job you want. What would your best friend say about you that would make the employer want to call you for an interview? _____

   Example: The best friend of a job hunter desiring an editorial position with a newspaper might say, "She even won the Pulitzer prize! I don't think anyone from the *Examiner* had ever done that before."

   Summary statement: First syndicated journalist from the *Examiner* to receive the Pulitzer prize.

   Example: The colleague of a CEO seeking a membership on the Board of Directors of a crisis-prevention nonprofit organization might say, "He led a group that helped the community recover from the 1989 earthquake."

   Summary statement: Known for leading a committee that took the first step toward community rehabilitation after the 1989 earthquake.

3. How is success measured in the position mentioned in your Job Objective? How do you measure up? _____

   Example: A salesperson reaching for a sales management job might write, "I have always sold more than my quota and tried to motivate other salespeople so my team could meet group goals."

   Summary statement: Consistently exceeded personal quotas and inspired sales team members to meet group goals.

   Example: A software developer wishing to make a move into technical writing might write, "Many different users have told me that my explanations are easy to understand."

   Summary statement: Reputation for writing clear and concise explanations for technical and nontechnical users.

4. What credentials do you have that are important for this job? _____

   Example: A fashion buyer looking for a position as a graphic designer might write, "My college degree was in design."

   Summary statement: Bachelor of Fine Arts with an emphasis on design.

   Example: A geology teacher seeking a position at a community college in California might write, "I have a Lifetime California Community College Teaching Credential in Earth Science."

   Summary statement: California Community College Teaching Credential, Earth Science, Lifetime.

5. What is it about your personality that makes this job a good fit for you? _____

   Example: A customer-service representative staying in the same field might write, "I am very diplomatic, so I get good results."

   Summary statement: Outstanding diplomacy that consistently produces win-win results for customers and the company.

   Example: An architect applying for a post in a professional organization could write, "I have natural problem-solving skills that lead to good solutions."

   Summary statement: Natural problem-solving skills that create both practical and agreeable solutions.

6. What personal commitments or passions do you have that would be valued by the employer? _____

   Example: Someone wanting to lead an environmental organization could write, "I am committed to educating people about industrial-waste hazards that are endangering the environment."

   Summary statement: Strong commitment to preserving nature through education about hazards to the environment.

   Example: A psychologist going for a job in human resources might say, "I like to help others achieve their potential through evaluation of their personal skills."

   Summary statement: Dedicated to maximizing others' potential through careful assessment and acknowledgment of their personal skills.

7. What other experience do you have that will be a bonus to the employer? _____

   Example: A new graduate seeking her first job as a nurse could write, "I volunteered in a medium-sized clinic."

   Summary statement: Volunteer experience in a clinic with an interdisciplinary staff of 12.

   Example: Someone trying for a position on the mayor's administrative staff might mention, "My family includes three generations of political professionals, so I'm used to debating controversial issues."

   Summary statement: Developed talent for debating controversial issues as a member of a family with three generations of political professionals.

8. Do you have any technical, linguistic, or artistic talents that would be useful on the job? _____

Example: Someone applying to be a teacher in a multilingual school might write, "I can speak Spanish, Italian, and Russian."

Summary statement: Fluent in Spanish, Italian, and Russian.

Example: An artist seeking a commission from the city's museum could write, "I have worked in just about every kind of medium."

Summary statement: Adept at working in a range of mediums, including paint, pen and ink, clay, metal, collage, and wood.

Not all the questions on the Summary of Qualifications Worksheet will work for your situation. Just answer the ones that do, and you're bound to come up with three or four good statements for your resume.

Your Mini-Resume

Put your best foot forward! After you've listed your Summary of Qualifications statements, prioritize them so that the most relevant and most impressive one comes first.

Now that you've written your Heading, Job Objective (see Chapter 6, "Step One: Heading Your Way"), and Summary of Qualifications sections, notice how the top of your resume is sort of a mini-resume. It tells the employer

➤ Who you are

➤ What you want

➤ Why you should have it

If you've done a good job, it should be enough to convince the employer to consider you for the position.

Career Casualty

Be careful not to list tasks you don't like to perform. Mentioning them is a sure way of finding them in your next job description.

Bonus Check

Your Heading, Job Objective, and Summary of Qualifications sections might be all you need to create a networking card (mentioned in Chapter 2, "A Resume for All Reasons") for your job search.

The Least You Need to Know

➤ A strong Summary of Qualifications section will grab an employer's attention and make him think, "Here's the person for the job."

➤ Your Summary of Qualifications summarizes your qualifications for your next job (your future); it doesn't summarize you past.

➤ Don't write overused phrases such as "Excellent communication skills."

➤ Prioritize your Summary of Qualifications statements so that the strongest one comes first.

Chapter 8

Step Three: Been There, Done That

In This Chapter

➤ Creating a work history that shows off your strengths

➤ Using dates on your resume to fight age discrimination

➤ Disguising gaps in your employment history

➤ Adding volunteer experience to your Work History section

➤ Making your promotions noticeable at a glance

Employers give a lot of attention to the Work History section of a resume. It's one of the first things they look for after they see your Job Objective. They want to know about your track record, where you've been and how long you stayed there. What they're trying to figure out is: Are you a stable person? What are your demonstrated talents? And most importantly, would you be a good fit for the job opening they have?

A well-presented Work History section is clearly important. Building one that maximizes your experience is what this chapter is all about.

Writing History

Where you list your previous positions depends on what type of resume format you're using. If you're a chronological resume writer (remember that lesson in Chapter 4, "Chronologically Speaking"?), your Work History will be distributed throughout the midsection of your resume. The following chronological template shows you exactly where it would appear.

If you're a functional resume writer, Work History will be listed in one section at the bottom of your resume. The following functional resume template highlights the area I'm talking about.

The next step is to put the Work History section in your resume. Sounds easy enough, doesn't it? But what if you have a situation that's tricky to present in your employment history? This situation could be any of the following:

➤ Dates that go back so far that they trigger age discrimination.

➤ So little employment history that you appear too young for the job.

➤ Gaps in your work history.

➤ Multiple positions at the same company.

Take a look at the following resume templates, with the Professional Experience and Work History sections highlighted. Let's take a closer look at some Work History issues and figure out ways you can resolve them.

Fight Age Discrimination

"How far back should I go in my work history?" is a good question to ask yourself as you set out to document your history. In general, you're not expected to go back more than 10 years, but you can if it's to your benefit. To help you figure out how far back to go in your work history, consider the following:

➤ How relevant your earliest positions are to your job objective

➤ How old you want to appear on your resume

Age discrimination is illegal, but like it or not, employers usually try to figure out your age using the dates you give. Most employers have an age range they consider to be ideal for a particular job, based on the following factors:

➤ Salary expectations

➤ Skill level

➤ Ability to supervise or be supervised

➤ Amount of life experience needed

➤ Company or industry image

(Work History in Chronological Resume)

Name
Street
City, State Zip
Phone, Fax, E-mail

JOB OBJECTIVE

The job you want next

SUMMARY OF QUALIFICATIONS

- How much experience you have in the field of your job objective, in a related field, or using the skills required for your new position.
- An overall career accomplishment that shows you'd be good at this job.
- What someone would say about you as a recommendation.

PROFESSIONAL EXPERIENCE

19xx-pres. **Company Name, City, State**
Job Title

- An accomplishment you are proud of that shows you're good at this profession.
- A problem you solved and the results.
- A time when you positively affected the organization, the bottom line, your boss, your co-workers, your clients.
- Awards, commendations, publications, etc., you achieved that relate to your job objective.

19xx-xx **Company Name, City, State**
Job Title

- A project you are proud of that supports your job objective.
- Another accomplishment that shows you're good at this line of work.
- Quantifiable results that point out your skill.

19xx-xx **Company Name, City, State**
Job Title

- An accomplishment you are proud of that shows you will be valued by your next employer.
- An occasion when someone "sat up and took notice" of your skill.

EDUCATION

Degree, Major (if relevant), 19xx (optional)
University, City, State

The Work History section of the chronological resume template.

(Work History in Functional Resume)

Name
Street
City, State Zip
Phone, Fax, E-mail

JOB OBJECTIVE
The job you want next

SUMMARY OF QUALIFICATIONS
- How much experience you have in the field of your job objective, in a related field, or using the skills required for your new position.
- An overall career accomplishment that shows you'd be good at this job.
- What someone would say about you as a recommendation.

RELEVANT EXPERIENCE
MAJOR SKILL
- An accomplishment you are proud of that shows you have this skill.
- A problem you solved using this skill, and the results.
- A time when you used your skill to positively affect the organization, the bottom line, your boss, your clients.
- Awards, commendations, publications, etc., you achieved that relate to your job objective.

MAJOR SKILL
- A project you are proud of that supports your job objective.
- Another accomplishment that shows you're good at this line of work.
- Quantifiable results that point out your skill.
- An occasion when someone "sat up and took notice" of your skill.

WORK HISTORY

19xx-present	Job Title	COMPANY NAME and city
19xx-xx	Job Title	COMPANY NAME and city
19xx-xx	Job Title	COMPANY NAME and city
19xx-xx	Job Title	COMPANY NAME and city

EDUCATION
Degree, Major (if relevant), 19xx (optional)
University, City, State

The Work History section of the functional resume template.

Bonus Check

Remember Resume Commandment II: Thou shalt not confess (the Resume Commandments were listed in Chapter 3, "Winning Resume Wisdom"). In other words, you don't have to tell everything. Stick to what's relevant and marketable. Rely on this commandment when resolving any issues with your Work History section.

A well-written resume uses dates to lead the employer to deduce that you are the ideal age for the job you're after, regardless of your actual age. The following two sections show you how to work with dates on your resume to create the ideal image.

Putting Your Younger Foot Forward

Sally, 35 years old, was applying for a job as a sales clerk in a clothing store that catered to young professional women. She thought the employer was probably looking for a woman in her mid-20s because the employer wanted someone who fit the image of the store and who wouldn't expect wages as high as someone who had been in the field for many years.

Terms of Employment

Age discrimination works in two ways. An employer may eliminate a job candidate because he is too old or too young.

To present herself as the ideal candidate, Sally decided to go back only five years in the Work History on her resume, because the employer would most likely

➤ Take 20 years of age as a starting point.

➤ Add the five years of work experience shown in her work history.

➤ Conclude that Sally was at least 25 years old.

Likewise, in her Education section, she stated her degree but did not give her graduation date because doing so would give away her age.

The dates on Sally's resume were all honest, they just didn't tell all. In the interview, she would have the opportunity to sell herself with her enthusiasm, professional manner, and appropriate salary request and thereby fulfill the employer's expectations of the ideal candidate.

Older Is Better

Sam is a new graduate who worked in his dad's business all through high school and college. He was a remarkable achiever and was ready for more responsibility in the workforce than most people his age. He applied for a position as a store manager, knowing that if he could just get his foot in the door he could convince the owner he could handle the job.

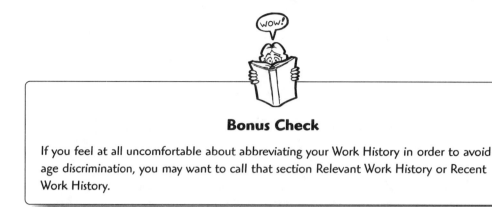

Bonus Check

If you feel at all uncomfortable about abbreviating your Work History in order to avoid age discrimination, you may want to call that section Relevant Work History or Recent Work History.

He decided that the employer was probably expecting to hire someone in his late 20s. So on his resume, Sam went back in his Work History section eight years to when he started working for his dad in low-level positions and showed his progression over the following years. He stated that he had a degree, but he did not give the date of completion, because it might indicate that he was only 22. Everything on Sam's resume honestly painted the picture of someone who had the experience and maturity of a 30-year-old without ever revealing his age.

Job-Hunt Hint

Dates in your Education section are optional. List them if they make you look the right age for the job you are going for. Delete them if they lead the reader to deduce that you are older or younger than you want to appear for the job application.

Down and Dirty Formula

Here's a quick and a easy method for understanding how dates on your resume make an impression about your age. I call it my EPT (Experience Plus Twenty) formula. Subtract the earliest date on your resume from today's date (using years only, no months). Add that number of years to 20 (as a ballpark figure for how old you might have been when your experience started) to get a total. Your perceived age is greater than or equal to this total. For example, a resume written in 2000 with a Work History that starts in 1984 tells the employer that the job applicant is at least 36 years old (16 years of experience + 20 = 36).

Unsightly Unemployment Blemishes

"What's wrong with a few gaps in my work history?" you might ask. "Isn't everyone entitled to a little time off?" Many responsible professionals have taken breaks in their careers to travel, take care of ill parents, recover from personal illnesses, or for other legitimate reasons.

But for some reason, employers don't like to see gaps in your work history. They would rather see the unemployed time explained, especially if the explanation is somehow connected to your job objective or at least shows strength of character. If you have a period of unemployment in your history, the following sections explain some ways of dealing with it.

Bonus Check

If you're a seasoned professional with a few careers under your belt, it may be to your advantage to mention only your most recent career on your resume in order to avoid age discrimination. This is a completely acceptable practice, one I recommend if it expedites your job search.

Years Go Solo

Use only years, not months, when referring to spans of time in your Work History. Using years makes it quicker for the potential employer to grasp the length of time and can eliminate the need to explain gaps of less than two years.

Notice the gap in this presentation:

12/95– 3/99	Manager	Friendly's Ice Cream Parlor, Trenton, NJ
2/92–12/94	Manager	Lyon's Restaurant, Milbrae, CA

Without the months, there is no apparent gap:

1995–1999	Manager	Friendly's Ice Cream Parlor, Trenton, NJ
1992–1994	Manager	Lyon's Restaurant, Milbrae, CA

Career Casualty

A void in your work history may cause an employer to think that you are hiding something or that you might have a past or current problem (such as substance abuse, incarceration, laziness, or instability) that would affect your ability to work. To gain the employer's trust, it's important to justify your employment gaps.

Filling in the Gaps

If your unemployment covers two calendar years or more, you need to explain the void. Consider all the things you were doing during that time (volunteer work, school activities, internships, schooling, travel, and so on) and present it in a way that's relevant to your job objective, if possible.

Someone looking for a medical sales position who took care of an ill parent for two years might list the following:

1996–98 Home Care Provider for terminally ill relative

An applicant for a travel agent position could refer to a vacation:

1998–99 Independent travel: Europe, Asia, and South America

A mother wanting to reenter the job market as a teacher's aide might say:

1993–99 Full-Time Parent and PTA Volunteer, St. John's Academy

115

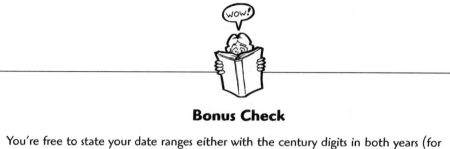

Bonus Check

You're free to state your date ranges either with the century digits in both years (for example: 1998–1999) or with the century digits in the first year and not in the second (for example: 1998–99). The key is to be consistent throughout your resume.

Job-Hunt Hint

Presenting only years in your Work History may not only save you from having to explain gaps of unemployment, but will also make your resume easier to read. Months complicate the presentation and make it harder (and therefore longer) for someone to figure out. Remember the eight-second scan? Providing just the years will help you pass that eight-second test.

Career Casualty

Don't refer to personal illness, unemployment, or rehabilitation in your Work History. These topics usually raise red flags, so avoid mentioning them at all cost.

Character That Counts

Even if your activities during your unemployment have no apparent relevancy to your job objective, you need to account for the gap. Explain what you were doing in a way that is honest and feels comfortable to you. If your main activity was something you don't want to talk about, think of something else you were doing during that time, even if it doesn't relate to your job objective, and refer to that activity instead of using a job title in your Work History. Some suggested substitutes for a job title include

Full-Time Parent

Home Management

Family Management

Family Financial Management

Independent Study

Personal Travel

Adventure Travel

Travels to (fill in the place you traveled to)

Professional Development

Freelance Work (replace Work with the type of work you did, such as writer, artist, or plumber)

Student

Consultant

Contractual Work (replace Work with the type of work you did, such as administrator, accountant, hair stylist)

Relocation from abroad

Volunteer

Civic Leader

There's no need to elaborate on your "filler" job title, unless doing so will support your job objective. For instance, if your Job Objective reads "Fundraiser," you might say "Volunteer (emphasis on fundraising)" in your Work History section.

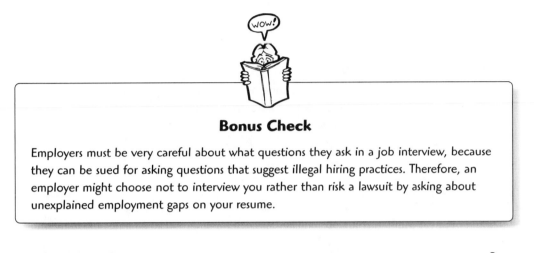

Bonus Check

Employers must be very careful about what questions they ask in a job interview, because they can be sued for asking questions that suggest illegal hiring practices. Therefore, an employer might choose not to interview you rather than risk a lawsuit by asking about unexplained employment gaps on your resume.

The Gapless Resume

Janet Bennett had a long period of recent unemployment. For that reason, she chose to use the functional format and filled in her gap with two job titles:

➤ Childcare Teacher (which was a volunteer position at her church)

➤ Full-Time Parent (for her two children)

Job-Hunt Hint

You may have two or three "job titles" that could fill an employment gap on your resume. If so, choose the title that is most relevant to your Job Objective.

These two titles not only demonstrate that she's a stable citizen, they also qualify her for her job objective. Can you see how she used both experiences in the achievement statements in the body of the resume?

If you include unpaid experience in your Work History section as Janet did, be sure that you call this section either Work History or History, not Employment History, because the word *employment* implies that you were paid.

Promoting Your Promotions

You can be especially proud of your work history if you've been promoted within a company. So go ahead, this is your chance to brag!

Potential employers will be impressed by your promotions because they indicate employment stability and high performance. Let's look at ways to show off your promotions in your Work History section.

Janet Bennett

123 Amboy Street • North Little Rock, AR 12345 • **(123) 123-1234**

JOB OBJECTIVE: A position teaching preschool and elementary age children.

SUMMARY OF QUALIFICATIONS

- More than 20 years teaching preschool and elementary age children.
- Good communication skills with children and adults.
- Capable of leading projects. Supportive team worker.
- Experience working in low-economic settings.

EXPERIENCE

WORK WITH CHILDREN

- Taught children of low-income families at State of Arkansas Preschool Program, a parent participation program.
- Incorporated parents into the preschool program, being sensitive to the parents' needs for shared responsibility.
- Planned the preschool's parent education programs and trained them in effective communications with children.
- Collaborated with fellow preschool teacher to share ideas and solutions, as well as to train teacher aide in classroom management style and curriculum.

SCHOOL-COMMUNITY RELATIONS

- Served on PTA Board as president (four years) and coordinator of parent services in the classroom (four years) of Briarcliff Elementary (my children's school).
- Taught Parent Educator Program (five years) at Briarcliff. Co-planned curriculum, and facilitated discussions on prevention of drug and alcohol abuse, and self-esteem.
- Volunteered extensively for classroom activities, field trips, etc. at Booker Baptist Church.
- As member of School Site Council, planned use of state funds for school.
  - Identified the area of need; built a consensus of how to address it.
  - Applied for funding.

WORK HISTORY

Childcare Teacher	Booker Baptist Church, North Little Rock, AR,	2000
Full-time Parent	North Little Rock, AR	1984-00
Classroom Teacher	State of Arkansas Preschool Program, Sherwood, AR	1977-84
Classroom Kindergarten Teacher	Pine Bluff Public Schools, Pine Bluff, AR	1975-77

EDUCATION AND CREDENTIALS

B.S., Elementary Education, University of Arkansas, Little Rock, AR, 1974
State of Arkansas Teaching Credential, K-9 and Early Childhood, lifetime

Janet Bennett's resume.

Imagine that you have been promoted three times within a company called Harrison Productions. Notice what kind of impression you might make if you used this format:

1998–present	President, Harrison Productions, Chicago, IL
1997–1998	Vice President, Harrison Productions, Chicago, IL
1994–1997	Producer, Harrison Productions, Chicago, IL

At first glance, the employer is likely to think you are a job-hopper who had three jobs in four years. (Ouch!) Only upon closer examination might she understand that your three jobs were at the same company. But what if the employer doesn't take the time to figure that out? You will have made a negative impression when you had an excellent opportunity to make a positive one.

I suggest organizing the same information in this way:

1994–present	HARRISON PRODUCTIONS, Chicago, IL
	President, 1998–present
	Vice President, 1997–1998
	Producer, 1994–1997

Notice how the second version makes it immediately clear that you were a loyal employee who had multiple promotions. The good news is that this concept applies to both the chronological and functional formats, as demonstrated by the following three resumes.

Zipping Along

When Shane Mathews wrote his resume in 1999, he wanted to show off his promotions at his last two companies. By grouping his job titles as subsets under each company heading he achieved two things:

➤ He made it easy for employers to see that he'd been promoted.

➤ He avoided having to go into detail about each job title.

The employer surely appreciated this smart move.

Career Casualty

If you've owned a business, don't say so on your resume. In the hiring world, it's often thought that once people have worked for themselves, they'll never make a good employee again, because self-employed people like being the boss and are driven by the profit motive. A way around revealing your self-employment is to give yourself a job title in your business, choosing a title that supports your current job objective, if possible.

Job-Hunt Hint

When lining up text in a column, always use tabs instead of the space bar. Then your words will align perfectly every time.

Shane Mathews

123 Bay Court • Columbus, OH 12345 • Home: (123) 123-1234 • Work: (123) 123-1234

JOB OBJECTIVE: Collections Administrator

SUMMARY OF QUALIFICATIONS

- 10 years business experience including eight years in the financial services industry.
- Proficient at utilizing computer systems to produce analytical reports.
- Enhance operations through strong organizational and problem solving skills.

EXPERIENCE

THE BANK OF OHIO, Columbus, OH, 1996-pres.
Corporate Operations Manager
Banking Officer
Banking Assistant

- Retrieved data, analyzed information and spread financial reports for management, using mainframe and PC systems. LAN Administrator for two years.
- Bank-certified to respond to credit inquiries using Robert Morris Associates criteria.
- Administered operational systems that satisfied auditors for four consecutive years.
- Reduced liability and standardized corporate banking operations by instituting risk management policies.
- Served as liaison to account officers, clients and bank departments, ensuring quality customer service through problem resolution.
- Supervised personnel; handled salary reviews, performance counseling and training.

GREAT MID-WESTERN BANK, Cleveland, OH, 1992-1995
Management Trainee
Administrative Assistant

- Compiled and calculated statistics for weekly and quarterly reports.
- Prepared human resources reports that included salary and turnover analyses.

UNIVERSITY OF CLEVELAND, Cleveland, OH, 1990-1991
Full-time MBA Student

WHITE MEADOWS CENTER, INC., Cleveland, OH, 1989-1990
Assistant Marketing Manager

- Assisted in development of annual calendar and budget for this large shopping center.
- Collaborated with merchants and management to produce joint promotions.

EDUCATION

MBA, Marketing, 1994, University of Cleveland, Cleveland, OH
BA, Administration and Legal Processes, 1989, Kent State, Kent, OH

Shane Mathews's resume.

Bonus Check

If you're running short on space, be creative in how you present your work history information. Check out the sample resumes in Appendix B, "Portfolio of Sample Resumes," and throughout the chapters in this book to find clever techniques that save a line here and there.

Grass Underfoot

Dianne Woo was concerned that a potential employer would view her as stagnant because she'd worked at General Electric for so many years. To avoid creating such a negative image, she separated her job titles under the company heading and inserted achievements for each one, as you can see in her resume. Doing so made it obvious the grass hasn't been growing under her feet!

If you have many years at the same organization, emphasize your promotions by placing bullet-point achievement statements under each job title. Doing so will give your Work History a sense of dynamism and diversity, thereby countering the image of being a stuck-in-the-mud that sometimes comes from exceptional longevity at one company.

Straight Up

Barry Rizkallah presented his comprehensive career at Chevron in a concise list in the Work History section of his functional resume. At a glance, the reader could see that Barry was an accomplished marketing professional—why else would he have been promoted through such a healthy tenure?

Job-Hunt Hint

When listing your promotions at one place of employment, organize the dates of your job titles so the reader understands at a glance that they are a subset of the overall dates at the company. In Dianne's resume, her overall dates are flush left, and her job-title dates are on the right, making it obvious that her job-title dates are detailing her overall time at the company.

Bonus Check

If your potential employer isn't likely to recognize a company you list in your Work History, you may want to give some explanation as to what industry it is in or what product it sells. You can do that by writing a short overview statement immediately beside or under the company name.

DIANNE WOO
12 Hollister Place, St. Louis, MO 12345, (123) 123-1234

OBJECTIVE

Office Manager

SUMMARY OF QUALIFICATIONS

- 12 years office management experience in one of the nation's leading corporations.
- Consistent record of increasing productivity by maintaining effective interdepartmental relations and office systems.
- Excellent IBM and Macintosh skills.
- International background. Bilingual: Mandarin/English.

PROFESSIONAL EXPERIENCE

1988-present   GENERAL ELECTRIC, INC., St. Louis, MO
Administrative Secretary to Director, Corporate Communications, 1993-present
- Independently streamlined this fast-paced department that generates annual, quarterly, and monthly publications with individual circulation of up to 120,000.
- Devised electronic network that facilitates immediate written communications with over 200 remote locations.
- Managed budgets totaling $1 million. Prepared estimates and proposals for new publications.

Secretary to Vice President, Merchandising, Office Products, 1991-1993
- Set up and managed office procedures for the Merchandising Department, which produced a national wholesale office products catalog.
- Provided office support for 13 managers.

Secretary/Assistant to Manager, Office Services, 1988-1991
- Increased quality of office services for the 750-person headquarters building by improving customer service and inventory systems.

Assistant to Managing Director, Missouri Training Academy, 1988
- Assisted Director in setting up training program for technical and media professionals.

1980-1988   FOREIGN OFFICE, REPUBLIC OF CHINA
Administrative Secretary to Consul General, St. Louis, MO, 1983-1988
Secretary to Ambassador, Beijing, China, 1980-1982
- Represented Republic of China to foreign diplomats and maintained strict confidentiality as "right-hand" to the Consul General and the Ambassador.
- Served as translator to Chinese officials during state visits.

EDUCATION

B.S. equivalent, University of Beijing, China, 1980
Certificates, Foreign Language Correspondent, Beijing, China

Dianne Woo's resume.

Barry M. Rizkallah

1234 Banana Drive • Wheeling, WV 12345 • (123) 123-1234 • rizkallah@thenet.net

Marketing Professional

Summary of Qualifications

- 13 years as a marketing professional for one of the nation's leading corporations.
- Expertise in project management, marketing, and vendor relations.
- Computer proficient: Excel, PowerPoint, MS Word, Vizio, Lotus Notes, Microsoft Project.

Selected Accomplishments
at Chevron U.S.A. Products, Inc.

PROJECT MANAGEMENT

- Led a team of operations, advertising, and product development managers for the $200,000 launch of a new product.
- Coordinated analytical team efforts to standardize quality of service in 8500 retail sites.
- Increased sales and improved customer relations by developing Chevron International's first co-op advertising program.
- Organized sales retreats in U.S. and overseas resorts for 50 agents from around world.
- Trained regional coordinators and outside consultants in new computer programs.

MARKETING

- Created "Who's Who," a 12-page, four-color brochure distributed world-wide that promoted Chevron as a valuable international player.
- Designed a $15,000 booth for international trade shows for Chevron's cultural diversity.
- Produced "Technical Tables and Charts," a detailed, 50-page publication used in the shipping industry. Updated content and image, dramatically increasing demand.

Work History

1987-present	**Chevron U.S.A. Products, Inc., Wheeling, West Virginia**
	Business Analyst, 2000-present
	Marketing Specialist, 1996-2000
	Senior Marketing Assistant, 1993-1996
	Marketing Help Desk Representative, 1992-1993
	Collections Representative, 1991-1992
	Customer Representative, 1987-1991
	Administrative Assistant, 1987
1986-1987	**Saudi Research & Marketing, Inc., Houston, TX**
	Publication Subscription Manager

Education

B.A., Public Relations, minor: Business, West Virginia State College, Wheeling, WV, 1985

Barry Rizkallah's resume.

123

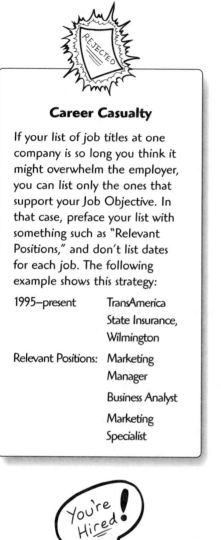

Career Casualty

If your list of job titles at one company is so long you think it might overwhelm the employer, you can list only the ones that support your Job Objective. In that case, preface your list with something such as "Relevant Positions," and don't list dates for each job. The following example shows this strategy:

1995–present	TransAmerica State Insurance, Wilmington
Relevant Positions:	Marketing Manager
	Business Analyst
	Marketing Specialist

Terms of Employment

The following titles are meant to convey temporary worker, as opposed to unemployed. **Contractor** is a title used in many fields such as construction, administration, and business management. **Freelance** is used in creative fields such as graphic design and interior decorating. **Consultant** is used in fields such as business management and technology development.

The Happy Job Hopper

Temporary employment or short-term assignments can make your Work History look complicated and sometimes create gaps in employment. If that's the case for you, don't worry. You have two solutions to choose from:

➤ List the name of the employment agency you worked for, followed by a subset of impressive clients, as in the following example:

Graphic Designer	Creative Power Employment Agency, 1998–pres.
Clients included:	Xerox Corp.
	IBM
	First Bank

➤ Justify the span of time with a professional title preceded or followed by a term like *contractor*, *freelance*, or *consultant*, whichever is appropriate for your field. The following examples show this strategy:

Freelance Graphic Designer, 1998–pres.	
Clients included:	Xerox Corp.
	IBM
	First Bank

Marketing Consultant, 1997–present	
	McMillan Financial Services
	Lewiston National Bank
	Prosperity Trust

By bundling your short-term assignments under a professional title in your Work History, you'll no longer look like a job hopper.

Go for It

Now that you're armed with solutions to some tricky problems, you're ready to fill out the following worksheet for your Work History.

Work History Worksheet

1. How far back do you want to go in the work history on your resume, based on the EPT formula you read about earlier in this chapter? _____

2. List all the jobs you've held from that time until now.

Dates (years only)_____

Job Title _____

Employer _____

City and State _____

Dates (years only)_____

Job Title _____

Employer _____

City and State _____

Dates (years only)_____

Job Title _____

Employer _____

City and State _____

Dates (years only)_____

Job Title _____

Employer _____

City and State _____

Dates (years only)_____

Job Title _____

Employer _____

City and State _____

Dates (years only)_____

Job Title _____

Employer _____

City and State _____

Dates (years only)_____

Job Title _____

Employer _____

City and State _____

Review the work history you wrote in the worksheet. Are there any gaps in your employment or other sticky issues? If so, remedy it with one or more of the tips mentioned in this chapter. After you've smoothed out all the wrinkles, you're ready to insert your work history information into either the chronological and functional resume template, whichever you have chosen.

The Least You Need to Know

➤ Use only years, not months, when presenting your work history.

➤ Avoid age discrimination by using the EPT formula.

➤ Disguise gaps in your Work History by giving yourself a job title that explains the unemployed span.

➤ Arrange your Work History section to show off your promotions within a company.

Chapter 9

Step Four: You're an Achiever!

In This Chapter

➤ Why achievement statements are a smart use of your resume real estate

➤ How to present major headings in your functional resume

➤ How to make the value of your experience obvious to an employer

➤ Why action verbs add power to your sentences

Most resumes are dry (so dry you need to drink a couple of glasses of water just to get through them) because they focus on boring job duties. Although your potential employer wants to know what you've done, she is even more concerned with whether you've achieved the desired results on the job. In this chapter, you determine what your relevant achievements are and learn how to put them on your resume, so you can get the most out of every word.

Chronologically Clear

The achievement statements in your chronological resume appear under the company name where you performed the achievement. To understand what section I'm referring to, look at the highlighted areas in the following chronological template.

(Achievement Statements in Chronological Resume)

Name
Street
City, State Zip
Phone, Fax, E-mail

JOB OBJECTIVE

The job you want next

SUMMARY OF QUALIFICATIONS

- How much experience you have in the field of your job objective, in a related field, or using the skills required for your new position.

- An overall career accomplishment that shows you'd be good at this job.

- What someone would say about you as a recommendation.

PROFESSIONAL EXPERIENCE

19xx-pres. **Company Name, City, State**
Job Title

- An accomplishment you are proud of that shows you're good at this profession.

- A problem you solved and the results.

- A time when you positively affected the organization, the bottom line, your boss, your co-workers, your clients.

- Awards, commendations, publications, etc., you achieved that relate to your job objective.

19xx-xx **Company Name, City, State**
Job Title

- A project you are proud of that supports your job objective.

- Another accomplishment that shows you're good at this line of work.

- Quantifiable results that point out your skill.

19xx-xx **Company Name, City, State**
Job Title

- An accomplishment you are proud of that shows you will be valued by your next employer.

- An occasion when someone "sat up and took notice" of your skill.

EDUCATION

Degree, Major (if relevant), 19xx (optional)
University, City, State

Chronological resume template with achievement bullet points highlighted.

If you're a chronological resume writer, skip past the next few sections about the functional resume and jump into "Dynamite Achievements" later in this chapter.

Functionally Sound

You're still reading, so you must be a functional resume writer. Your achievement statements should appear under the appropriate skill headings in the body of your resume. Check out the next functional resume template to see what I mean.

Do you have a feel for where your achievements are going to be listed? Good. Now read on to learn some important things about creating the skill headings for your functional resume.

Functional Help

One of the key advantages to using a functional resume is that you define yourself by your skills, rather than by your former job titles. That's why it's an especially good format for career changers and those with tricky employment histories.

The way to put the spotlight on your skills in the functional resume is to create skill headings, which appear in the body of the resume. The purpose of using the skill headings is to help the potential employer quickly identify you as someone with the talents needed to do the job. (Don't forget you have to make a good impression during an initial eight-second scan!) If you keep your skill headings brief and put them in bold or large print, the employer will quickly define you by your skills, rather than by your previous job titles.

One Plus One Is Enough

To figure out what skill headings to put on your functional resume, imagine that you are an employer who is writing an ad for the job mentioned in your Job Objective statement. What skills would you list as requirements?

Let's say you're the manager of a retail store, and you're looking for a Director of Customer Service. Your help-wanted ad might read: "Applicant must be skilled in supervision and customer service." Now step back into the shoes of the job seeker. Supervision and Customer Service would be the two skill headings you should use on your resume.

Terms of Employment

Professional Experience is the name of the midsection in the chronological template shown in this chapter (which contains your work history and achievement statements). That section may also be called

> Professional Accomplishments
>
> Career Achievements
>
> Achievements
>
> Selected Accomplishments
>
> Experience

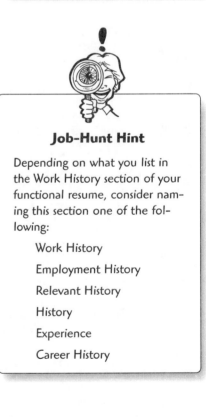

Job-Hunt Hint

Depending on what you list in the Work History section of your functional resume, consider naming this section one of the following:

> Work History
>
> Employment History
>
> Relevant History
>
> History
>
> Experience
>
> Career History

(Achievement Statements in Functional Resume)

Name
Street
City, State Zip
Phone, Fax, E-mail

JOB OBJECTIVE

The job you want next

SUMMARY OF QUALIFICATIONS

- How much experience you have in the field of your job objective, in a related field, or using the skills required for your new position.
- An overall career accomplishment that shows you'd be good at this job.
- What someone would say about you as a recommendation.

RELEVANT EXPERIENCE

MAJOR SKILL

- An accomplishment you are proud of that shows you have this skill.
- A problem you solved using this skill, and the results.
- A time when you used your skill to positively affect the organization, the bottom line, your boss, your clients.
- Awards, commendations, publications, etc., you achieved that relate to your job objective.

MAJOR SKILL

- A project you are proud of that supports your job objective.
- Another accomplishment that shows you're good at this line of work.
- Quantifiable results that point out your skill.
- An occasion when someone "sat up and took notice" of your skill.

WORK HISTORY

19xx-present	Job Title	COMPANY NAME and city
19xx-xx	Job Title	COMPANY NAME and city
19xx-xx	Job Title	COMPANY NAME and city
19xx-xx	Job Title	COMPANY NAME and city

EDUCATION

Degree, Major (if relevant), 19xx (optional)
University, City, State

Functional resume template with achievement bullet points highlighted.

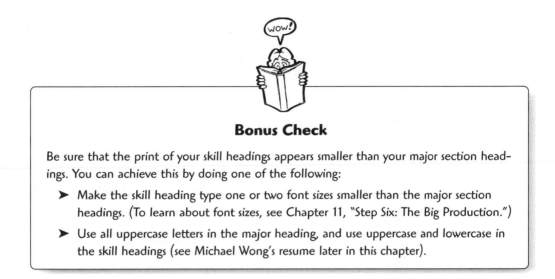

Bonus Check

Be sure that the print of your skill headings appears smaller than your major section headings. You can achieve this by doing one of the following:

➤ Make the skill heading type one or two font sizes smaller than the major section headings. (To learn about font sizes, see Chapter 11, "Step Six: The Big Production.")

➤ Use all uppercase letters in the major heading, and use uppercase and lowercase in the skill headings (see Michael Wong's resume later in this chapter).

Let's role-play again: As a supervisor in a software-development firm looking for a technical supervisor, you might write, "Applicant must be proficient in computer programming and team leadership." As a job seeker, you understand that Programming and Leadership would be good skill headings to use on your resume for this job.

Take a look at the following resume for Michael Wong. Notice how his skill headings define his Job Objective, which differed from his Work History. This resume is an excellent example of how a resume should be about a job-seeker's future, not his past.

Skills for Sale

Some functional resume writers have trouble coming up with skill headings. When selecting the skill headings for your functional resume, be sure to choose ones that define your future (your Job Objective), not your past (your Work History). If you feel stuck, take a look at the following list of skills. Notice that I've categorized this list according to four general occupational areas: business management, education, engineering/technology, and nonprofit management. Although you may want to focus on an area that's close to your job objective, I suggest you read through the entire list. Maybe a word in another category will inspire you to define your skill set in a way that is uniquely yours.

Career Casualty

Don't overwhelm your reader by having too many skill headings. Two (at most three) headings are usually plenty to make a good first impression.

Career Casualty

Don't write lengthy skill headings in your resume. Limit them to no more than three words each. Otherwise they become too difficult to read in the employer's typical initial eight-second scan.

Michael Wong

001 Adams Street, #1 • Somerville, MA 12345 • (123) 123-1234

JOB OBJECTIVE: A position in Public Relations with an emphasis on Event Planning.

SUMMARY OF QUALIFICATIONS

- Experienced at public relations for a provider of promotional merchandise for national and international concert tours.
- Success in producing events for up to 8,000 people.
- Reputation for achieving goals using a professional yet personable approach.

EDUCATION

MBA, International Marketing, Boston University, Boston, MA, 1991
BA, Marketing, Northeastern University, Boston, MA, 1989

RELEVANT ACCOMPLISHMENTS

Public Relations

- Represented promotional merchandise providers to concert hall managements, bands, and the public. Tours included: Melissa Etheridge   KD Lang
  The Plain Janes   The Indigo Girls
- Saved as much as 6% of revenues when negotiating venue contracts for promotional merchandise sales of up to $25,000 per night.
- Developed positive rapport between band and merchandise company by creating a team atmosphere rather than a strictly business relationship.
- Commended for establishing strong working relationships with bands and management companies. Consistently requested by bands for repeat and new tours.
- Acted as tour public relations person, handling questions and comments from fans.

Event Planning

- As event planner on the Arts Board, produced sell-out musical and theatrical programs for up to 8,000 attendees.
- As hospitality director for Musical Event Board, negotiated contracts, supervised catering, and managed backstage accommodations for concerts including:

The Who	Boston	Talking Heads
Jackson Browne	Genesis	Willie Nelson

WORK HISTORY

1996-present	**Tour Manager for Merchandise**	DAVIS ENTERTAINMENT, nationwide, 1997-present
		CARMICHAEL GROUP, nationwide, 1997 tour
1997	**Executive Assistant** (contractual)	AXTELL GROUP (advertising/promotions), Boston
1994-1996	**Department Manager**	SHOE SHOPS INC., Cambridge

Michael Wong's resume.

Business Management

Accounting

Accounts Payable

Accounts Receivable

Administration

Advertising

Benefits

Budget Management

Business Development

Client Relations

Community Relations

Conflict Resolution

Consulting

Copy Writing

Corporate Giving

Customer Service

Executive Management

Financial Management

Human Resources

Insurance

International Relations

Inventory Control

Inventory Management

Investor Relations

Leadership

Legal

Management Consulting

Marketing

Media Relations

Mediation

Meeting Planning

Negotiations

Office Management

Operations

Order Fulfillment

Organizational Development

Personnel

Presentation Coaching

Presentations

Product Development

Production

Project Management

Promotions

Public Relations

Purchasing

Quality Assurance

Re-engineering

Recruitment

Retail Management

Sales

Shipping

Speech Writing

Strategic Planning

Supervision

Training

Vendor Relations

Writing

Education

Administration

Admissions Evaluation

Classroom Management

Committee Leadership

Counseling

Curriculum Development

Bonus Check

A thesaurus is a great tool for coming up with just the right word. One of my favorite sources is *The Synonym Finder* by J.I. Rodale (Warner Books). There are also some excellent thesaurus software applications that you can buy for your computer.

Job-Hunt Hint

Visit your industry's Web sites to learn what skill sets are sought after in your field.

Interdisciplinary Teamwork

Parent Relations

Program Development

Research

Teaching

Tutoring

Engineering and Technical

Analysis

Computer

Customer Support

Data Collection

Database Management

Design

Development

Documentation

Engineering

MIS

Planning

Presentations

Programming

Research

Survey Coordination

System Design

System Evaluation

Systems Analysis

Team Leadership

Teamwork

Technical Support

Technical Writing

Nonprofit Management

Advocacy

Board Relations

Calendar Management

Community Outreach

Consensus Building

Counseling

Development

Event Planning

Financial Management

Fundraising

Grant Proposal Writing

Bonus Check

College career centers are happy to help alumni with their job searches. Call or visit yours to get help in defining the skills required for the type of work you seek.

Leadership

Major Donor Giving

Media Relations

Needs Assessment

Program Coordination

Program Development

Project Coordination

Public Relations

Public Speaking

Recruiting

Service Delivery

Solicitations

Staff Management

Volunteer Management

Volunteer Recruitment

Writing

Career Casualty

All caps are hard to read when used in skill headings that have long words. If a heading contains two words, and one of those words has more than eight letters, use upper- and lowercase letters so that it's easy to grasp at a glance.

Getting Down to Business

Are you ready to declare the two or three skill headings for your functional resume? Great! Here's a worksheet to help you out.

Functional Skill Headings Worksheet

1. My Job Objective (see Chapter 6, "Step One: Heading Your Way"):

_____

2. The two (maybe three) skills required to perform my Job Objective:

➤ _____

➤ _____

➤ _____

Having stated your skill headings, you're ready to move on to creating dynamite achievement statements for each heading.

Career Casualty

When you create your achievement sentences, be careful not to emphasize any aspect of the experience that you don't enjoy doing. Only stress the parts of the achievement that you would like to repeat.

Job-Hunt Hint

Talk about your experience in terms of achievements instead of monotonous job descriptions. Achievements will impress the reader, make your resume far more interesting to read, and stimulate productive conversation during the interview.

Job-Hunt Hint

Build a strong foundation for your salary negotiations by writing powerful achievement statements that speak to the employer's bottom line.

Dynamite Achievements

Nab the employer's interest right away with an achievement-oriented resume. By writing about your experience in terms of achievements, not job descriptions, you'll convey three things:

➤ You have the experience and skills to do the job.

➤ You're good at this work and at using these skills.

➤ You like your work. (You must! There's pride in your statements.)

Who's Your Audience?

Keep in mind while you write your resume that your audience is the hiring manager for the position mentioned in your Job Objective statement. In order to sell yourself to this potential employer, talk about yourself in ways that are meaningful to her. In some cases, you may need to do one or more of the following:

➤ Translate terminology to downplay differences between your past experience and your job objective.

➤ Select only aspects of your achievements that paint a picture of you at your next job.

➤ Prioritize your points so that your most relevant achievements are emphasized.

Downplay Differences

Avoid job-specific jargon in order to downplay the differences and emphasize the similarities between your previous position and your Job objective. For example, Elizabeth was a nurse who was applying for a customer service position at a department store. She used general terms when referring to her hospital work so the employer would see that her customer service skills were just what was needed in the department store.

Instead of writing: Explained medical procedures and equipment to Hamilton Medical Center patients and their families to enable them to make wise decisions regarding surgery, care, and discharge.

Elizabeth wrote: Educated clients about new products and procedures at the medical center and assisted them in making personal decisions based on financial, lifestyle, and timeline concerns.

When Charles's military service ended, he wanted a job in corporate public relations, so he phrased his statements using civilian terminology to de-emphasize his career transition.

Instead of writing: Managed public relations for the U.S. Navy's Fleet Week, a $1.5 million celebration that drew 50,000 civilians.

Charles wrote: Managed public relations for a $1.5 million celebration sponsored by the Bay Area's largest employer and attended by some 50,000 people.

Always make it simple for an employer to understand how you fit into her organization. If necessary, translate your experience into terminology that she will identify with easily.

Keep It Relevant

Your achievements consist of several ingredients, some of which may have nothing to do with what you will offer your next employer. Make an impression that you're a good fit by presenting only the aspects of your achievements that relate to your job objective.

For example, Henry was an excellent event planner who wanted to use his organizational skills in a new field: graphic layout for a daily newspaper. He knew he could not assume the employer would conclude that Henry was capable of laying out newspaper copy just because he knew how to plan events, so Henry took extra care to draw the parallels between the two occupations.

> **Instead of writing:** Produced social and business events for up to 2,000 people, managing budgets, catering, entertainment, and logistics.

> **Henry wrote:** Maintained a perfect record of on-time delivery of at least 20 projects a month, involving time, budget, and space constraints.

As a horticulturist, Patty realized that the part of her job she liked the most was answering clients' questions. When she wrote her resume for a job as a travel agent, she emphasized her customer service skills and downplayed her scientific expertise.

> **Instead of writing:** Provided scientific information on thousands of plant species as the lead horticulturist of the country's most prestigious botanical garden.

> **Patty wrote:** Assisted customers in selecting from more than 2,000 options by patiently answering questions and educating them about costs and benefits.

In order to have effective achievement statements, refer to the aspects of your experiences that paint the picture of your job objective, and therefore have meaning to your prospective employer.

First Things First

Prioritize your statements, so the achievement most relevant to your job goal is first. For example, as a former office manager, 75 percent of Andrea's time was spent processing administrative paperwork, and less than 25 percent of her time was spent on training and

Career Casualty

Obey the seventh Resume Commandment: Thou shalt not lie. You can be creative, as long as you're honest.

Job-Hunt Hint

Select from your past only those parts of an achievement that describe you at your next job.

Career Casualty

Don't go on and on with details that aren't relevant to your job objective. Space is limited on your resume and the employer's clock is ticking the whole time she's reading it.

supervision. However, she wanted to get a job as a corporate trainer. So she prioritized her achievement statements to stress the training experience, even though it was not her primary responsibility.

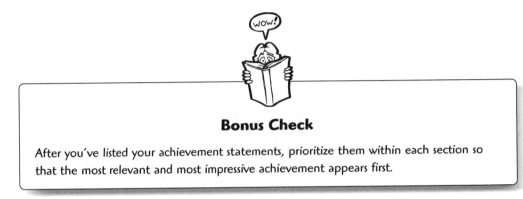

Bonus Check

After you've listed your achievement statements, prioritize them within each section so that the most relevant and most impressive achievement appears first.

The following order reflects the amount of time Andrea spent on each achievement:

- Supervised administration of firm's largest litigation department with more than 300 cases per week.
- Led office to achieve "#1 Team" award by motivating staff to take a customer service approach to all internal and external interactions.
- Trained 13 employees on new automated accounting system, providing classroom sessions, individual coaching, and written instructions.

This order reflects which achievements are most important to Andrea's job goal:

- Trained 13 employees on new automated accounting system, providing classroom sessions, individual coaching, and written instructions.
- Led office to achieve "#1 Team" award by motivating staff to take a customer service approach to all internal and external interactions.
- Supervised administration of firm's largest litigation department with more than 300 cases per week.

The order in which you list your achievements should indicate what tasks you like best and which ones you wish most to perform on your next job.

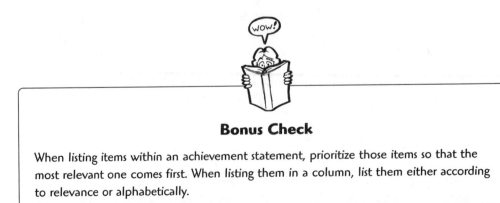

Bonus Check

When listing items within an achievement statement, prioritize those items so that the most relevant one comes first. When listing them in a column, list them either according to relevance or alphabetically.

Lights, Camera, Action Verbs!

A film crew may have lights and cameras, but there's no movie until there's action. Likewise, your resume needs dynamic language to make it move. To deliver the most punch in your achievement statements, use an action verb at or near the beginning of each line. Action verbs make your resume more powerful by emphasizing how you accomplished your goals.

The following list of verbs is categorized under two headings: Management and Communication. Which verbs most powerfully describe your achievements?

Terms of Employment

Responsible for is a slippery phrase that doesn't clearly describe your level of involvement. Did you think of an idea that others carried out, or did you work overtime to implement every detail of a project? Either way, be sure to give yourself full credit by using action verbs (instead of "responsible for") to indicate exactly what your role was.

Management	
accelerated	caused
accomplished	centralized
achieved	certified
activated	chaired
added	championed
administered	collaborated
advanced	completed
allocated	conceived
analyzed	concentrated
anticipated	conducted
appointed	consolidated
appropriated	contracted
approved	controlled
arranged	converted
assigned	coordinated
attained	corrected
augmented	cultivated
authorized	cut
bid	decided
boosted	defined
budgeted	delegated
built	delivered
capitalized on	designated
carried out	determined
	developed

Job-Hunt Hint

Using action verbs on your resume is one of the easiest ways to tell the employer that you're a go-getter!

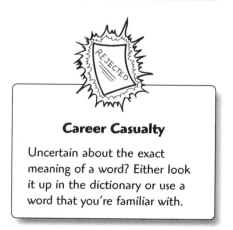

Career Casualty

Uncertain about the exact meaning of a word? Either look it up in the dictionary or use a word that you're familiar with.

Job-Hunt Hint

Read each line on your resume out loud. If you stumble over a word, consider changing it to one that's more comfortable for you. After all, in the job interview, you'll be expected to discuss what's on your resume with ease.

Career Casualty

Avoid using the same word many times in your resume. For instance, if you say "Managed a software project" in one bullet-point statement, say that you "Supervised a team of engineers" in another statement so as not to repeat the word "managed."

devised

directed

dominated

doubled

downsized

drove

earned

empowered

endorsed

engineered

enhanced

enlarged

enlisted

established

evaluated

exceeded

executed

expanded

expedited

facilitated

financed

focused

forced

forged

fostered

founded

fulfilled

gained

generated

governed

guided

handled

headed

heightened

hired

implemented

improved

incorporated

increased

induced

initiated

installed

instituted

integrated

intensified

introduced

invested

launched

led

lowered

magnified

maintained

managed

marketed

maximized

merged

met

minimized

mobilized

modernized

modified

monitored

motivated

multiplied

Bonus Check

Simple sentences are usually more effective than complicated sentences. Shorter words are often more powerful than longer ones. For hints on good writing technique, turn to Chapter 16, "You've Got Style." Although I wrote that chapter with letter writing in mind, there are several tips that apply to resume writing as well.

Career Casualty

Don't be redundant in your use of verbs within one statement. For instance, "created" and "developed" mean essentially the same, so write "Developed a software program," instead of "Created and developed a software program."

netted

obtained

opened

orchestrated

organized

oversaw

performed

piloted

pioneered

planned

positioned

precipitated

presided

prioritized

processed

produced

promoted

proposed

purchased

ran

ranked

rated

re-engineered

reached

realized

recommended

recruited

reduced

regulated

rejuvenated

remedied

renewed

represented

resolved

restored

restructured

revamped

reviewed

revitalized

revived

revolutionized

scheduled

secured

served as

set

shepherded

Job-Hunt Hint

Think of your resume as a sample writing piece that you're sending to a potential employer. If necessary, get help from someone who is prodigious in grammar and spelling to help with your composition so that your resume makes a good impression.

Career Casualty

If you're changing careers, be sure you're using the correct terms on your resume for the industry you're going into. For instance, an associate in the legal field is an attorney. An associate in retail is a salesperson. Big difference!

sold
solved
started
steered
stimulated
streamlined
strengthened
structured
succeeded
supervised
synchronized
systematized
targeted
trained
tripled
triumphed
turned around
underwrote
unified
united
upgraded
upheld
verified
won

Communication

addressed
adjudicated
advertised
advised
advocated
annotated
announced

answered
appeased
arbitrated
argued
articulated
asserted
assuaged
assured
authored
bargained
briefed
campaigned
canvassed
clarified
coached
coined
collaborated
communicated
compelled
compiled
composed
compromised
conversed
converted
convinced
corresponded
counseled
created
defined
delivered
demonstrated
demystified

depicted

described

detailed

developed

dictated

discussed

drafted

edited

educated

elucidated

encouraged

explained

expounded

expressed

facilitated

formulated

guaranteed

guided

illustrated

impressed

influenced

informed

inspired

instigated

instructed

interpreted

intervened

interviewed

intonated

lectured

litigated

lobbied

mediated

moderated

motivated

negotiated

ordered

outlined

persuaded

phrased

pitched

preached

prepared

presented

pressured

proclaimed

promoted

prompted

proofread

proposed

publicized

reassured

recommended

reconciled

remarked

represented

settled (disputes)

specified

spelled out

spoke

stated

stimulated

stipulated

stressed

Job-Hunt Hint

It's okay to use slang as long as it's understandable and appropriate. For instance, you could say that you "beat the competition" on a resume for a sales position; whereas it would be more appropriate to say that you "placed first in fundraising" in a resume targeted for nonprofit organizations.

Career Casualty

Avoid gerunds (verbs that end in "ing") in your writing whenever possible. For instance, say "Wrote 10 reports that proposed the value of carpooling," instead of "Wrote 10 reports proposing the value of carpooling."

swayed	verbalized
taught	voiced
trained	won over
translated	wrote
urged	

Bonus Check

If you get stuck figuring out how to phrase a line, browse through the resumes in Appendix B, "Portfolio of Sample Resumes," and throughout the chapters of this book. You're bound to come across a few lines that will work for you, even if they come from resumes with different job objectives than your own.

How'd the Other Guys Say It?

A quick look at what others have written might give you the jump start you need for writing about your own accomplishments. The following achievement statements were taken from several different resumes:

➤ Restructured entire Service Department, resulting in more efficient outreach programs.

➤ Initiated procedures to increase employee productivity while reducing stress levels.

➤ Successfully explained and demonstrated technical products in lay terminology to prospective buyers.

➤ Negotiated the sale of $100,000 worth of unprofitable inventory.

➤ Created sales and marketing programs that increased shopping center profits by 33 percent.

➤ Won more than 80 percent of cases, delivering persuasive arguments as legal representative for corporate clients in administrative law hearings.

➤ Increased MediSave's stock value five-fold in nine months by repositioning the product and company.

➤ Convinced more than 400 commuters to carpool, reducing the number of vehicles on the road by 225 per year.

Career Casualty

Most chronological resume writers make a big mistake: Because they're creating a history-based resume, they write job descriptions instead of dynamic achievements. Don't fall for that logic! By writing achievement statements, you'll turn a stereotypical document into a winning sales piece.

➤ Managed a national and international sales force of 32 manufacturers' representative companies for Teekel Press, a publisher.

➤ Exceeded delivery performance by 10 percent, taking it from 85 percent to a record 95 percent in an industry where the norm is 75 percent.

➤ Managed the sales and full Profit & Loss for 20 stores in Northern California region.

➤ Handled daily news coverage of the San Francisco 49ers and Oakland A's, which involved extensive travel.

➤ Authored two published pieces on international touring, which demystified the hardships and emphasized the rewards of independent travel.

➤ Reconciled differences among personnel, creating a more cohesive team spirit.

Bonus Check

Achievement statements on your resume can trigger some good conversation about your strengths during the interview.

Brainstorming

The questions on the following worksheet will help you think of relevant achievements for your resume. Not all of the questions will apply to your situation, so answer only the ones that do.

Achievement Statements Brainstorming Worksheet

1. What work-related projects are you proud of that relate to your job objective?

   Example: Increased productivity 20 percent as lead engineer on Hewlett-Packard's HMS technical team.

2. What are some quantifiable results that point out your ability?

   Example: Drove profits from $20 million to $34 million by directing a national celebrity marketing campaign.

3. When have you demonstrated PAR (Problem, Action, Result)? What was the problem, what was your action to remedy it, and what was the result?

   Example: Reduced theft 47 percent by instituting Shoppers' Spy, a tight yet discreet security program.

4. When did you positively affect the organization, the bottom line, your boss, your co-workers, or your clients?

   Example: Enhanced staff morale through a six-month incentive program that also prompted a major increase in sales.

5. What awards, commendations, or publications have you achieved that relate to your job objective?

   Example: Awarded "Top Salesperson" for three consecutive years.

6. How is success measured in your field? How do you measure up?

   Example: Selected by the NIH to represent the United States at the International AIDS Conference in Brazil.

7. Are you good at using the skills required for this job? When have you demonstrated that to be true?

   Example: Used advanced CAD tools to create a totally new look in video game modeling.

8. What activities, paid and unpaid, have you performed that used skills you'll be using at your new job?

   Example: Offered academic counseling to 40 students at "Make It Happen," a volunteer program at Sanford High School.

9. When did someone sit up and take notice of how skilled you are?

   Example: Commended for achieving 97 percent of production goal in an industry where 85 percent is considered high.

In addition to filling out this worksheet, you might want to browse through the resumes in Appendix B and other chapters to see which phrases trigger ideas in you.

Bonus Check

Name-dropping is the name of the game. Look for opportunities to enhance your image by slipping in names of impressive people, companies, or organizations.

Warning! Functional Resume Ahead

Many times functional resume writers make the mistake of writing accomplishment statements without indicating where the achievements took place. This practice makes potential employers uneasy because they have no way of confirming the experience. The solution? Give each accomplishment credibility by saying where it happened. Here are three ways to indicate where your success took place:

1. Incorporate the name of the organization or your position into the sentence:

   Managed Harrington Department Store's $1.5 million budget.

   Collaborated with executives to create a new marketing strategy, as member of the St. Francis Board of Directors.

2. Reference the organization or your position at the end of the statement:

   Managed budget of $1.5 million. (Harrington Department Store)

   Collaborated with executives to create a new marketing strategy. (St. Francis Board of Directors)

3. Group achievements together according to where they happened, still keeping them within skill categories. This kind of organization, in effect, becomes a hybrid resume based on a functional format (explained in Chapter 14, "A Functional Hybrid That Makes Sense").

Bonus Check

A well-crafted functional resume that makes it clear where the job seeker's achievements took place can win over employers, even those who claim not to like functional resumes.

You'll notice all three of these techniques as you peruse the sample functional resumes in Appendix B.

The Least You Need to Know

➤ In a chronological resume, place your achievement statements under the appropriate job title in the body of your resume.

➤ In a functional resume, your skill headings become subheadings under the Relevant Experience section in the body of your resume.

➤ Write powerful achievement statements instead of boring job descriptions.

➤ Use action verbs at or near the beginning of your achievement statements.

➤ Prioritize bulleted points within each section so the statement with the most impact comes first.

➤ Include the information on where an achievement took place in functional resumes.

Chapter 10

Step Five: Education and Extra Credit

In This Chapter

➤ How to create a proper Education section

➤ Where to put professional affiliations, community service, and other information on your resume

➤ How to deal with an employer's request for your salary history

➤ What not to put on your resume

Your resume is looking pretty good, isn't it? You've resolved your work history problems, written dynamite achievement statements, made claims that blow your competition out of the water—you're on a roll! You need to consider only a few more things, and then you'll be ready to drop your resume in the mail.

In this chapter, I'll share some helpful hints on how to make the most of your academic, professional, and vocational training, as well as other activities that support your job objective. I'll also explain why some information, such as references, salary history, and personal data, may not belong on your resume at all.

Finish Lines

At this point, you may be left with laundry lists of technical, personal, and professional details that don't fit into the primary sections of your resume discussed so far. Lingering lists might include the following information:

➤ Education

➤ Professional training

➤ Community service

➤ Professional affiliations

Career Casualty

Don't feel pressure to have lots of extra sections on your resume. If your resume is complete with your Heading, Job Objective, Summary of Qualifications, Professional Achievements, Work History, and Education sections, stop right there. After all, look at how many of the sample resumes in Appendix B, "Portfolio of Sample Resumes," have just those six sections.

Job-Hunt Hint

Instead of listing all the classes and workshops you ever attended, list only the ones that support your job objective.

➤ Publications

➤ Awards

➤ Computer skills

➤ Personal pursuits

Even if you feel like just throwing them in a big pile at the bottom of the page, don't! Instead, create one or more logical sections that will spark the employer's interest. Sneak a peek at the following template to see where you might place your extra goodies.

Education 101

Your education is almost always a point of interest to a prospective employer. The Education section is usually positioned at or near the end of the resume, as noted on the previous template.

In some cases, however, it's better to place the Education section under the Summary of Qualifications section near the beginning of the resume. You might want to put it here if one or more of the following conditions applies:

➤ Your education is highly relevant to your new position.

➤ You're a new graduate and you want to show off your degree.

➤ You have no employment experience in the field you are going into, but you have a degree or training in that field.

What If?

Education comes in many forms (formal, independent, professional training, and experiential), and there are as many ways to measure its results (degrees, credentials, certifications, equivalencies, years of experience, lists of acquired skills).

You probably fall into one of the following categories:

➤ You have one or more college degrees.

➤ You are about to achieve your college degree.

➤ You have a college degree equivalent.

➤ You went to college but didn't complete your degree program.

➤ You just graduated from high school.

➤ You graduated from high school some time ago and never went to college.

(Extra Resume Sections)

Name
Street
City, State Zip
Phone, Fax, E-mail

JOB OBJECTIVE: The job you want next

SUMMARY OF QUALIFICATIONS

- How much experience you have in the field of your job objective, in a related field, or using the skills required for your new position.
- An overall career accomplishment that shows you'd be good at this job.
- What someone would say about you as a recommendation.

PROFESSIONAL EXPERIENCE

19xx-pres.   Job Title   **Company Name, City, State**
- An accomplishment you are proud of that shows you're good at this profession.
- A problem you solved and the results.
- A time when you positively affected the organization, the bottom line, your boss, your co-workers, your clients.
- Awards, commendations, publications, etc., you achieved that relate to your job objective.

19xx-xx   Job Title   **Company Name, City, State**
- A project you are proud of that supports your job objective.
- Another accomplishment that shows you're good at this line of work.
- Quantifiable results that point out your skill.

19xx-xx   Job Title   **Company Name, City, State**
- An accomplishment you are proud of that shows you will be valued by your next employer.
- An occasion when someone "sat up and took notice" of your skill.

EDUCATION
Degree, Major (if relevant), 19xx (optional), University, City, State

PROFESSIONAL AFFILIATIONS

Association	Position (optional)	Dates (optional)
Association	Position (optional)	Dates (optional)

COMMUNITY SERVICE

Volunteer position	Organization	Dates (optional)
Volunteer position	Organization	Dates (optional)

Template of chronological resume with Education and other sections highlighted.

151

Career Casualty

If you don't have a college degree, don't let that discourage you from applying for jobs that require one. If you have the right life experience and you present it effectively in your resume, you might very well win a chance at the job.

Job-Hunt Hint

If you've earned a graduate degree and are applying for an academic or scientific position, you probably want to create a curriculum vitae. Turn to Chapter 15, "When You Really *Are* a Brain Surgeon: The Curriculum Vitae," to learn the ins and outs of writing a CV, including how to create your Education section.

Let's look at how to present each one of these situations.

Hot College Degrees

Perhaps the most common listing for the Education section on a resume is a college degree. (Don't let the lack of a college degree stop you from applying for a job that requires one; life experience often grabs an employer's attention and lands the applicant a job!) Let's begin by talking about degrees and related information. If you have one or more college degrees, keep the following points in mind:

➤ State where each degree (graduate and undergraduate) was received. You don't have to list all the different schools you attended leading up to achieving your degree, just list the one where you obtained your degree.

➤ Dates are optional. They sometimes indicate how old you are and how current your knowledge is, so be conscious of that when you decide whether to include dates.

➤ Majors, minors, theses, dissertations, internships, projects, papers, and coursework should be listed only if they are relevant to your job objective.

➤ You can spell out a degree (for example, Bachelor of Arts) or use the representative letters (BA or B.A.).

Phillip Reikels listed his Education section near the top of his resume (following) because his degrees are so important to his Job Objective.

Getting Credit for Your Pending Degree

If you are currently in a relevant educational or training program but have not yet finished, list the program and name of the institution you are attending, followed by the date you intend to finish or one of the following phrases:

➤ Currently enrolled

➤ Anticipated completion: Spring 2001

➤ In progress

➤ Six months completed

Robyn Jones's resume demonstrates this point.

Phillip Riekels, RN, MS, CNA

12 Palmer Avenue • Muskegon, California 12345 • (123) 123-1234 • PhRiekels@holt.com

Health Care Administrator with 20 years combined experience:
Project Management
Standards Development/Quality Assessment and Improvement
Staff Training and Development
Client Services

EDUCATION

MS, Nursing Major with dual focus: Administration and Education, 1991
Thesis: Identification of Family Problems During the Treatment Stage of Cancer
University of Oklahoma, Oklahoma City, Oklahoma

BS, Nursing, 1979, University of Arizona, Tucson, Arizona
BA, History of Art, 1973, University of Michigan, Ann Arbor, Michigan

Continuing Education
Numerous courses to maintain **Certified Nurse Administrator** status, 1995-present
Western Network for Nurse Executives, 1994, University of California at Berkeley

PROFESSIONAL EXPERIENCE

1992-present **St. Agnes Medical Center,** Fresno, California
DIRECTOR PATIENT CARE SERVICES, 1997-present
DIRECTOR MEDICAL/SURGICAL, 1992-1997

Managed operating budgets up to $14M, 382 FTEs, and 272 patient beds for this 326-bed accredited, not-for-profit, regional, acute care facility.

- Revitalized Quality Assurance Program by developing high standards, establishing interdepartmental problem solving, and transitioning to Quality Assessment and Improvement.

- Played primary role in achieving JCAHO accreditation and placement within top 10% of facilities nationwide.

- Improved staff productivity, patient satisfaction, and quality of care.

  - Empowered staff by decentralizing management and decision making within patient-care services. Reorganized, trained, and supported staff.

  - Restructured systems for delivery of care, including staff roles and interdepartmental reporting.

  - Introduced communication and computer technology involving 20 departments.

  - Aligned FTEs with volume and cost variations by introducing staffing by Hours Per Patient Day (HPPD) to replace staffing ratios and static patterns.

  - Improved communication and conflict resolution by providing 20-hour training program, Increasing Personal Effectiveness, for over 500 personnel.

(Continued)

153

Phillip Riekels, Page 2

St. Agnes Medical Center (Continued)

- Recruited 13 British nurses (five of whom have stayed for more than five years) as a result of three trips to London. Worked with advertising agency, State Board of Nursing, and immigration attorney.

- Represented the hospital through newspaper and TV interviews about innovative solutions to health care problems.

- Oversaw remodeling of three major units. Merged intensive and cardiac care into one critical care unit.

1989-1992   **HCA Northwest Hospital,** Tucson, Arizona
MANAGER SURGICAL/ORTHOPEDICS

Played major role in the start-up of this new 150-bed, for-profit, acute care community hospital.

- Developed and managed a 28-bed surgical unit.

- Managed a 24-bed ortho/neuro unit and hospital-wide messenger service.

- Started the nursing Quality Assurance Program and chaired its committee.

- Implemented the HCA Patient Classification System.

- Established HPPD staffing guidelines for all nursing units.

1988-1989   **University of Oklahoma, College of Nursing,** Tulsa, Oklahoma
TEACHING ASSISTANT

1987-1988   **CSI Productions,** Tulsa, Oklahoma
RESEARCHER AND WRITER

Wrote narratives for this producer of health care training materials on Cardiac Monitoring, Medicating the Patient, and Antiembolism Stockings.

1984-1987   **Gila Pueblo College,** Globe, Arizona
NURSING INSTRUCTOR

- Saved the nursing program by achieving 100% graduate passing rate on State Board Exams, a drastic improvement from previous years' unacceptably low rates.

- Redeveloped entire content of first year associate degree nursing program to update information and improve presentation.

1980-1984   **Hospitals in Arizona and Oklahoma**
CLINICAL PATIENT CARE positions: Charge Nurse, IV Therapist, Staff Nurse

AFFILIATIONS

World Affairs Council

Nursing Administrators Council (NAC) of Central San Joaquin Valley
- As President, established NAC as a voice of influence on nursing and health care in the valley.

Organization of Nurse Executives, California (ONE-C)

Sigma Theta Tau, National Nursing Honorary Society

Phillip Riekels's resume.

ROBYN JONES
1234 Primavera Ct., Portland, ME 12345, (123) 123-1234

JOB OBJECTIVE

A position in organizational systems management

PROFILE

- Expertise in developing and managing organizational systems that:
  Facilitate efficiency   Encourage creativity
  Promote responsible behavior   Respond to change
  Optimize the group's diversity   Build team spirit

- Committed to improving the environment through research and education.

- Particular skill in empowering others to acknowledge and articulate their value and role in an organization/society.

EXPERIENCE

1993-present **Facilitator, Navy Program for Personal Responsibility**
The Prevent Office, University of Maine, NAS Biddeford, ME

- Facilitate weekly classes for 20 Navy personnel from diverse cultural backgrounds, promoting personal responsibility through communication and appropriate lifestyle behaviors. Topics include:
  Decision Making and Problem Solving Strategies   Interpersonal Skills
  Personal and Organizational Values and Conflicts   Resistance to Addictions

1989-1993   **Manager, Project Management and Contracts**
Accounting Manager
Loonery & Crosby, Inc., Saco, ME

An international consulting firm specializing in projects that address energy efficiency.

- Facilitated forums for organizational dialogue, encouraging excellent communication among all levels of personnel (president through support staff).

- Improved client relations by establishing procedures and training staff to develop strong consultant-client rapport.

- Worked with staff to provide tools and resources needed to manage projects.

1984-1989   **Independent Bookkeeping Contractor**

1981-1984   **Paralegal**
Raddison, Maloney & Powers, Portland, ME

EDUCATION

Candidate, Master's Program, Social and Cultural Anthropology
Maine Institute of Multicultural Studies, Portland, ME

B.A., Anthropology and Social Studies
Macalester College, St. Paul, MN

Robyn Jones's resume.

Bonus Check

If you have just one or two entries for a section, you might combine two similar sections with a double heading, as in the following examples:

Education and Training

Training and Credentials

Awards and Presentations

Career Casualty

Don't look overqualified for the job. For some positions, your master's or doctoral degree might scare the pants off an employer because you look too expensive or intimidating. When in doubt, leave the degree off.

Job-Hunt Hint

If a job posting requires a particular degree that you don't have, don't let that stop you from applying. On your resume, emphasize your relevant life experience, education, and training. If you present your case well, the employer may see your qualifications as a degree equivalent.

Interpreting Degree Equivalents

If you achieved a degree equivalency through a less traditional or non-American system, state your experience in terms of its equivalency, for example, "B.A. equivalent, St. Paul University, Rome, Italy." Grace Deminier's resume presents her degree equivalent.

Don't Have a Degree?

If you went to college, but you do not intend to get your degree in the immediate future, write your area of study and the name of the college, for instance: Liberal Arts, Oberlin College. If you attended several schools without completing your degree requirements, list only one or two schools. Listing more than that might make the reader think you tend to move around a lot without finishing things. Leonora Braun's resume shows how you can present a partial college education.

Yahoo! Just Got My High School Diploma

If you are a new high school graduate, write the name of your high school and year of graduation. If you have enrolled in a college, say so, for example, "Enrolled in St. Mary's College, Moraga, CA." Frank Jordan's resume (following) lists his high school diploma.

Grace Deminier

123 California Street, Fort Wayne, Indiana 12345   (123) 123-1234

JOB OBJECTIVE: Director of Customer Service

SUMMARY OF QUALIFICATIONS

- 10 years as department manager with experience in internal and external customer service.
- Excellent supervisory skills which enhance employee skills to produce quality work.
- Computer literate: Windows and Macintosh.

PROFESSIONAL ACCOMPLISHMENTS

MANAGEMENT
Paramount Credit Services, Corp.

- Monitored $500,000 per month in expenses and compiled data for upper management.
- Decreased expenditures 35% by standardizing purchasing procedures.
- Created and directed all administrative procedures for this 58-person financial firm affiliated with Xerox Corporation.
- Wrote six manuals (70-100 pages each) to clarify responsibilities of accounts payable, telecommunications, records, check processing, and administrative support.

Public Information Group

- As manager of 28 employees, increased productivity, morale, and individual and team initiative by fostering employee career development within the company.
- Improved staff performance evaluations by upgrading job descriptions.
- Created and administered an $850,000 annual budget.

CUSTOMER SERVICE
Public Information Group

- Created system for identifying and notifying past-due accounts, recovering $236,000 of uncollected premiums from previous years.
- Used diplomatic yet firm approach to resolve disputes with customers, agents, and sales staff.
- Encouraged interdepartmental cooperation through excellent internal customer service.

Paramount Credit Services, Corp.

- Resolved client issues promptly as liaison to branch offices and attorneys.
- Anticipated and handled hardware and software problems, achieving minimum of downtime for six departments that work with offices in other time zones.

WORK HISTORY

2000	Administrative Assistant	Environmental Review Group, Fort Wayne, IN
1995-99	Supervisor, Administration	Paramount Credit Services, Fort Wayne, IN
1989-95	Manager, Policy Administration	Public Information Group, Toledo, OH
1987-89	Family Management	Les Sables d'Olonne, France

EDUCATION
B.A. equivalent, French, Sorbonne, Paris, France, 1986

Grace Deminier's resume.

Leonora Braun

123 Sea Cliff Drive • San Diego, CA 12345 • (123) 123-1234

JOB OBJECTIVE

Bookkeeper/Accountant

HIGHLIGHTS OF QUALIFICATIONS

- Experienced Bookkeeper/Accountant for small and medium-sized businesses.
- Ability to work independently.
- Strong list of references.

PROFESSIONAL EXPERIENCE

1982-present BOOKKEEPER/ACCOUNTANT

Selected Clients/Projects

Michael Smith, CPA, San Diego, CA
Blue Nile Cafe, San Diego, CA
Star Mountain Texaco, La Jolla, CA
The Walters Marketing Group, San Diego, CA
Paintings '80, La Jolla, CA
Fleur D'Alsasce Restaurant, San Diego, CA
Mark-Thomas Corporation, San Diego, CA

Michael Smith, CPA

- Prepared federal and state tax returns for corporations, partnerships, individuals, and estates.
- Maintained general ledgers and prepared financial statements for assigned clients.
- Prepared payrolls, quarterly federal and state payroll tax returns, and state sales tax returns.

Blue Nile Cafe and Star Mountain Texaco

- Set up company books, maintained general ledgers, and prepared Schedule C and partnership returns.

The Walters Marketing Group

- Maintained general ledger, accounts receivable, and accounts payable. Prepared financial statements.
- Prepared payroll, federal and state payroll tax returns, and sales tax returns.
- Assisted in the conversion to computer generated accounting.

EDUCATION

Accounting: University of California, Berkeley Extension, San Francisco, CA
Healds Business College, San Francisco, CA
San Diego State University Extension, San Diego, CA

Computer: Computer Options, San Diego, CA

Leonora Braun's resume.

Frank Jordan
P.O. Box 12
Bayview Meadow, ND 12345
(123) 123-1234

OBJECTIVE: Bus Driver

SUMMARY OF QUALIFICATIONS

- Dependable, hard worker who can be counted on to "get the job done."
- Excellent driving record; always give first priority to safety.
- Friendly and well liked; good at customer relations.
- Available to relocate.

EXPERIENCE

Driver/Tour Guide   **Trolley Tours, Bay Meadows, ND, 1998-2000**

- Drove small tour bus through scenic parts of this resort, pointing out sites, providing friendly service, and assisting senior citizens.
- Did light repair work as needed.
- Recognized as #1 employee within this company of 15.

Sales Representative   **Recycled Tractor Parts, Townsend, ND, Summer '98**

- Sold used tractor and equipment parts by phone and over the counter.
- Handled inventory, shipping, and nationwide teletype service.

Driver   **Paris Oil Recycling, Paris, ND, Summer '97**

- Picked up and delivered waste oil (until business was sold).

EDUCATION

Diploma, Wells High School, Wells, ND, 1999

Frank Jordan's resume.

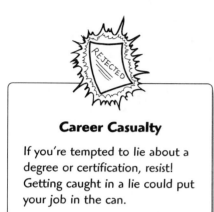

Career Casualty

If you're tempted to lie about a degree or certification, resist! Getting caught in a lie could put your job in the can.

The Not-So-New High School Diploma

If you received your high school diploma more than two years ago and have no additional schooling, you do not need to have an Education section on your resume unless the job you are applying for specifically asks for a high school diploma. If it does, put "Graduate" or "Diploma," followed by the name of your high school. State your graduation date only if it doesn't blow your cover with regard to your age (as explained in Chapter 8, "Step Three: Been There, Done That"). If you have a high school diploma but no formal higher education, one option is to create a section titled Professional Development. In this section, you can list any training, workshops, seminars, or classes you have attended. Another option is to simply omit the Education section on your resume. Rose Manson didn't put an Education section on her resume (following) because she didn't have a college degree, her high school graduation was many years ago, and her professional experience is all that she needs to qualify for her objective.

Bonus Check

Presenting your material so that it looks appropriate for the company and position you're applying for is one way of telling the reader that you understand the industry and will fit in. For instance, Frank Jordan's resume is a very simple one-pager that makes him look like a straightforward, easy-to-approach guy. That's appropriate for his job objective (bus driver).

Bonus Check

If you don't have any formal higher education, consider having a section called Training or Professional Development, where you list relevant workshops, seminars, and classes.

ROSE MANSON
1234 Fourteenth St., #123
Birmingham, AL 12345
(123) 123-1234

OBJECTIVE: To retain insurance company relations, as new owner of Highland Insurance Agency

★ Reliable reputation among Birmingham attorneys.

★ Proven ability to work profitably with home office.

★ Currently developing underwriting practice at Highland Insurance Agency.

PROFESSIONAL ACCOMPLISHMENTS

CLIENT RELATIONS

As Branch Manager, Bonding Service, American Insurance:

- Developed and serviced a loyal client base, almost doubling branch premium dollars from $190,000 to $365,000 per year.
    - Gained a reputation among attorneys for providing timely service/markets.
    - Recaptured accounts lost during departure of previous branch manager.
    - Offered additional services to gain accounts.
    - Generated new business through regular court appearances.

As Vice President, Highland Insurance Agency:

- Secured clientele, based upon my established reputation among local attorneys.

UNDERWRITING

As Branch Manager, Bonding Service, American Insurance:

- Authorized to execute under power of attorney in all counties in Alabama, with underwriting authority up to $50,000. Branch bond amounts ranged from $6,000 to $3,000,000.

- Simplified application form to more effectively gather underwriting data.

- Established and implemented more efficient procedures for home office approval, reducing turnaround time from three days to eight hours.

- Dealt directly with surety home office in Springfield, IL.

- Gained extensive knowledge of litigation process as it relates to judicial bonds.

- Negotiated with brokerage firms to perfect surety positions.

MANAGEMENT

As Branch Manager, Bonding Service, American Insurance:

- Developed a user-friendly billing system that increased efficiency of premium collections.

- Managed office relocation, keeping down-time to a minimum.

WORK HISTORY

1999-pres.	**Vice President**	Highland Insurance Agency, Birmingham, AL
1994-1999	**Branch Manager**	Bonding Service, American Insurance, Birmingham, AL
1986-1994	**Operations Manager**	Windows Plus, Inc., Birmingham, AL

Rose Manson's resume.

The Last Word

Your destination is within sight; you don't even need binoculars to see the resume shore anymore! A few more sections might appear on your resume, such as professional affiliations, community service, computer skills, and personal interests. Let's talk about them.

Job-Hunt Hint

Dates are optional under the Volunteerism section. If you list them, you should present your volunteer work in reverse chronology (your most recent work first). If you don't use dates, list your community service according to impact (the most relevant first).

Volunteerism That Pays Off

What you do in your unpaid time may say as much about what kind of person you are than what you do for employment. If you feel that your volunteerism makes a statement about your dedication, character, or social awareness, or in any way enhances your qualifications for your next job, a section called Community Service, Civic Leadership, or Volunteerism is the place to list it.

Professional Schmoozer

Professional associations to which you currently belong or have once belonged can be listed either alphabetically or in order of relevance to your profession under a section called Professional Affiliations. If you currently hold or have held an office, that should also be noted.

Getting Published

Articles, books, chapters in books, and research papers that you have authored or coauthored belong in a section called Publications. Usually, dates accompany this information, requiring presentation in reverse chronology (the most current date first).

Career Casualty

Don't exaggerate your achievements when it comes to listing team awards. If you try to take entire credit for the award, it could backfire if it is discovered, because you'd look like a cheat. The solution: Be up front in your listing and state that it was a team award. By doing so, you'll also get credit for being a team player.

Standing Up for Your Award

In the Awards section, list honors, awards, and grants you have received that support your job objective. You can arrange this list according to date received (if you give the date) or by relevance to your next job (if you don't provide the date).

Flaunting Your Computer Skills

If you have computer skills that are important to your next job, you can highlight them under a special section called Computer Skills. Your list might include hardware, software, languages, systems, and networks with which you have experience.

Making a Hobby of It

Some job seekers like to have a section called Personal Pursuits, Personal Interests, or Personal Activities in which they can list travel, sports, religious, political, and other personal activities. The Personal Pursuits section is optional and should be included only if you feel your personal activities

➤ Add to your qualifications as a candidate for your job objective.

➤ Say something about your character that might be valued on the job.

Professional resume writers disagree as to whether personal interests are appropriate on a resume. Some employers find them interesting and valuable; others find them irrelevant. Although many employers have said they wouldn't hold it against a job seeker for including that sort of information, consider whether stating your personal activities might create undesired conflict with your employer's views and preferences. A potential conflict of interest could arise over issues such as race, religion, unions, and other controversial topics.

Bonus Check

Some employers like the Personal Pursuits section of an applicant's resume. They look there hoping to find an interesting non–work-related topic for the interview and often use such a topic as an ice-breaker.

Here are some assumptions an employer might make from the following listings on resumes:

➤ An applicant who lists "Board of Trustees, St. Anne's Episcopal Church" is indicating that she is actively involved in her church. Although some employers may welcome this involvement, others may feel uncomfortable with it.

➤ An applicant who writes "Member, Gay and Lesbian Couples United" on his resume tells the reader that he is probably homosexual. Such a disclosure may create a problematic impression with a hiring manager.

➤ The owner of a nonunion company might feel threatened by an applicant who lists "Organizer, Teamsters, Local Chapter 47092," because he may be worried the applicant will want to unionize his company.

Job-Hunt Hint

Every word on your resume, even those listed in your extra sections, should paint the picture of you on your next job.

Job-Hunt Hint

If you're questioning whether to add another section to your resume, weigh the pros and cons. Does it warrant the extra space it will take, especially if it means the resume will spill onto a second page?

Anything Missing?

Other headings that might appear on your resume include Exhibitions, Research, Lectures, Licenses, and Certifications. Cruise through the many resumes in Appendix B to see how various professionals have presented their laundry lists of achievements.

On the Line

It's time to get your lists in order. Use the following worksheet to jot down what laundry lists you might have on your resume and what you'll call each section. You're not expected to have all these sections on your resume, so if one doesn't work for you, skip it and go on to the next one.

Laundry List Worksheet

Education

Other name I might give this section:

_____

Laundry list for this section:

_____

_____

_____

_____

_____

Community Service

Other name I might give this section:

_____

Laundry list for this section:

_____

_____

_____

_____

_____

Professional Affiliations

Other name I might give this section:

_____

Laundry list for this section:

_____

_____

_____

_____

_____

Publications

Other name I might give this section:

_____

Laundry list for this section:

_____

_____

_____

_____

Awards

Other name I might give this section:

_____

Computer Skills

Other name I might give this section:

_____

Laundry list for this section:

_____

_____

_____

_____

_____

Personal Pursuits

Other name I might give this section:

_____

Laundry list for this section:

_____

_____

_____

_____

_____

Other Sections

The name for this section:

_____

Laundry list for this section:

_____

_____

_____

_____

_____

Excellent! You've now completed the contents of your resume.

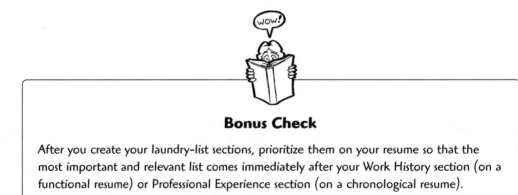

Bonus Check

After you create your laundry-list sections, prioritize them on your resume so that the most important and relevant list comes immediately after your Work History section (on a functional resume) or Professional Experience section (on a chronological resume).

Getting by with Nothing

Knowing what to leave off your resume can be just as important as knowing what to include. Do not include the following:

➤ Salary history or requests

➤ Reference information

➤ Personal data

Let's talk about why these items are best left off your resume.

Money Talk

Although some job advertisements ask for a resume and salary history, the two do not go together. Discussion about salary belongs in the interview, not on the resume. It is to your advantage not to make a monetary request before an interview. Indicating salary requirements before the interview may increase your chances of being screened out and decrease your bargaining power during salary negotiations.

If you feel obligated to address salary in order to fulfill the employer's initial application requirements, do so in your cover letter, not on your resume. Turn to Chapter 17, "The Cover Letter Connection," to get ideas for talking about money in your letter.

Referring to References

Addresses and phone numbers of references should not be a part of your resume. They belong on a separate sheet of paper that you bring to the job interview.

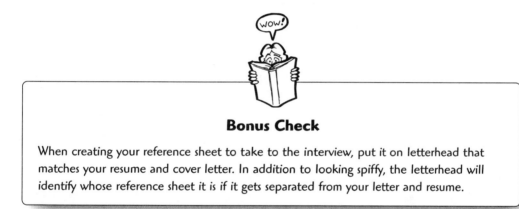

Bonus Check

When creating your reference sheet to take to the interview, put it on letterhead that matches your resume and cover letter. In addition to looking spiffy, the letterhead will identify whose reference sheet it is if it gets separated from your letter and resume.

Also, a big thumbs-down on writing "References available upon request" at the bottom of your resume. It's unnecessary, because employers will assume that you have references, and they know to ask for them when the time comes.

Forget the Personal Stuff

Including information about your age, sex, marital status, and health is not appropriate for resumes being used in the United States (but you might want to include some personal information on your resume if something in your personal life supports your job objective). If you're applying abroad (in Europe or the United Kingdom), however, it might be expected.

Job-Hunt Hint

Although personal information doesn't usually appear on a resume, you may want to make an exception if something in your personal life supports your job objective. For instance, if you're applying for a position designing content for a Web site on diabetes, you might mention on your resume (perhaps in your Summary of Qualifications) that you have diabetes if you think it will increase your chances for an interview.

The Least You Need to Know

➤ List only the degrees, courses, training sessions, and workshops that are relevant to your job objective.

➤ If you have a degree or credential that makes you look overqualified for the job, don't put it on your resume.

➤ If dates within the Education section tell the reader more than you want to reveal, leave them out.

➤ Take inventory of the relevant information that you still want to include and list that data in appropriate sections such as Community Service, Professional Affiliations, and Awards.

➤ Do not include salary history, references, and personal data on your resume.

Chapter 11

Step Six: The Big Production

In This Chapter

➤ Making sure your resume is in order

➤ Looking spiffy on paper

➤ Using the right type

➤ Getting your resume to the employer

See, it didn't take you 34 days to reach your goal, unlike Columbus. I knew you could do it. But before you start stuffing envelopes and announcing your career move to the world, take one more minute to review the checklist in this chapter as well as the tips on printing and circulating your resume. Then you'll be armed with a winning strategy for getting your resume out to the job market.

Designer Resumes

These few design tricks will help to ensure that your resume looks spiffy once it gets into the hands of the employer:

➤ Use an appropriate typeface.

➤ Use the right size of type.

➤ Use bullet points for your achievement statements.

➤ Add vertical or horizontal lines. (This is completely optional and should only be used if the lines increase ease of reading or the aesthetics of the resume.)

➤ Make sure you have enough white space.

➤ Keep a clean master copy.

➤ Make sure your reproductions are clean.

➤ Use good paper.

Following are instructions for how to take advantage of some of these design concepts using Microsoft Word (MS Word). If you're working in an application other than MS Word, consult your manual to learn how to get the job done.

Bonus Check

A nice touch for your resume presentation is matching letterhead, and it's easy to create. On your computer, duplicate your resume and delete all the text except the Heading in the duplicate. Instant letterhead!

Fancy Fonts and Practical Print

Choosing the style of type for your resume can be fun. You have several choices, and each one has a slightly different look and feel. To help you pick one for your resume, let me explain the ABC's of type styles.

Job-Hunt Hint

To find the right typeface for your resume, try on a few by printing out several versions of your resume, each with a different font, so you can see which one you like most.

There are two categories of type (or *font*, as it's called in the business):

➤ Serif

➤ Sans serif

Either a serif or sans serif font is okay for your resume, but most graphic designers say that serif type is easier to read.

Serif's Up!

Serif type has little feet on its characters (see examples following). There are many serif fonts, ranging from super fancy scripts to basic typewriter print. For your resume, stay away from the two extremes and pick one that's mid-range so that your resume is easy to read and pleasing to the eye.

The following serif fonts are found on most word processing programs and are suitable for the job. As you can see from the resume samples in this book, serif fonts are what I use most of the time. Notice that I've printed each name in the font it represents so you can compare them all.

New Century Schoolbook

AGaramond

Palatino

Times

Bonus Check

If you travel and need to be able to print your resume on the run, store it on your laptop computer, on a floppy disk, on a ZIP disk, or in your e-mail system, so you can access it from remote locations. Most public computers and printers (such as those at libraries and copy centers) can produce your document with no problem if you've used the standard fonts listed in this section.

Simply Serif

Sans serif characters don't have little feet on them. Following are some sans serif fonts that I like.

> Helvetica
>
> Univers

To change the font in your MS Word document

1. Select the particular text you want to change, or choose Select All from the Edit menu.

2. Choose Font in your pull-down toolbar at the top of your screen.

3. Highlight the font you want.

Once you get the hang of changing fonts, you'll be able to do it in the blink of an eye.

Does Size Matter?

Font sizes are measured by points, and with a few exceptions, those measurements are standard among the various fonts. Use either 11 or 12 point for the text of your resume. Don't be tempted to use 10 point or smaller in order to make it all fit on one page; it'll be too hard to read.

The type size for your major headings (Job Objective, Summary of Qualifications, Professional Experience, and Education) should all be equal to each other and may be as small as 11 point and as large as 13 point. Choose the point size to please your taste, staying within the 11- to 13-point limit.

Although there is no standard size of type for your name on your resume, a good rule of thumb is that it should be no larger than 18 points and no smaller than 12 points.

You can adjust a font's *point size* by pulling down the Format menu from the toolbar. Then click Font and choose a size from the Size box.

Terms of Employment

Fonts are typefaces, which come in two styles: **serif** (with the little feet on the characters) and **sans serif** (without the feet).

Terms of Employment

Point size is a measurement used by typographers to gauge the size of type. The larger the number of the point, the larger the letter, number, or symbol is.

Career Casualty

Watch out for the family of fonts called Times (Times New Roman, New York Times, or any font with Times in its name). These fonts look great, but they tend to print small. If you are using a Times font, go no smaller than 12 point in the text of your resume.

Job-Hunt Hint

If you export your text into a graphics program such as PageMaker or QuarkXpress, you can really have fun with the layout options.

Sharp-Shooting Bullets

Bullet points are little dots placed at the beginning of a statement, which help the reader move swiftly through your resume. They let you present your information in bite-sized pieces and avoid unwanted paragraphs (as mentioned in Chapter 3, "Winning Resume Wisdom"). Here's how to create the bullet point in MS Word:

➤ On the Macintosh, press the Option and 8 keys at the same time.

➤ In MS Word for Windows, select the bullet icon on your toolbar or go to the Format menu and select Bullets and Numbering.

There are symbols other than bullet points that can be used to separate statements on your resume. Here are some that I like:

→

■

☐

You can elaborate on a bullet-point statement by adding sub-bullet statements. Sub-bullet statements should be indented and should start with a symbol other than the bullet point, perhaps a dash, plus sign, or one of the untraditional symbols mentioned above.

The following resume by Joanne Rainey demonstrates the use of dashes to create indented sub–bullet-point statements under her achievements.

Shady Bars

You may like the look of lines, double lines, bars, or shaded bars running across or up and down your resume. Here's how to do those nifty extras if you're working in MS Word:

1. Put your cursor where you want to insert a line or bar into your resume.
2. In your toolbar, access the Format pull-down menu.
3. Select Borders and Shading.
4. Under Setting, choose Box.
5. Under Style, choose the width.
6. Under Preview, click on the icon representing the bottom of the box.

It's that simple, and the results will make you look like a desktop-publishing pro.

Horizontal lines and shaded bars can help an employer immediately identify the different sections of the resume allowing him to move through your document quickly. Too many lines, however, can make a resume look cluttered. So use your judgment or consult a friend who has an artistic eye to create the right balance.

JOANNE RAINEY

123 Essex Street • Healdsburg, CA 12345 • (123) 123-1234

OBJECTIVE: A position in the alternative health field
with a focus on communication, administration, and client relations

HIGHLIGHTS OF QUALIFICATIONS

- A clear and straightforward communicator, skilled in establishing strong, long-term client relationships and cultivating productive teams.
- Highly organized, directed, and detail-oriented; able to juggle multiple responsibilities simultaneously and maintain calm in fast-paced environments.
- Committed to a healthy and balanced lifestyle; passion for conveying the wisdom of alternative healing.

RELEVANT ACCOMPLISHMENTS

COMMUNICATION & CLIENT RELATIONS

- Provided comprehensive in-person and telephone assistance to clients and prospects at Fast Forward:
  - Acted as initial contact for new and prospective members.
  - Advised clients regarding individual counseling and workshop options specific to their career goals.
  - Responded to client concerns with directness, and used diplomacy to resolve problems equitably.
- Coordinated with other Fast Forward Client Services Representatives to ensure smooth scheduling transitions and effectiveness in daily operations and client satisfaction.
- Answered phones and scheduled acupuncture appointments for Sung Lee, L.Ac.
- At Sonoma Realtors, consulted with clients to assess needs and match requirements with properties.

ADMINISTRATION

- Registered new clients for membership, counseling sessions, seminars, and workshops at Fast Forward.
- Updated records and maintained efficient office organization for Sung Lee's active acupuncture practice.
- Researched, synthesized, and edited relevant articles for publication in 20th Century Publishing's weekly international newsletters, with circulation of over 2,000.

PROFESSIONAL EXPERIENCE

1996-pres.	**Client Service Representative**	Fast Forward, Sebastopol, CA
1994-96	**Office Manager**	Sung Lee, L.Ac., Occidental, CA
1993-94	**Office Manager**	20th Century Publishing, Novato, CA
1991-93	**Sales Agent**	Sonoma Realtors, Santa Rosa, CA

EDUCATION

B.A., Psychology & English Literature, Mills College, Oakland, CA
Counseling Internship with Family Service Agency of Sonoma County
Ongoing independent research into numerous alternative health modalities

Joanne Rainey's resume.

173

Check out the lines Sean Goodridge used on his resume, and flip through Appendix B, "Portfolio of Sample Resumes," to see how others have incorporated shaded bars and lines into their documents.

Bonus Check

When designing your resume, stay within appropriate boundaries for your profession and industry. For instance, the CEO for a conservative insurance company should have a traditional-looking resume. A graphic designer for a greeting-card company could have a more creative layout that shows off her aesthetic tastes.

Job-Hunt Hint

In addition to making your resume handsome, white space on your resume may be used by the interviewer as a place to make notes (or possibly doodle) during the interview.

Spacing Out

Think of your resume as a valuable piece of Manhattan real estate where every increment of space must be used. As land is used for buildings, signs, and pathways, use your resume real estate for headings, phrases, and lists. And just as landscaping and parks are appreciated in congested urban areas, white space gives relief to the resume reader's eye.

One way to create white space on your resume is to set generous margins. Here's how:

1. In your MS Word toolbar, select the File pull-down menu.
2. Select Page Setup.
3. Click Margins.
4. Set the left and right margins to no less than 1 inch each.
5. Set the top and bottom margins to no less than .5 inch each.

Bonus Check

Ever wonder why newspapers use one-inch columns instead of printing across the full width of the page? Short lines are quicker to read than long ones. That's a tip you can use in formatting your resume. Keep your line lengths short, no more than five inches across if possible.

Sean Goodridge

123 La Cage Ave.
Miami Beach, FL 12345
(123) 123-1234
sean@goodridge.com

PROFILE
- Aspiring Interior Designer with experience in design development and drafting.
- Produced preliminary drawings and construction documents for commercial and residential projects.
- Creative approach to problem solving.

EDUCATION
BS, Interior Design, Rhode Island School of Design, Providence, RI

Conceptual Design	Architectural Lighting Design
Creative Problem Solving	Model Making
Space Planning	Computer Design: MiniCAD, Adobe Illustrator

RELEVANT ACCOMPLISHMENTS
INTERIOR DESIGN
- Designed residential addition. Drafted preliminary drawings and construction documents. Worked with architect who followed plans through to completion.
- Completed drafting for projects:
  Water treatment plant
  Housing developments
  Apartment complexes
- Developed floor plans and elevations for commercial and residential projects.
- Conceptualized and created design for a cafe. Completed a specification book and made material selections for presentation boards.

CLIENT RELATIONS
- As part of space planning class, met with business owners to discuss their ideas and needs for developing conceptual plans.
- Built a clientele at Hayward's by providing personal attention to customer needs and comprehensive product knowledge.

WORK HISTORY
1999-present	Salesperson	Hayward's, Miami Beach, FL
1998-1999	Junior Designer	Burton & Duncan Architects, Tallahassee, FL
1995-1998	Assist. to Interior Designer	Brown & Walton Associates, Johnston, RI

— Portfolio available —

Sean Goodridge's resume.

Adjusting the *leading* (the space between your lines) is another clever way to add white space without eating up too much real estate. For example, you may want to have just a little space (but not a full line space) between each bullet-point statement to set them apart. Customizing space before or after lines (which are considered *paragraphs* for formatting purposes) is easy:

1. Highlight the paragraph (or bullet-point statement) you want to add space before or after.

2. In your MS Word toolbar, select the Format pull-down menu.

3. Select Paragraph.

4. Click Indents and Spacing.

5. Under the heading Spacing, you'll see boxes next to Before and After. Insert a number, such as 6, in either the Before or After box to add space before or after a paragraph. (The smaller the number, the smaller the space will be.)

6. Click OK to see the results of your work.

Terms of Employment

Leading (rhymes with bedding) is the space between lines of text. Adjust the leading of individual lines to accent headings and increase ease of reading.

Bonus Check

There are standard tabs programmed into a Microsoft Word document. You can change those tab settings by using the ruler on the screen at the top of your document. Take time to learn how to use the various types of tabs by consulting your word-processing manual.

Terms of Employment

In word-processing jargon, a **paragraph** is any text that begins after a hard return (pressing Return or Enter on your keyboard) and ends with the next hard return. That means that technically a bullet-point statement is a paragraph.

A third white-space technique is to use the Tab key to indent text in order to create columns or sub–bullet-point statements, as demonstrated in the Job Objective statement in the following resume by Francine Ling.

Resume Reality

Now that you've learned what a good resume design and type style are, it's time to get your resume printed and out in the real world where it's going to work wonders for you. Let's move on to the nuts and bolts of getting your resume out of the printer and into the hands of your next employer!

Francine M. Ling

123 Frontier Avenue, #2 • Madison, Wisconsin 12345-1234 • (123) 123-1234

ADMINISTRATIVE PROFESSIONAL
with strengths in:

Project Management	Executive Support
Office Management	Team Building

PROFESSIONAL EXPERIENCE

1991-present **XEROX CORPORATION - MADISON RESEARCH CENTER**
Executive Secretary/Member Support Staff, Madison, WI 1993-present
Office Manager/Member Support Staff, Milwaukee, WI, 1991-1993

➤ One of first five members of research team that consults with corporate and institutional clients regarding their document creation and publishing problems.

➤ Logistics manager of research team awarded for completion of educational project for Harvard Business School.
  - Honorary MBA from Harvard Business School.

➤ Excellence in Science and Technology Award plus $1,000, Xerox's second highest employee award.

➤ Co-planned "Vision & Values" and "Milestones & Goals" statements for the team.

➤ One of five originators of "Office of the Future," a successful pilot project involving two sites connected by audio/visual communications through a gateway.

➤ Supervised construction/remodeling and furnishing of offices in Milwaukee and Madison. Set up administrative operations for both 10-person sites.

➤ Managed the physical facilities including compliance with corporate requirements.

➤ Office manager for 10 research and marketing professionals. This included customer contact, consultant contracts, accounting, budgets, purchasing, travel, and conferences. Commended for best record keeping in the corporation.

1987-1991 **PELLEY & CO.,** Milwaukee, WI
Executive Secretary
➤ Provided office management and administrative assistance to President and Vice President of this lumber equipment manufacturer.

EDUCATION
Honorary MBA, Harvard Business School, Cambridge, MA
Business and Business Law, Milwaukee State College, Milwaukee, WI
Xerox Training: Leadership Through Quality

WINDOWS AND MACINTOSH SKILLS

MS Word	Excel
PowerPoint	FrameMaker

Francine Ling's resume.

Career Casualty

The print on a sheet of paper from an inkjet printer runs when it gets wet, so don't send an inkjet master copy to an employer. Instead, send a photocopy of the inkjet master to ensure that the print will survive a rainstorm or coffee spill.

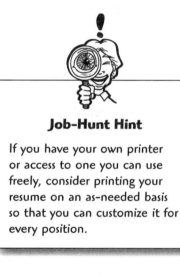

Job-Hunt Hint

If you have your own printer or access to one you can use freely, consider printing your resume on an as-needed basis so that you can customize it for every position.

Job-Hunt Hint

Your resume needs to be ready to survive a long process of faxing and photocopying. That means you should use black print on white or very light paper.

Mastering Your Resume

After the content of your resume is written and laid out in either the chronological or functional format, you need to print and copy it. Print your master resume on a laser or inkjet printer. Don't use a dot-matrix printer, even if that's all you have hooked up to your computer; you'd be better off hiring a professional word processor to do the printout or renting time on a computer and printer at your local copy shop. Your master printouts should be on white paper of any weight.

In the Mood to Reproduce

After you have printed your master, it's off to a copy center, unless you have access to a high-quality copier elsewhere. Don't order a whole slew of copies; start with the number you think you'll need for one or two weeks of your job search.

By copying your resume in short runs, you'll be a lot more inclined to adjust your marketing approach as you pursue your ideal job. That's important because you need to be prepared to change your Job Objective statement and tweak your resume, if necessary, as you get feedback from employers along the way.

Looking Classy on Paper

Your next step is to select paper that's appropriate for the type of work you're after. It makes sense that someone going for a CEO position is going to have higher-end paper than someone seeking a clerical position.

Personally, I don't like fancy textured or parchment sheets—to me they look pretentious. I like plain white that has just a little more weight than the standard 20-pound paper used for copying. That extra weight sends a subconscious message of quality to the reader without screaming out, "This is expensive paper!"

But don't go overboard on the weight. As one administrative assistant pointed out to me, "When the paper is too thick, it jams up the copier. That makes me mad, and I'm apt to throw the resume away." Oops! You better not get on the wrong side of an administrative assistant who, at that moment, wields the fate of your career. Solution: Choose something a little heavier than 20-pound but not as thick as card stock.

I can just see you now—your chin lifted high and chest puffed out as you walk out of the copy center with your stack of fresh resumes. You're ready to conquer the world!

The Top Ten Checklist

Now that you're finished writing, designing, and printing your resume, give yourself a standing ovation for your hard work. Then grab your pencil (or get out a box of gold stars) and take credit for each one of the items on the following list that you've completed. No need to get nervous—it's not a test. It's just a way to assure yourself that you've done the best job possible with your resume.

- ☐ **1.** Your name appears in the top center or on the upper right-hand side (not in the upper left-hand corner) of the page.

- ☐ **2.** Your resume starts with a brief and clear Job Objective statement or a strong indication of what position you are seeking.

- ☐ **3.** Everything on your resume supports your Job Objective.

- ☐ **4.** Achievements, rather than job descriptions, are stressed.

- ☐ **5.** Achievement statements start with action verbs and do not contain vague terms such as "responsible for."

- ☐ **6.** There are no paragraphs anywhere on the resume. Bulleted statements make achievements quick and easy to read.

- ☐ **7.** Statements and sections are prioritized so the most impressive information comes first.

- ☐ **8.** Your resume fits on no more than two pages. The exception to this two-page limit applies to resumes (also called curriculum vitae) for the academic and scientific communities.

- ☐ **9.** If you have a two-page resume, "Continued" appears on the bottom of page one, and your name and "Page Two" are placed at the top of the second page.

- ☐ **10.** There are no misspellings, grammatical errors, or other mistakes.

If you've checked off everything on the list, you're in good shape. Now it's time to get your masterpiece onto the employer's desk.

Getting It out the Door

Just a few more steps and your resume will be in your new boss's hands. Here's what's left to do:

➤ Wrap it up

➤ Send it out

Although sending out a resume is not rocket science, it's worth taking a few minutes to look at the following hints to ensure a smooth send-off and landing.

Stuffing Envelopes

Instead of stuffing your cover letter and resume into the standard 4 × 9-inch business envelope, mail your marketing duo in a large 9 × 12-inch envelope (white, manila, or gray will do). In the larger envelope, your documents will lie flat, allowing them to arrive without creases that can crack the print. (Imagine how badly cracked print will look after the resume is photocopied and faxed a few times—a common paper trail in corporate America.)

Career Casualty

Don't staple your cover letter and resume together. Clip them together with a paper clip instead so the recipient can easily separate them for copying and filing.

Terms of Employment

There are several cool ways to communicate with folks during your job search:

snail mail What the U.S. Postal Service delivers

e-mail Mail sent electronically over the Internet

fax Memos and attachments delivered over a facsimile machine

voice mail Messages left on someone's telephone answering machine or service

If your printer doesn't accept a 9 × 12-inch envelope (and most don't), it's perfectly fine to hand-address your envelope. Or you could type or print out the address on a plain white label, if you have sticky labels for a typewriter or computer printer.

Snail Mail

If you have plenty of time before the application deadline, the U.S. Postal Service (increasingly referred to as snail mail) is a great and fairly reliable way to send your resume and cover letter. There's no need to send your packet certified or registered; simply put a stamp for first-class delivery on that big envelope I suggested and head for a mailbox.

Special Delivery

If you're in a hurry to get your resume and cover letter to an employer, use one of the overnight or two-day courier services such as FedEx, UPS, or the U.S. Postal Service's Express Mail. Most of these services will pick up your packet at your address, or you can take it to their dispatch center and have it sent from there.

Here's how to prepare your packet:

1. Print out your cover letter and resume.
2. Place your material in a 9 × 12-inch envelope with the employer's name and address on it (just in case your stuff escapes the courier's packaging).
3. Put your envelope into the courier's cardboard delivery envelope.
4. Fill out the courier's form, pay him his money, and you're done!

Fax Magic

When you're up against a tight deadline or the job posting says to fax the resume, go straight to a fax machine and start pushing those buttons. Your faxable cover letter and resume should be created exactly like the ones you would send via the U.S. mail. But they need one more ingredient—a fax cover sheet, which simply states the following information:

1. The date
2. The recipient (to whom the fax is being sent)
3. Who is sending the fax (that's you!)
4. The total number of pages being faxed and the general contents of those sheets

Here's what a typical fax cover sheet looks like:

Date: September 13, 1999

To: Brad Thompson

From: Susan Ireland

Pages: Three: cover letter

resume

fax cover sheet

If you fax your cover letter and resume, call the employer and ask whether you should also send your resume by mail. Some companies are so inundated with paperwork that they prefer not to receive duplicate resumes. Others appreciate having the real thing sent on nice paper, especially if they don't have high-quality fax machines or copiers.

Job-Hunt Hint

Figure out when your resume and cover letter are likely to land on the employer's desk (depending on whether you send it via U.S. mail, courier, fax, or e-mail). Then make a note to follow up by phone one day after you think your packet has arrived.

E-mail Flash

If your potential employer is expecting your resume and cover letter to arrive by e-mail, check out Chapter 21, "It's all a Scan: Scannable Resumes," where I explain how to format a resume that will survive and thrive in the world of e-mail.

The Least You Need to Know

➤ Limit your resume to one page, if possible, and no more than two pages.

➤ No paragraphs! Use bullet points to make your material look quick and easy to read.

➤ Choose an appropriate font, set wide margins, adjust line spaces, and indent text to make the body of your resume inviting to read.

➤ Print your resume on a laser or inkjet printer.

➤ Reproduce your resume on a high-quality copier using appropriate paper.

➤ Send your cover letter and resume via U.S. Post, express/courier service, fax, or e-mail, depending on how quickly it must arrive and which way the employer would like it to be delivered.

Part 3

So, You Need a Special Resume

When I go to the grocery store, I like lots of variety, especially when it comes to the cookie aisle. I like to choose from as many different kinds of chocolate chip cookies as possible, just to be sure I'm getting the best. When I get my package home, I examine each cookie and pick the one that has the most chocolate chips. I've been persnickety since I was a kid, and I probably always will be.

That's the kind of discriminating attitude I expect you to have when it comes to deciding which resume format to use. Now that you know all about chronological and functional resumes from Parts 1 and 2, I'm going to tell you about some spin-offs on these two formats. By the end of this part, you'll be able to pick the format that's right for you.

Chapter 12

The Big Winner: An Achievement Resume

In This Chapter

➤ Why employers like achievement resumes

➤ When to let your achievement statements do the talking

➤ Why your achievement resume will make you look like a winner

➤ How to create your own achievement resume

Of all the resume formats, the achievement resume is the one I find to be most powerful. It doesn't fit all job seekers' situations, but if it fits yours, it can have tremendous impact. The achievement resume is frequently the most effective way to stop potential employers in their tracks and get the salary dollars rolling in an upward direction. I bet you'd like that to happen to you! This chapter explains what an achievement resume is and helps you decide whether it's the right format for you.

This Resume Packs a Punch!

Saying less is more effective than saying a lot, and that's what the achievement resume is all about: brevity and punch! With a few strong accomplishments, an achievement resume can generate more questions and interest than pages of details. This type of resume works well for sales professionals, top-level executives, and those who want to keep the spotlight on just a few successes from their whole career.

Imagine how short and powerful a former U.S. president's resume could be. Take Jimmy Carter. Although he could fill pages and pages with his achievements, he doesn't need multiple pages to make his point. At most, two lines such as the following will get him in the door for any interview he's after.

➤ 39th President of the United States

➤ Negotiator of 1979 Camp David Accords between Egypt and Israel

Career Casualty

Don't think that a one-page resume makes you look like a lightweight. On the contrary, a heavyweight professional can make a strong impression with just a few carefully chosen lines of print.

Terms of Employment

Bottom line means different things to different folks. In for-profit organizations, the bottom line is measured by revenue, savings, and profit. In nonprofit organizations, the bottom line may be program effectiveness, enroll-ment, or budget growth. The key to writing effective achievement statements on your resume is to understand the reader's bottom line.

Likewise, Ronald Reagan's resume might read:

➤ 40th President of the United States

➤ Known as the "Great Communicator" who drastically improved U.S. relations with the Soviet Union

The achievement resume is also a marvelous way to throw attention onto your strengths while de-emphasizing a weak or complicated employment history. Using this format, I've created dynamite resumes for many a client whose career history was a mess.

Asking the Right Question

The key question to ask yourself when writing your achievement state-ments for this type of resume is "How does the potential employer define success for the position I'm seeking?" Let the four or five achievement statements in the body of your resume answer that all-important question. When you've done that, you've snagged employ-ers into calling you for an interview to talk about how your new job would impact their *bottom line*.

Oooh, You're Going to Look Great!

An achievement resume looks like a functional resume except that it doesn't have skill headings (in other words, you aren't going to cate-gorize your skills) in the body of the resume. Instead it just lists five or six strong, relevant achievements under a main heading such as Professional Accomplishments or Selected Achievements. Look through your old performance evaluations to find references to relevant achievements and quotable quotes for your resume.

The following template represents an achievement resume. It's followed by five achievement resumes by real job seekers. A scan of these resumes will tell you that the job seeker in each case is a winner in his or her field. That's the beauty of this format!

Bonus Check

Use the following template as a springboard to launch your one-of-a kind achievement resume. You can do that by answering only the questions that fit your situation, brain-storming on your own to come up with dynamite statements, and being creative with the layout so that it reflects your personality.

(Achievement Resume Template)

Name
Street
City, State Zip
Phone, Fax, E-mail

JOB OBJECTIVE

The job you want next

SUMMARY OF QUALIFICATIONS

- How much experience you have in the field of your job objective, in a related field, or using the skills required for your new position.
- An overall career accomplishment that shows you'd be good at this job.
- What someone would say about you as a recommendation.

SELECTED ACHIEVEMENTS

- An accomplishment you are proud of that shows you'd be a valuable employee.
- Another achievement that demonstrates you have the skills to produce results.
- A project you are proud of that supports your job objective.
- A problem you solved using the skills required for your job objective.
- A time when you used your skill to positively affect the organization, the bottom line, your boss, your clients.
- Awards, commendations, publications, etc., you achieved that relate to your job objective.

WORK HISTORY

19xx-present	Job Title	COMPANY NAME and city
19xx-xx	Job Title	COMPANY NAME and city
19xx-xx	Job Title	COMPANY NAME and city
19xx-xx	Job Title	COMPANY NAME and city
19xx-xx	Job Title	COMPANY NAME and city

EDUCATION

Degree, Major (if relevant)
University, City, State, 19xx (optional)

Achievement resume template.

The Perfect One-Pager

Anthony Wright, whose resume follows, had an achievement-packed, 20-year career in management, which he distilled down to one page using an achievement format. This concise format did two things for him:

➤ It allowed him to state his relevant experience in just five bullet-point statements.

➤ It downplayed his career in the military and government by listing his work history near the end of the resume.

You'll also note that because he had so few statements on the page, he was able to write some pretty hefty ones, sometimes taking three lines each.

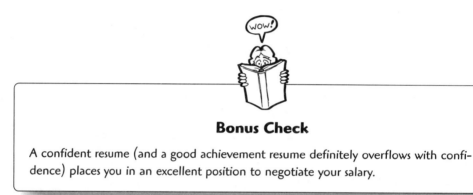

Bonus Check

A confident resume (and a good achievement resume definitely overflows with confidence) places you in an excellent position to negotiate your salary.

Quality vs. Quantity

There isn't a lot of quantity on Cliff McMillan's achievement resume (following), but there's plenty of quality. His achievement resume's impressive statements made him shine. He not only hit the nail on the head when it came to the type of experience and skills the employer was seeking, Cliff also demonstrated his good taste in the layout of his resume. Good idea!

Your achievement resume doesn't have to be only one page; your information can spill onto a second page if necessary. Whether it's a one- or two-pager, be sure it contains only the very best you have to offer a prospective employer.

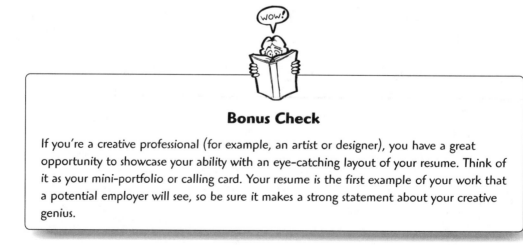

Bonus Check

If you're a creative professional (for example, an artist or designer), you have a great opportunity to showcase your ability with an eye-catching layout of your resume. Think of it as your mini-portfolio or calling card. Your resume is the first example of your work that a potential employer will see, so be sure it makes a strong statement about your creative genius.

Anthony Wright

123 Whitehall Place • Austin, TX 12345 • (123) 123-1234 • anthony_wright@thenet.net

ADMINISTRATIVE MANAGER

- 20 years experience directing complex organizational and technological changes.
- Recognized leadership skills and a natural talent for relating to people of various ethnic, socioeconomic, and educational backgrounds.
- Customer-focused management style.
- Ability to find innovative solutions to resource constraints.

QUALITY MANAGEMENT ACCOMPLISHMENTS

- Implemented two major organizational changes in the U.S. Air Force personnel and human resources management administration. Commended for relocating and retraining personnel while maintaining quality customer service.
- Directed the conversion from hierarchical to relational information systems at the U.S. Air Force Facilities. Recognized by technical team for using effective training and internal marketing to achieve management and staff "buy-in" of this major change.
- Developed a self-directed team to conduct process analysis in preparation for decentralization of 35 Medicare process operations. Trained staff in the practical and theoretical aspects of process improvement.
- Reduced U.S. Airforce Airbase's unreconciled material costs $1.5M by reorganizing administrative procedures, introducing a new information system, and directing the first complete physical inventory certified by the GAO.
- Improved goal tracking at U.S. Air Force Facilities by analyzing the workload evaluation process, assessing its validity, and convincing headquarters to revise the methodology.

WORK HISTORY

1997-present	Medicare, Austin	Program Manager, 1999-present Senior Budget Analyst, 1997-1999
1980-1997	U.S. Airbase, Austin	Director Workload Analysis, 1986-1997 Program Analyst, 1983-1986 Accounting Manager, 1980-1983

EDUCATION

B.S., Organizational Behavior, Austin State College, 1993

Anthony Wright's resume.

Cliff McMillan

123 Ocean Street, #3 • Rocky Hill, NC 12345 • (123) 123-1234 • cliff@mcmillan.com

JOB OBJECTIVE

Member of Creative Team with emphasis on Graphic Design

SUMMARY OF QUALIFICATIONS

- Skilled fine artist with experience in applied graphics.
- Competent in:
  - QuarkXpress
  - PageMaker
  - Adobe Illustrator
  - Design Studio
  - Freehand
- Designed promotional pieces for clients including:
  - Coffee-O-Rama
  - University of North Carolina
  - We-R-Juice
  - Pack & Ship

GRAPHICS PROJECTS

- Designed several of Coffee-O-Rama's promotional T-shirts, worn by all North Carolina store employees.
- Team-developed promotional materials for Pack & Ship used in 30 stores.
- Combined computer and applied graphics in designing the cover for *The Finnegan Corporation Plans Book* for the University of North Carolina.
- Designed POP standup card for We-R-Juice, displayed in stores throughout the New York metropolitan area.
- Created numerous promotional pieces for university and community events.

WORK HISTORY

1996-pres.	Freelance Graphic Designer	Rocky Hill, NC
1992-1996	Store Manager	Coffee-O-Rama, Rocky Hill, NC
1991-1992	Desk Top Publisher	Copies Ink, Eugene, OR

EDUCATION

B.A., Graphic Design/Fine Arts, University of North Carolina, Rocky Hill, NC, 1996
Internship: Project Coordinator, RRM Marketing, New York, NY

— Portfolio available —

Cliff McMillan's resume.

Professional Titles Count

Thomas Redding cleverly highlighted his professional roles throughout his achievement resume by doing the following:

➤ He put "P.E." next to his name in the Heading to show that he's a certified civil engineer.

➤ He stated his professional title immediately below his heading.

➤ He stated his professional title immediately below his heading.

➤ He highlighted his professional roles at the beginning of each achievement statement in the body of his resume.

➤ He listed his former job titles in his Work History, all of which support his job objective.

One can't help but identify Thomas's expertise in civil engineering from the highlighted titles that pop out all through his resume.

Be a Celebrity

You may not be a celebrity in your field (yet), but you can sometimes make a darn good impression by listing industry celebrities that you know. In the following resume, Marlon James prominently mentioned some well-known folks he worked for as a bodyguard. "You mean Forrest Gump and Jerry McGuire?" you ask in disbelief. Okay, for security reasons, I had to make this resume anonymous by taking out the famous names and inserting fictitious characters.

List a well-known person (or short list of them) on your resume if doing so enhances your perceived worth. In other words, your list should tell employers at least one of the following:

➤ You have a Rolodex of contacts that will be valuable on your next job.

➤ You've carried a high level of responsibility and therefore can do the same for your future employer.

➤ You understand the protocol required to operate at high levels in your field.

By "well-known person" I mean anyone who is either world famous, recognized in the employer's field, or an associate of the employer to whom you are applying.

Number One in Sales

The achievement resume is often an excellent format for the sales professional. With four or five dashing accomplishment statements, the salesperson can sweep an employer off her feet and close the deal. I've seen many sales professionals win an interview in record time using an achievement resume. Take a look at Wendy Fowler's resume to see how effectively it sold her.

Job-Hunt Hint

Think of your resume as a brochure of the type of work you want to do next. What hats would you like to wear on that job? Make those hats stand out on your resume by using bold, uppercase letters, bullet points, and white space. Chapter 11, "Step Six: The Big Production," has more information on resume production.

Job-Hunt Hint

My unofficial survey shows that when given two lists side-by-side to read, most people will read down the list on the left, and then down the list on the right. For that reason, I recommend prioritizing your lists vertically instead of horizontally.

Thomas Redding, P.E.

001 Sylvan Avenue • San Francisco, California 12345 • (123) 123-1234

Civil Engineer

Project Management   Construction Estimating

SUMMARY OF QUALIFICATIONS

- Wide variety of construction engineering experience ranging from heavy vessel transportation to commercial interior wall construction.

- Estimator and project manager for some of the most profitable specialty subcontracting jobs in the San Francisco Bay Area.

- Strong communication and analytical skills.

SELECTED ACCOMPLISHMENTS

- **Estimator and Interior/Exterior Wall Design Coordinator** for Highland Hospital, Oakland. Project consisted of 135,000 sq. ft. of EIFS material on built-in-place light-gauge metal framing. Coordinated structural analysis and shop drawing production for integration into project drawings by engineer-of-record.

- **Project Engineer, Scheduler, and Subcontract Administrator** for Exxon Oil refinery modernization in Fremont, CA. Project involved transportation and erection of multiple refinery process vessels up to 600 tons.

- **Project Manager** for highly profitable interior/exterior wall design and construction for the San Francisco Shopping Center. Project included 20,000 sq. ft. of built-in-place EIFS wall and detailed interior atria.

- **Estimator and Project Manager** for the $1.5 million structural fireproofing, load-bearing wall framing, and massive drywall and plaster ceiling construction for the redesign of San Francisco's Warfield Theatre. Maintained strict critical path schedule.

WORK HISTORY

2000-present **Estimator/Engineer**
             Phillips Construction Contractors, Inc., Hayward, CA
1996-1999   **Estimator/Project Manager**
             Browning and Dunn Contractors, San Mateo, CA, 1998-1999
             Calabasas, Inc., San Francisco, CA, 1996-1998
1994-1996   **Estimator/Project Engineer**
             Reynolds Construction, Inc., Oakland, CA
1991-1994   Project Manager/Engineer
             Brendan Walsh Rigging, San Leandro, CA

EDUCATION AND CERTIFICATION

Registered Professional Civil Engineer, certified 1991, State of California
Bachelor of Science, Civil Engineering, 1990, University of California, Santa Cruz

Thomas Redding's resume.

Marlon James
Security Professional

---

123 Mercy St., Highland Park, MI 12345   (123) 123-1234

QUALIFICATIONS

- 20 years as a Security Professional who has demonstrated the ability to research, evaluate, and implement procedures that encompass all levels of security.
- Track record of handling privileged and sensitive situations discreetly, maintaining a level of respect and dignity for all involved.
- Extensive network of professional contacts in all areas of public and private security.
- Superior interpersonal skills with the ability to work with all levels of personnel.

PROFESSIONAL SECURITY EXPERIENCE

- Provided executive protection to a wide range of clients from corporate executives to music celebrities, remaining prudent and discreet in both formal and informal settings.
- Designed corporate and estate security programs, utilizing CCTV, physical security, and access control systems.
- Developed and implemented security programs ($1.2M annual budget) for three luxury hotels in the Cadillac Square area of downtown Detroit.
- Served as team leader for many foreign and domestic assignments, handling all travel assignments.
- Successfully discharged potentially explosive workplace violence through crisis intervention.
- Infiltrated and broke a large criminal team accounting for the sabotage, theft, and embezzlement within a major corporation.
- Assisted in personal matters including shopping, errands, and domestic assignments, frequently managing large amounts of cash.
- Directed the maintenance and management of a private auto collection to uphold full functionality and optimum market value ($4.1M).

SELECTED CLIENTS

American Auto Corp., Office of the Chairman	Sutherland Steel
Hitella Inc., Office of the Chairman	Jay Gatsby
Rainy Tree Productions, Office of the Chairman	Marvel Co.
Forrest Gump	General Transportation
Jerry McGuire	Motown History Museum

— Continued —

Marlon James
Page 2

WORK HISTORY

1994-present	Executive Protection Specialist	H.M. Evans & Assoc., Grosse Point, MI
		Safety Specialists, River Rouge, MI
		Belle Isle Security, Belle Isle, MI
		Lock & Key Inc., Warren, MI
1991-1994	Investigator	LTD Properties, Westland, MI
1989-1991	Director of Security Operations	United Retail, Sterling Heights, MI
1983-1989	General Manager	Rockland Protection Services, Inc., Detroit, MI
1982-1983	Retail Loss Investigator	Maltese Group, Detroit, MI
1980-1982	Area Supervisor	Prism Inc., Garden City, MI

EDUCATION

University of Michigan at Dearborn:	Hotel and Restaurant Management
	High-Rise Fire and Life Safety Certified
Lawrence Technical University:	Criminal Justice, Correctional Sciences

TRAINING

POST Certified #1234, Detroit Police Academy
American Red Cross Certified, CPR, Emergency First Aid
Executive Protection, MM #123, Henry Watts Protective Training Center
Defensive Driving Skills, The Ladbroke School
Evasive, Anti-Kidnapping Driving, Fredrick Rintoul Executive Driving School
Terrorism, Institute for Specialized Security
Executive Protection, Institute for Specialized Security, NLA#123

LICENSES

Michigan Concealed Weapons Permit, LN #123456789
Certified Protection Specialist, MM123 & NLA123
Michigan Consumers Affairs Registered, PPO #PQ 12345 - Weapons #123456

PROFESSIONAL ACHIEVEMENTS

Qualified Expert in Security, United States Supreme Courts
Co-author, *Specialized Security Manual*, Institute for Specialized Security

Marlon James's resume.

Wendy Fowler

001 Coolidge Road • Santa Monica, CA 12345 • (123) 123-1234 • fowlerw@thenet.net

JOB OBJECTIVE

Sales Consultant/Representative

SUMMARY OF QUALIFICATIONS

- Nine years as a business development manager, using a collaborative approach to build an international clientele.
- Intuitive interpersonal skills. Ability to think on my feet and use humor to mix with people.
- Comfortable working with cross-cultural and multi-functional teams.

RELEVANT ACHIEVEMENTS

- Generated international business by developing TraxNet promotional material that was included in Writeword's developers' package.
- Managed TraxNet's broker relations, which generated accounts with Fortune 500 clients including: Bank of America   Cincom
  Disney   First Interstate Bank
- Solicited donations within an affluent community for organizations including the Sierra Club, National Organization for Women, and the Los Angeles SPCA.
- Served as active member of fundraising team which doubled contributions for Echo Park School through donor solicitations and event planning.
- Made persuasive presentations before multi-city councils in Los Angeles which influenced tax funding of public school bussing.

WORK HISTORY

1995-present	Business Development Manager, TraxNet, Inc., Century City, CA
1994-1995	Business Manager, The Shopper's Weekly, Pasadena, CA
1991-1994	Sales Representative, Open Door Travel Agency, Pasadena, CA
1988-1991	Full-time parent/fundraising volunteer

EDUCATION

B.A., Psychology, University of California at Los Angeles, 1987
M.A. Program, Social Work, City College of Los Angeles, 1988-1990

Wendy Fowler's resume.

Career Casualty

Saying too much on a resume can be fatal. You want to say enough to entice the employer to ask questions (in an interview) without giving away the juicy details.

It's Your Turn to Shine

It's time to sit down at your computer (or get out your pencil and paper) and use the template found earlier in this chapter to create your achievement resume. All the principles discussed in Part 2, "Six Steps to a Perfect Resume," apply here (using action verbs, writing punchy summary statements, and so on). The only difference is the midsection of the resume, where you're going to write just a few smashing accomplishments that shoot you light-years ahead of your competition. That's right: no boring job descriptions, no skill headings, just the cream from the top of your career. Like I said, you're going to look great!

The Least You Need to Know

➤ An achievement resume that exudes confidence is hard for any employer to resist.

➤ Emphasize only selected achievements that say you're the best person for the job.

➤ De-emphasize a tricky employment history by placing it concisely at the bottom of the page.

➤ Because your resume presents you as one of the best in your field, you can start salary negotiations at a higher level.

Chapter 13

A Chronological Hybrid That Adds Up

In This Chapter

➤ When to use a chronological hybrid resume

➤ Where to add skill subheadings

➤ How to bring out the dynamism of a lengthy career

➤ How to create your own chronological hybrid resume

You're stuck! You've considered the chronological and functional resume formats, but neither one is quite right for your situation. Here's an idea: Combine the benefits of both formats to develop a hybrid. Creating a hybrid resume is kind of like borrowing from two recipes to come up with a wonderful new entré. In this chapter, I'll explain how to put together a resume that is a chronological hybrid. Then, in Chapter 14, "A Functional Hybrid That Makes Sense," I'll show you how to create a functional hybrid.

It's Got Structure

Let's say your career transition fits the criteria for using a chronological resume (see Chapter 4, "Chronologically Speaking"), but you want to highlight your transferable skills the way a functional resume would. You could start with the chronological structure and then add skill subheadings under the job titles in your Professional Experience section. To see this hybrid in action, take a look at the following template, which represents a *chronological hybrid* resume.

At first glance, the chronological hybrid looks like the traditional chronological format because the job seeker's achievements are presented as part of the work history in the body of the resume. The difference is that the achievement statements under each job heading are listed under skill subheadings.

(Chronological Hybrid Resume Template)

Name
Street
City, State Zip
Phone, Fax, E-mail

JOB OBJECTIVE
The job you want next

SUMMARY OF QUALIFICATIONS
- How much experience you have in the field of your job objective, in a related field, or using the skills required for your new position.
- An overall career accomplishment that shows you'd be good at this job.
- What someone would say about you as a recommendation.

PROFESSIONAL EXPERIENCE
19xx-pres.   Company Name, City, State
Job Title

MAJOR SKILL
- An accomplishment you are proud of that shows you're good at this profession.
- A problem you solved and the results.
- A time when you positively affected the organization, the bottom line, your boss, your co-workers, your clients.

MAJOR SKILL
- A project you are proud of that supports your job objective.
- Another accomplishment that shows you're good at this line of work.
- Quantifiable results that point out your skill.

19xx-xx   Company Name, City, State
Job Title

MAJOR SKILL
- An accomplishment you are proud of that shows you will be valued by your next employer.
- An occasion when someone "sat up and took notice" of your skill.

EDUCATION
Degree, Major (if relevant), 19xx (optional)
University, City, State

Template for chronological hybrid resume.

Take a look at the following sample Professional Experience section of a resume. The applicant has created the two skill subheadings Management and Marketing, under which she placed relevant achievement statements.

PROFESSIONAL EXPERIENCE

1989–pres.   Marketing Director, Fairfield General Company, Franklin, MA

           MANAGEMENT
- Started the company's marketing department, which now creates promotional strategies for all 46 national branches.
- Directly supervised 16 managers who oversaw the work of 14 graphic designers, 10 copywriters, and 12 vendors.

           MARKETING
- Increased sales by 40 percent by launching three new products in the first year.
- Achieved significant return on advertising by creating a campaign that made "Fairfield" a household name.

Sample of Professional Experience section.

Once you've created two or three skill subheadings under a job title on your chronological hybrid resume, prioritize those subheadings according to how relevant they are to your Job Objective statement.

Now that you have a handle on what the chronological hybrid looks like, let's see whether it's the right format for you.

Are You the Hybrid Type?

When should you consider using a chronological hybrid instead of the regular chronological format? If you fit into one of the following circumstances, a chronological hybrid might be the way to go:

➤ You're looking for a promotion.

➤ You're switching industries.

➤ Your job titles are nondescript.

➤ Your Work History looks stagnant. That is, you've been in the same position for many years.

Let's see how real job seekers used chronological hybrids to handle these situations.

Terms of Employment

The **chronological hybrid** is a chronological resume with skill subheadings (similar to the skill headings in a functional resume) incorporated into the Professional Experience section.

Climbing Higher

If you want to use your resume to get a position that's a rung higher on your career ladder, use the chronological hybrid. Its skill subheadings will help the employer understand right away that you've already acquired and used the skills required for your job objective. There's no set number of bullet-point statements that should follow a skill subheading, but here's my rule of thumb: You can have as few as one or as many as eight.

For example, Gireesh Vaid had worked her way up to vice president within a prominent nonprofit organization. When the position for president opened up, she decided to go for it. Using a chronological hybrid (following), she showed off her recent success in the company and used skill subheadings to demonstrate that she had the skills for the new job.

Variations on a Theme

If you want to continue with the same kind of work you've been doing but you want to change industries, the chronological hybrid can be a great promotional tool for you. This format will encourage the employer to identify you by your job titles and skills, even though your work history is from a different industry.

Tyler Zahn had been in management positions in the newspaper business for years. When he decided to transfer his management skills to a new industry, he chose the chronological hybrid format (following). In a flash, the employer saw that Tyler had honed valuable leadership abilities, even though he had not held typical manager titles.

Gireesh Vaid

001 Mark Twain Ave. • St. Louis, MO 12345 • (123) 123-1234

JOB OBJECTIVE: President, St. Louis Community Health Association

SUMMARY OF QUALIFICATIONS

- Accomplished Assistant Vice President in The St. Louis Community Health Association.
- Doubled donations during the '96 Campaign, achieving stretch goal of $500K.
- Allocated $750K to community service agencies.
- Enjoy motivating and establishing rapport with volunteers, donors, and co-workers.

PROFESSIONAL EXPERIENCE

1997-present THE ST. LOUIS COMMUNITY FOUNDATION, Saint Louis, MO
ASSISTANT VICE PRESIDENT
Manage a wide range of activities within the organization, including:

Fundraising • Manage four fundraisers with a $750K goal - 25% over last year. • Manage 110 existing corporate accounts; develop new accounts with high potential for giving. • Develop leadership giving. • Speak to community and corporate groups to solicit funds.

Allocations and Agency Relations • Allocated $750K after reviewing fiscal stability, board governance, and program services of 43 St. Louis Community Health-funded agencies. • Serve as liaison to coordinate activities.

Staffing Committees • Staff the Marketing, Agency Relations, Special Events Committees, creating effective teams of volunteers.

Volunteer Management • Recruit, develop, and manage high-level volunteers.

Special Events • Conceive and produce special events throughout year, including public relations events and prestigious fundraising galas.

LOANED EXECUTIVE
• Sponsored by Fossil Fuels Inc. to fundraise for the '96 St. Louis Community Health campaign.
• Personally doubled annual donations, raising more than $250,000 from local businesses, schools, and city officials. • Contributed 1/2 of overall stretch goal of $500K.

1996-97 CROSS & CROWDER CORPORATION, Kansas City, MO
PUBLIC RELATIONS ASSISTANT
• Assisted in corporate and product public relations during leveraged buy-out.
• Collaborated on PR strategies. • Co-managed sensitive internal issues such as layoffs and restructuring due to buy-out.

1992-96 Jiffy Business Services, Kansas City, MO
CONTRACTOR
• Provided sales and administrative assistance to nonprofit and for-profit organizations.

EDUCATION
B.S., Psychology, Rockhurst College, Kansas City, MO

Gireesh Vaid's resume.

Tyler Zahn
Executive Management Professional
123 Steep St. • Denver, CO 12345 • (123) 123-1234 • Tyler@Zahn.com

QUALIFICATIONS

- 11 years progressive leadership experience for a Denver company recognized as the best in its field.
- Success in managing 75% of organization's total revenue and expenditure, affected by multiple markets and fluctuating economy.
- Excellent supervisor who motivates staff by instilling confidence and dedication.

PROFESSIONAL EXPERIENCE

1989-present **Daily Journal**, Denver, CO
Associate Publisher, 1997-present
General Manager, 1993-1997
Director of Legal Information Services, 1991-1993
Calendar Manager, 1989-1991

BUSINESS

- Manage a $1.5M annual print budget, requiring creative negotiations with vendors to maintain quality, despite 40% rise in paper costs.
- As director of a $300K legal budget, achieve consistent sales in a declining market.
- Approve all capital acquisitions (approximately $50K per year) for the entire company.

PROJECT INITIATION

- Cut costs 35% by creating a 25-user, in-house editorial and production system.
- Doubled subscriptions by establishing a daily stand-alone supplement that provides crucial legal information to over 25,000 industry professionals.
- Increased sales market 45% by expanding courtroom coverage from one to six counties.

SUPERVISION

- Hired, trained, and supervise 10 art, production, MIS, advertising, and clerical personnel, using a management style of staff empowerment and delegation.
- Motivate an interdepartmental team of 25 to consistently meet two publication deadlines per day (500 per year).
- Maintained excellent retention rate, experiencing turnover only due to employee advancement or education.

1985-1988 **Peace Corps**, Brazil, South America
Volunteer, Medical Services Officer

EDUCATION

B.A., Anthropology, Nebraska Wesleyan University, Lincoln, NE, 1985
Internship, The Omaha Free Press, Omaha, NE, 1983

Tyler Zahn's resume.

The Hidden Functional Message

You may have job titles in your Work History that don't express the level of responsibility you held. (This is frequently the case for government and university employees, where titles such as Assistant, Level III tell the reader almost nothing about the job.) If you have tons of achievement statements under a job heading in a chronological resume, consider breaking them into smaller groups according to skills. Inserting skill subheadings makes your many achievements easier to read. Futhermore, inserting skill subheadings into your Professional Experience section will help the employer understand what your responsibilities were and give you the credit you deserve.

A case in point: From some of his job titles (such as "specialist" and "coordinator"), it was hard to understand where Robert MacIntyre stood in the organizational hierarchy where he worked. So he presented his work history in a chronological hybrid format (following) so that he could use skill subheadings to define his previous positions according to the skills needed in his job objective. That way, the employer saw that he had the qualifications for the job.

Standing Still

Longevity at an organization is something to feel proud of. But if you've spent many years in one spot, you might look stagnant in the eyes of a new employer. How can you highlight that you developed new skills, increased your industry knowledge, and took on more responsibility, even though your job title remained the same throughout your many years of dedication to the company? Use the chronological hybrid format. Your loyalty will ring clear in the Work History section, and the subheadings that categorize your achievements will demonstrate growth.

In Christine Whitley's resume (following), she divided her accomplishments according to the type of law she was involved with as a legal secretary. Her resume tells the story of diversity and stability—two attributes of an excellent legal secretary.

Career Casualty

When applying to a conservative employer, use a chronological or chronological hybrid format if at all possible, because they are the most traditional formats.

Terms of Employment

Stagnant work history is defined differently by hiring managers, depending on what industry they're in. For instance, a job seeker's eight-year stint at a company might seem healthy and stable to a prospective employer in biotechnology, whereas an engineer's eight-year stay at one company might seem stagnant to a hiring manager in multimedia.

Putting Words on Paper

If you've decided the chronological hybrid is the right format for you, it's time to put your thoughts on paper. Follow the step-by-step guidelines in Part 2, "Six Steps to a Perfect Resume," for creating each section of your resume, using the hybrid template presented earlier in this chapter as your foundation. It's that simple!

Robert MacIntyre

001 Long Shore Street • Evanston, IL 12345 • (123) 123-1234 • MacIntyre@thenet.net

JOB OBJECTIVE

Environmental Health & Safety Coordinator

SUMMARY OF QUALIFICATIONS

- 10 years as an Environmental Compliance Professional with recent experience in Environmental Protection and OSHA compliance.

- Demonstrated ability to build rapport and resolve complex issues among multiple entities with conflicting interests.

- Working knowledge of industrial and research settings.

PROFESSIONAL EXPERIENCE

1995-present **Environmental Compliance Specialist**
SIDNEY LABS (SL) , Chicago, IL

Leadership
- As Facility Coordinator for a building on the University of Chicago campus, closed out 85% of 1800 deficiencies, turned around maintenance and custodial standards, implemented a recycling program, and improved security.

- As Chairperson of the Life Sciences Division Safety Committee, revitalized the group, improved productivity, increased recognition within SL, and facilitated a self-assessment inspection program.

- Served as liaison between Principle Investigators and Environmental Health and Safety (EH&S) Division. Developed strategies for EH&S compliance including OSHA and waste management.

- As Manager of the Medical and Biohazardous Waste Program, developed a comprehensive compliance document including a generator's guide and training plan. Program was fully implemented in only five months.

Compliance Enforcement
- Conducted advice visits to hazardous and mixed waste generators to review procedures, labeling practices, and adherence to accumulation time limits.

- Updated and managed the Underground Storage Tank (UST) Program, which included the creation of four-page Monitoring Plans that were used as models by the Department of Energy (DOE).

- Coordinated certification of tanks and secondary containment for six Permit-by-Rule (PBR) Hazardous Waste Treatment Units. Ensured upgrades were in compliance and directed the permit writing effort.

— Continued —

Robert MacIntyre
Page 2

1994-1995   **Environmental Compliance Consultant**
SafeTech, Springfield, IL
An environmental consulting firm providing support to DOE facilities.
- Developed and wrote the first-ever Quality Control Inspection Plan/Procedure to monitor quality assurance of Pleasant Hills Laboratories' Hazardous Waste Management storage and treatment facilities. Plan was incorporated into their Part B Permit.

- Audited hazardous waste management facilities and Waste Accumulation Areas (WAAs) for compliance with EPA and Cal-EPA regulations, and DOE policies. Waste included: Hazardous
              Radioactive, high and low level
              Mixed

1990-1994   **Environmental Program Manager**, 1993-1994
Environmental Compliance Specialist, 1993
Chemist, Materials Engineering, 1990-1993
U.S. AIR FORCE, Wichita, KS
An aircraft re-work facility comprised of 125 manufacturing shops and a materials engineering laboratory.
- Ensured EH&S compliance in 75 WAAs by performing frequent surveillance and enhancing the training program.

- Co-developed directives for issues including waste minimization, solvent substitution, recycling, chemical storage, fire safety, and OSHA standards.

- Directed preparation of individual shop contingency plans for the site Hazardous Material Management Plan.

1987-1989   **Physical and Inorganic Chemistry Advanced High School Teacher**
MARLON RIGGS HIGH SCHOOL, Topeka, KS

1984-1987   **Chemist**, 1987
Lab Technician, 1984-1987
TOXMOX INC., Topeka, CA
A hazardous waste disposal company.

EDUCATION
B.S., Biochemistry, Emporia State University, Emporia, KS, 1985

Seminars:	OSHA/RCRA	Hazardous Materials
	Hazardous Waste	Medical Waste
	Emergency Preparedness	Radioactive and Mixed Waste
	Fire Safety	Underground Storage Tanks

Robert MacIntyre's resume.

Christine C. Whitley

123 Tall Tree Drive • San Diego, CA 12345 • (123) 123-1234

JOB OBJECTIVE: Legal Secretary

SUMMARY OF QUALIFICATIONS
- 13 years as a legal secretary for two prominent law firms.
- Specialization in litigation support.
- Experienced at integrating interpersonal and professional skills to facilitate the objectives of a legal team.

PROFESSIONAL EXPERIENCE

1988-present   **Legal Secretary**
VALENCIA & STEIN, San Diego, CA

Litigation, 1995-present
- Provided legal and administrative support for two partners and three associates who specialized in underwriters' insurance and international securities litigation.
- Managed voluminous amounts of paperwork, gaining a reputation for providing information accurately and promptly.
- Frequently asked by co-workers to clarify litigation procedures.

Estate Planning/Administration, 1988-1995
- Played supportive role on legal team comprised of an attorney, a paralegal, and myself.
- Commended for accuracy in preparing and assembling legal documents and correspondence for large complicated estates.

1987-1988   **Legal Secretary**
WILLARD & PORTER, San Diego, CA

Maritime Law
- Handled correspondence and prepared legal documents for two partners specializing in sexual harassment cases.
- Gained basic knowledge of legal procedure including litigation.

EDUCATION
Degree: Legal Secretary
Lane College of Business, Los Angeles, CA
Legal Secretary Procedures
University of California at Riverside, Riverside, CA

Christine Whitley's resume.

Be creative in developing a hybrid resume that promotes you as the best candidate for the job. You can mix and match ideas from this book's guidelines, templates, and sample resumes to create your own special format.

If you still haven't decided which resume format to use, turn to the next chapter and learn all about the functional hybrid resume. It just might be the best format for you.

The Least You Need to Know

➤ The chronological hybrid emphasizes your career history while highlighting skills that are particularly relevant.

➤ The chronological hybrid is ideal if you're looking for a promotion within your current place of employment.

➤ The chronological hybrid is great for a professional who wants to switch industries.

➤ Skill subheadings help define vague job titles.

➤ The chronological hybrid gives life to a long work history at one company.

A Functional Hybrid That Makes Sense

There aren't any limits to how creative you can be with your resume format. Sure, there are guidelines of what to do and what not to do, but it's your marketing piece, and you can be innovative with it!

So far, you've learned about four resume formats: functional, chronological, achievement, and chronological hybrid. Hang on to your marketing hats a little longer—you're about to discover one more: the functional hybrid. In this chapter, you'll see how to design a functional hybrid resume and figure out whether it's the right format for you.

The Skillful Hybrid

You might be the ideal candidate for using the functional resume (based on what you learned in Chapter 5, "Get Functional"), but you may be worried that the functional resume won't be well received by a conservative employer. In that case, you could start with the basic functional layout and add subheadings composed of the name of the company where your achievements took place. This *functional hybrid* has enough of the characteristics of the traditional chronological resume to please your conservative potential employer.

The functional hybrid looks very much like a straight functional format. Its Work History section is concise and placed at the bottom of the page; achievement statements are categorized according to skill headings in the body of the resume. What makes it a hybrid is that

(Functional Hybrid Resume Template)

Name
Street
City, State Zip
Phone, Fax, E-mail

JOB OBJECTIVE

The job you want next

SUMMARY OF QUALIFICATIONS

- How much experience you have in the field of your job objective, in a related field, or using the skills required for your new position.

- An overall career accomplishment that shows you'd be good at this job.

- What someone would say about you as a recommendation.

PROFESSIONAL EXPERIENCE

MAJOR SKILL
Company where the following achievements took place
- An accomplishment you are proud of that shows you have this skill.
- A problem you solved using this skill, and the results.

Company where the following achievements took place
- A time when you used your skill to positively affect the organization, the bottom line, your boss, your clients.
- Awards or commendations you achieved that relate to your job objective.

MAJOR SKILL
Company where the following achievements took place
- A project you are proud of that supports your job objective.
- Another accomplishment that shows you're good at this line of work.

Company where the following achievements took place
- Quantifiable results that point out your skill.
- An occasion when someone "sat up and took notice" of your skill.

WORK HISTORY

19xx-present	Job Title	COMPANY NAME and city
19xx-xx	Job Title	COMPANY NAME and city
19xx-xx	Job Title	COMPANY NAME and city

EDUCATION

Degree, Major (if relevant), 19xx (optional)
University, City, State

Template for functional hybrid resume.

under the skill headings there are subheadings that indicate where the achievements took place. Take a peek at the following template to get a picture of how a functional hybrid is structured.

Looking the Part

As I mentioned in Chapter 5, one of the biggest objections employers have about functional resumes is that most of them unwittingly fail to say where each achievement took place. The functional hybrid identifies this information loud and clear through subheadings in the body of the resume (similar to the job subheadings in the chronological format). That's the advantage—the hybrid resembles the chronological resume (and therefore feels familiar to the employer), yet it has the structural advantage of the functional resume. The functional hybrid is a great format for job seekers who fit the criteria for the functional format and who have several achievements from one place of employment.

To understand this better, look at the way the achievement statements are categorized in the following excerpt from the body of a job seeker's functional hybrid resume. See how the subheadings make it easy to understand where the achievements took place? That's the beauty of this format.

Conservative Employer Alert!

Let's imagine you're applying to a conservative company (such as insurance or banking) where you assume that the hiring manager will expect a traditional chronological resume. But for reasons discussed in Chapter 5, you're leaning toward using the straight functional format. The problem is that your prospective employer may think you don't fit in if you send a functional resume, because it's an atypical format for the field. What should you do? Try the functional hybrid. By adding subheadings that indicate where your achievements took place, the hybrid format will look enough like the chronological resume to ease the employer into trusting that you're a stable worker with valuable skills.

Check out Dennis Beauregard's resume. He wanted to use the functional format because he was transferring his skills from the legal field to the public service arena. Because he was applying to a conservative organization (the Chicago Police Department), he created a functional hybrid resume. By using company names as subheadings under his skill headings, his resume looked enough like a chronological resume to gain his potential employer's respect.

Terms of Employment

The **functional hybrid** is a functional resume with company subheadings included in the Relevant Achievements section to indicate where the achievements took place.

Career Casualty

Don't assume that the employer will spend a lot of time figuring out what happened where on your resume. If it's not immediately clear, the employer may give up and throw your resume in the trash.

RELEVANT ACHIEVEMENTS

MANAGEMENT

Fairfield General Company
- Started the company's marketing department, which now creates promotional strategies for all 46 national branches.
- Directly supervised 16 managers who oversaw the work of 14 graphic designers, 10 copywriters, and 12 vendors.

Indigo International Inc.
- Introduced an automated resume-scanning system that eliminated 20 work-hours per week.
- Improved team spirit by including department representatives in corporate decision-making.

MARKETING

Fairfield General Company
- Increased sales 40 percent by launching three new products in the first year.
- Achieved significant return on advertising by creating a campaign that made "Fairfield" a household name.

Indigo International Inc.
- Wrote a 25-page proposal to outline strategies for reaching long- and short-term goals.

Sample of Relevant Achievements section.

Dennis Beauregard

001 Fairmont Street • Chicago, IL 12345 • (123) 123-1234

JOB OBJECTIVE: President of Civilian Oversight Board, Chicago Police Department

SUMMARY OF QUALIFICATIONS
- More than 20 years as an executive manager in the legal and business fields.
- Excellent researcher with ability to manage a heavy caseload.
- Skilled supervisor who knows how to build consensus among personnel.
- Strength in public relations. Experienced public speaker and spokesperson.

RELEVANT ACCOMPLISHMENTS
MANAGEMENT / SUPERVISION
Get Down Music
- Served as one of five members on the Executive Management Committee, which resolved harassment, discrimination, labor relations, and public relations issues.
- Enhanced departmental and interdepartmental teamwork by fostering strong company-wide communication.
- Managed Business Affairs and Legal Department comprised of attorneys, paralegals, secretaries and contract administrators from diverse cultural backgrounds.

LEGAL
Leder & Porzio, Esqs.
- Conferred with and advised clients with respect to claims against them or their organizations.
- Researched and evaluated validity of claims.
- Conducted conciliation meetings and made concrete recommendations for disposition of claims.
- Scheduled and participated in hearings.

Get Down Music
- Served as legal advisor to management regarding claims by artists, distributors, and employees.
- Conducted and supervised research of claims and prepared evaluations and recommendations.
- Provided statistical reports with respect to departmental operations.

WORK HISTORY
1999-pres Legal Consultant, Chicago, IL
1986-99   Attorney (private practice), Brooklyn, NY
1983-86   Vice President, Business Affairs and Legal Dept., Get Down Music, Inc., New York, NY
1974-83   Associate, 1980-83, Paralegal, 1978-80, Director, International Music Dept., 1974-78, Leder & Porzio, Esqs., New York, NY

EDUCATION
J.D., Columbia University, New York, NY, 1980
B.A., Columbia University, New York, NY, 1973

Dennis Beauregard's resume.

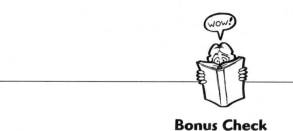

Bonus Check

Telling the reader where an achievement took place increases the credibility of your resume. If your resume has many achievements within a skill heading, avoid repeating the same company name over and over. An efficient way to handle the "where" of your achievements is to list them together under a subheading of the company name. After you create company subheadings under your skill headings, prioritize your subheadings so the most relevant one comes first.

Job-Hunt Hint

Subheadings of the functional hybrid can be either the names of the organizations where your accomplishments took place or the job titles that you held when you completed your achievements.

Terms of Employment

A **red flag** is anything on your resume that looks fishy to employers and might cause them to discard your resume.

Red Flags Down

Some employers don't like functional resumes. They worry that a job seeker who uses one is trying to hide something, and if they're not careful, they'll end up with a problem employee on their hands. *Red flags* on a resume might include the following:

➤ Unexplained gaps in employment, which could indicate instability due to personal problems

➤ A hard-to-follow presentation, which could be an attempt to hide something in the applicant's past

➤ An inappropriately long resume, which could mean the job seeker is unorganized

To relieve the fears of the employer and still use the functional format, categorize the achievement statements under your skill headings according to where they happened. That way the employer can easily reference your subheadings with your Work History at the bottom of the page.

Carmen Bishop's functional hybrid (following) took advantage of the functional format and put the reader's mind at rest by organizing her achievements under job-title subheadings. Her resume clearly shows that she has the sales and project management skills to fulfill the employer's expectations.

Giving Order to Chaos

Having a complicated work history (one that has concurrent employment, short-term jobs, or gaps) is one reason to use a functional resume, because it downplays the sequence of events and throws the spotlight on the important stuff: your transferable skills.

Carmen Bishop

001 Fairmount Street • Santa Barbara, CA 12345 • (123) 123-1234

JOB OBJECTIVE: A sales position

SUMMARY OF QUALIFICATIONS

- Enthusiastic and motivated; sincerely enjoy developing and maintaining excellent customer relations.

- Outstanding ability to understand others' needs and offer solutions.

- Resourceful and innovative; proven talent to adapt quickly to challenges.

- Commended for top-notch organizational skills.

RELEVANT ACCOMPLISHMENTS

SALES/INTERPERSONAL RELATIONS

Word Processing Contractor:
- Consistently developed new business despite slow economy through prospecting, persuasive presentations, and persistent follow-up.

- Easily developed rapport with clients, quickly assessing needs and responding effectively to pressure and deadlines.

Assistant to Executive VP of Production, Magic Movies:
- Handled phones for this successful VP working with celebrities and politicians. Used diplomacy to accommodate demanding schedules and powerful personalities.

- Negotiated terms with vendors for special events.

Inside Sales Representative, Vermont Makes It Special:
- Resolved customer service problems, i.e., deliveries, quality control.

PROJECT MANAGEMENT

Assistant to Executive VP of Production, Magic Movies:
- Planned private screenings for 50-100 VIPs. Evaluated needs for the event, personally invited guests and handled on-site logistics.

- Maintained an extremely high-profile appointment schedule with prominent directors, producers and actors. Managed correspondence, film proposals and expenses.

- Supervised immediate support staff.

WORK HISTORY

1995-present	Word Processing Contractor	West Hollywood
1993-1994	Assistant to Executive VP of Production	Magic Movies Inc., Los Angeles
1991-1992	Booking Assistant	Actors-Plus Agency, Los Angeles
1989-1991	Inside Sales Representative	Vermont Makes It Special, Santa Monica

EDUCATION

B.A., Political Economics, St. Francis College, Mosswood, CA
Culinary Program, Fine Foods Institute, San Luis Obispo, CA

Carmen Bishop's resume.

Todd C. Grey

001 Coolbrith Street • Berkeley, CA 12345 • (123) 123-1234

JOB OBJECTIVE: A position in Fundraising

SUMMARY OF QUALIFICATIONS

- Experienced at fundraising work for nonprofit organizations and political leaders.
- Talent for generating support for causes that increase community involvement.
- Skilled at fostering relationships with people from diverse backgrounds.

EXPERIENCE

FUNDRAISING / PUBLIC RELATIONS

Fundraiser for Access Education, a nonprofit organization dedicated to getting and keeping disabled youth on the college track.

- Played key role in focusing the fundraising committee. Clarified goals, set priorities, and created action plans.
- Organized a pubic relations/fundraising event that attracted 250 disability rights supporters/donors who saw the need to "make a difference" through education.

Public Relations for Political Figures

- Represented Congressman Hanley to the public, explaining his platform, answering questions, and responding to complaints by phone and through correspondence.
- Prepared packets for public appearances, debates, and press conferences for Governor Kunin during her presidential campaign, frequently responding to public controversies.
- Served as front-end person for Senator Dooley, handling hundreds of phone calls per day from a diverse constituency of 20 million.

ADMINISTRATION

- Created and maintained donor database for Access Education which has recently experienced a dramatic expansion.
- As assistant to political figures, managed extremely busy calendars that juggled numerous meetings, press conferences, and media events.
- Wrote commemorative announcements and letters on behalf of Senator Dooley.

RELEVANT WORK HISTORY

1997-present	Fundraiser	Access Education, Berkeley, CA
1996-1999	Financial Aid Advisor	San Francisco State College, San Francisco, CA

(Mostly concurrent with education)

1988-1992	Assistant to political figures:	Congressional Office of Andrew Hanley
		Kunin/Sanders Campaign
		Office of Senator Stanley Dooley

EDUCATION: B.A., San Francisco State, San Francisco, CA, anticipated 2000
Grant Proposal Writing, The Support Center, San Francisco, 2000

Todd Grey's resume.

But eventually the reader is going to notice that your Work History is complex. By using the functional hybrid with company subheadings (which don't have dates in them), you can help the employer easily make sense of an otherwise confusing presentation. For example, Todd Grey used subheadings under his skill headings (see preceding resume) to clarify what took place where and to gather several projects under one logical subheading ("Public Relations for Political Figures"). Nice touch!

Getting Down to It

Now that you've learned the ins and outs of the functional hybrid, you're ready to create yours. Follow the steps for creating the sections of a resume in Part 2, "Six Steps to a Perfect Resume," and use the hybrid template that appears earlier in this chapter, and you'll be all set!

Career Casualty

Never underestimate the importance of graphic appeal. A resume that looks time-consuming to read is an ineffective marketing piece and probably won't be read. Use headings and subheadings to break up the text of your hybrid so that it will be a winner!

The Least You Need to Know

➤ By using the functional hybrid format, you can de-emphasize your work history and spotlight your transferable skills in a structure that resembles a chronological resume.

➤ Create subheadings in the Relevant Experience section to indicate where groups of achievements took place.

➤ You can use organization names or job titles as subheadings in your functional hybrid resume.

➤ Within a skill heading, prioritize the subheadings so the most relevant one comes first.

When You Really Are a Brain Surgeon: Curriculum Vitae

In This Chapter

➤ How a curriculum vitae differs from a resume

➤ Who needs a curriculum vitae

➤ How to write an interesting and dynamic curriculum vitae

➤ Why more is more on a curriculum vitae

➤ How to create your own curriculum vitae

Curriculum vitae have been called the brainy resumes because they're used by scholars, scientists, and, yes, brain surgeons. But you don't have to have a degree in brain surgery to write one. In fact, now that you understand the principles behind good resume writing, you're almost ready to write your curriculum vitae.

A quick run through this chapter will teach you a few tricks of the curriculum vitae trade and will get you on track. Pretty soon you'll have a curriculum vitae you can present with pride.

Curriculum Vitae vs. Resume

When seeking a faculty, research, or leadership position at an academic or scientific organization, you need a special resume called a *curriculum vitae* (vita or CV for short). If you think a curriculum vitae sounds like a formal document, you can relax; there's no need to put on your evening gown or tuxedo to write your CV! Writing one will be a casual event for you because you've already learned the principles behind an effective resume. (Remember the Resume Commandments from Chapter 3, "Winning Resume Wisdom," and the Top Ten Checklist from Chapter 11, "Step Six: The Big Production"?)

To create a CV, there are three exceptions to the resume guidelines you read about in Parts 1, "Plan to Succeed," and 2, "Six Steps to a Perfect Resume":

Terms of Employment

Curriculum vitae is Latin for "life's course." In the academic and scientific worlds, it's a document used as a resume. A curriculum vitae is also referred to as **vita** or **CV.**

Job-Hunt Hint

Make it a habit to review your CV every six months or so to see whether it needs updating. Since updating your CV usually means you will be adding information about the projects you've completed, your CV will grow in length over time.

1. Most CVs are more than two pages long.

2. The information on a CV tends to be detailed, providing extensive data about your publications, presentations, and other academic activities.

3. CVs don't necessarily contain Job Objective statements, although it's perfectly all right to include them.

Let's look at each of these exceptions more closely.

When More Is More

The length of a CV may vary. A CV for a recent Ph.D. graduate would normally range from three to eight pages. For someone with extensive professional experience, a CV could run as long as 20 pages. That's a lot of paper, but in the academic world, that's a good thing. The people reading CVs seem to live by the slogan "more is more." (That's the CV twist on the "less is more" theme I've been espousing all along for resumes.)

Just the Facts

Your CV audience is more interested in the facts and details of your career than it is in hype (that is, language that sounds exaggerated in order to impress). Data such as reference information, dates, and exact titles are important, because they give a means for verifying information. Providing technical descriptions also gives you a chance to show that you know what you're talking about without sounding like a braggart.

Bonus Check

Your CV can be used for more than just getting a job. It will also come in handy when you

➤ Market yourself for a consulting position.

➤ Apply for positions on boards and committees.

➤ Need autobiographical information for proposals, publications, or lectures.

Each time you send out your vita, check to see that it contains the necessary elements for its specific purpose.

Here's an example of what I mean. Instead of saying

> Prominent scientist who has been honored at universities around the world for ground-breaking discoveries.

Use a more modest tone:

> Organic chemist who has presented discoveries and research at universities in Russia, Mexico, Canada, and the United States.

No Objections

Many CVs don't include Job Objective statements, especially if the applicant intends to stay in the same field. Between the college degree and the work history, it's usually obvious what type of position is being sought. However, if you're planning to change careers (for example, from research to teaching), a Job Objective statement at the top of your CV would be helpful to the potential employer.

The Person Behind the Paper Mask

Even though the language of your curriculum vitae will be low-key compared to, say, a salesperson's resume, your CV doesn't have to be devoid of personality. I suggest having a section near the top of your CV that tells the reader a little bit about who you are and what you're looking for (similar to the Summary of Qualifications section in a resume). Give this section a title such as Profile, Professional Statement, Summary of Qualifications, or Career Summary.

Use three to six bullet points to describe attributes such as

➤ How much experience you have in your field.

➤ Where your special strengths lie.

➤ What your particular professional philosophy is.

➤ Any of your immediate career goals that might affect the person reading your CV.

These statements should not be dramatic; they should simply summarize the pages of lists to follow and give the CV reader a sense of who you are (for instance, what your career passions are and what constitutes your work ethic).

Job-Hunt Hint

To portray a sense of personality in your CV, get a friend to help you write it. Ask your buddy to jot down the exact phrases you use to spontaneously describe your accomplishments. Then polish those carefree expressions into business-speak that captures a hint of your character.

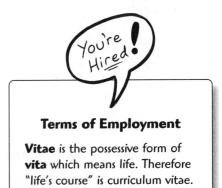

Terms of Employment

Vitae is the possessive form of **vita** which means life. Therefore "life's course" is curriculum vitae. Life is just plain **vita**.

Career Casualty

Don't bury your most prized achievement in the middle or at the end of your CV. Place it on the front page, if possible, so that it'll be seen right away by a potential employer.

Job-Hunt Hint

Combine two similar sections if you have only one or two items to list in each one. Then create a section heading to reflect your combination, such as Education and Training, Honors and Awards, or Exhibitions and Presentations.

Freedom of Format

Because the CV usually addresses a conservative reader, many people assume that it needs to follow a standard, rigid format. Not so! You can be creative in presenting your strengths while respecting the expectations of the academic, scientific, or institutional employer. That means you can consider using any one of the five formats I've suggested so far:

➤ Chronological (see Chapter 4, "Chronologically Speaking")

➤ Functional (see Chapter 5, "Get Functional")

➤ Achievement (see Chapter 12, "The Big Winner: An Achievement Resume")

➤ Chronological hybrid (see Chapter 13, "A Chronological Hybrid That Adds Up")

➤ Functional hybrid (see Chapter 14, "A Functional Hybrid That Makes Sense")

Use the guidelines in each respective chapter to determine which format is best for your CV.

Hanging Out Your Laundry

Following are headings of laundry-list sections commonly found on CVs:

➤ Education

➤ Publications

➤ Presentations

➤ Committees and Appointments

➤ Affiliations

The following sections cover what should be listed under each of these headings. If a heading isn't applicable to you, disregard it.

Good Schooling

The Education section almost always appears near the top of the first page. It should provide information about each degree you have acquired:

➤ Your major

➤ The date you received your degree

➤ The institution where you received it

➤ The city and state of the institution

➤ Titles of your thesis and dissertation

You might also list course titles if they demonstrate relevant knowledge and aren't obvious from the major you declared. You can place internships under the Education heading, in a section of their own (called Internships), or under Experience, depending on which strategy makes the most sense for your situation.

Are You Published?

You need a Publications section if you've authored or coauthored material such as articles, books, or chapters in books. When listing publications, mention

➤ the author (that's you!) or coauthors (you and your colleague).

➤ the title of your article or chapter (if one of these applies).

➤ the title of your book or the publication in which your article or chapter appeared.

➤ the date of publication.

➤ the publisher.

➤ the ISBN (if it applies).

This information appears in sentence format (as shown in the book section of Appendix C, "Other Cool Resources") with commas placed between each element. There are a few standards for order in which you place the elements within the sentences, so check a style manual such as *The Chicago Manual of Style* or *The Gregg Reference Manual* to find one that's right for you.

Be sure to list your published work properly; some employers will want to see that you know how to follow strict guidlines for academic writing.

Putting on a Show

You may have presented papers at conferences. If so, you could have a section called Presentations, Lectures, Symposia, Conferences, or Seminars. In this section, state the following information:

➤ Titles of papers you presented

➤ Names of conferences

➤ Locations

➤ Dates

It is a good idea to elaborate on other roles you played at the conferences (such as serving on panels) if doing so will add to your qualifications.

Career Casualty

Some employers will want to see that you know how to follow strict guidelines for academic writing. Be sure to list your published work properly. To learn the appropriate style for your industry, consult the bibliography section of a style guide that's commonly used in your field, or look at how bibliographies are presented in your trade publications.

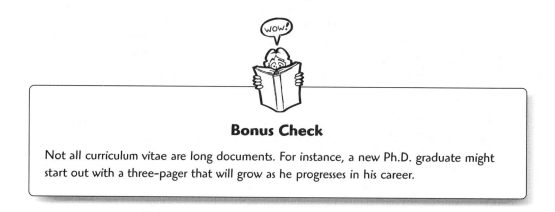

Bonus Check

Not all curriculum vitae are long documents. For instance, a new Ph.D. graduate might start out with a three-pager that will grow as he progresses in his career.

Joining the Team

If you've been selected to serve on one or more committees, consider creating a section entitled Committees, Appointments, Boards, or the like. Under your heading, list the following:

➤ Your titles

➤ Names of committees

➤ The city and state of each committee

➤ Dates you served on the committees

If appropriate, you could include bullet-point statements that say what results were achieved during your tenure. For instance

President, University of Colorado Alumni Association, 1997-99

➤ Designed the organization's first Web site, which enabled online member giving.

➤ Collaborated with Board to develop the Annual Alumni Scholarship Award.

Hangin' with the Right Folks

The associations that you belong to can be listed alphabetically, chronologically, or in order of relevance to your profession. You could call this section something like Professional Affiliations, Professional Associations, or Professional Memberships. If you held or currently hold an office, note that in this section also.

Forget Anything?

Here are some other headings that might appear on your CV:

➤ Exhibitions

➤ Awards and Honors

Job-Hunt Hint

In your CV, list organizations to which you previously belonged, along with the ones you currently participate in.

➤ Research

➤ Studies

➤ Grants

➤ Lectures

➤ Teaching

➤ Licenses

➤ Media Appearances

Remember, more is more when it comes to your CV, so think hard about all that you can include.

High Marks for a University Instructor

Ruth Schwartz used the following curriculum vitae to apply for college-level positions teaching Creative Writing. She realized that her main strength lay in her numerous publications and awards, and her weakness was that she had only one year of teaching at the university level. Therefore, she highlighted her list of publications by putting it on the first page of her CV. That way readers would already be impressed by the time they reached her rather meager teaching section, which began near the bottom of page four.

Create Your CV

Now that you have your feet wet, it's time to jump in. Create strong sections in your CV by using the concepts presented in Part 2. With the additional sections mentioned in this chapter, your CV is likely to run several pages, all of which should have the following information:

➤ Your name at the top of each page

➤ The page number (placed on either the top or bottom of each page)

➤ "Continued" at the bottom of each page (except the last one)

When you've done all of this, sit back, read through your CV, and admire how accomplished you are!

Career Casualty

If you have just one item to list under a heading, make sure the name of the heading is singular, not plural (for example, Professional Affiliation, not Professional Affiliations).

Job-Hunt Hint

To indicate that a laundry list on your CV does not include every single item in that category, add "Selected" or "Relevant" in the heading, for instance, Selected Presentations or Relevant Presentations.

Ruth L. Schwartz

1234 123rd Avenue   ◆   Lakewood, OH 12345
123/123-1234   ◆   Ruth1234@thenet.net

Education

M.F.A. in Creative Writing, 1985 - University of Michigan, Ann Arbor, MI

B.A. in Writing and Womens' Studies, 1983 - Wesleyan University, Middletown, CT

Selected Honors & Awards

◆ **Winner,** Associated Writing Programs Poetry Book Competition, 1994 *(Judge: William Matthews)*

◆ **Fellowship,** National Endowment for the Arts, 1993

◆ **Fellowship,** Astraea Foundation, 1992

◆ **Fellowship,** Wisconsin Institute for Creative Writing, 1992

◆ **Fellowship** to attend M.F.A. Program at the University of Michigan, 1983-85

◆ **First Prize,** Pablo Neruda Award (Nimrod Magazine), 1999 *(Judge: Mark Doty)*

◆ **First Prize,** Sue Saniel Elkind Poetry Contest (Kalliope), 1998 *(Judge: Maxine Kumin)*

◆ **First Prize,** Chelsea Magazine Poetry Competition, 1994

◆ **First Prize,** Randall Jarrell Poetry Contest (North Carolina Writers Network), 1993 *(Judge: Maxine Kumin)*

◆ **First Prize,** Americas Review Poetry Contest, 1992

◆ **First Prize,** New Letters Literary Award for Poetry, 1991 *(Judge: Charles Simic)*

◆ **First Prize,** Pablo Neruda Award (Nimrod Magazine), 1991 *(Judge: James Ragan)*

◆ **First Prize,** S.F. Bay Guardian Poetry Contest, 1991

◆ **International Merit Award Winner,** Atlanta Review International Poetry Competition, 1999

◆ **Reader's Choice Award,** Prairie Schooner Magazine, 1998

◆ **Second Prize,** George Bogin Memorial Award (Poetry Society of America), 1998 *(Judge: Marvin Bell)*

◆ **Second Prize,** Eclectic National Poetry Prize, 1998 *(Judge: Eavan Boland)*

◆ **Second Prize,** Ann Stanford Award (So. California Literary Anthology), 1993 *(Judge: Diane Wakoski)*

◆ **Third Prize,** South Coast Poetry Journal Contest, 1989 *(Judge: Mark Strand)*

◆ **Fourth Prize,** Marlboro Review Poetry Contest, 1997 *(Judge: Ellen Bryant Voight)*

◆ **Honorable Mentions,** National Poetry Competition (Chester H. Jones Foundation), 1999, 1998

◆ **Honorable Mention,** Eve of St. Agnes Competition (Negative Capability), 1998 *(Judge: Rodney Jones)*

- continued –

Ruth L. Schwartz
Page Two

Selected Honors & Awards *(continued)*

◆ **Finalist,** Glimmer Train Poetry Open Competition, 1999; Mudfish Poetry Prize, 1999 *(Judge: C.K. Williams);* National Poetry Series, 1998; Paumanok Visiting Writers Program / Farmingdale State University of New York, 1997; Alice Fay Di Castagnola Award (Poetry Society of America), 1992

◆ **Commendation,** National Poetry Competition (Chester H. Jones Foundation), 1990

◆ **Residency,** Centrum Arts Center, 1990

◆ **Listed** in <u>Who's Who of American Women</u>, <u>Contemporary Author,</u> and <u>Who's Who in Entertainment</u>

Poetry Publications

Book:

University of Pittsburgh Press, 1996   <u>Accordion Breathing and Dancing</u>

Poetry Publications: Anthologies

Pending
> **Southern Illinois University Press** - <u>New Young American Poets</u> (Four poems)
> **Carnegie Mellon Press** - <u>American Poetry: Next Generation</u> (Five poems)
> **St. Martin's Press** - <u>The World in Us: Lesbian and Gay Poetry</u> (Four poems)
> **National Poetry Competition Winners, 1999**   "Proof"

1999	**Ashland Poetry Press** - <u>And What Rough Beast: Poems at the End of the Century</u> - "The City"	
1998	**National Poetry Competition Winners, 1998**	"Why You Listen"
1997	**W.W. Norton** - <u>The Poet's Companion</u>	"Bath"
1996	**Crown Press** - <u>The Zenith of Desire</u>	"January Vineyards"
1996	**Ballantine Books** - <u>My Lover is a Woman</u>	"Midnight Supper," "January Vineyards"
1995	**St. Martin's Press** - <u>The Key To Everything</u>	"The Offering"
1992	**Sidewalk Revolution Press** - <u>Sister/Stranger</u>	"The Same Moon"
1990	**National Poetry Competition Winners Book**	"By Asking"

Poetry Publications: Journals

1999	**Nimrod**	"Millennium Love Poems," "Shrine," "Belief"
	Atlanta Review	"Important Thing"
	Mudfish	"All-Night Crisis Line"
	Cleveland Plain Dealer Sunday Magazine	"Cirque du Soleil" (reprint)
	Eckerd College Review	"Land," "Rafting the Illinois," "Landing"

- continued –

Ruth L. Schwartz
Page Three

Poetry Publications: Journals *(continued)*

1998	**Prairie Schooner**	"The Roses," "Flood Winter"
	Marlboro Review	"Albuquerque B&B," "Can Pigeons Be Heroes?"
	Sow's Ear Poetry Review	"Turkey Vulture, Cove Beach"
	Kalliope	"Gravity"
1997	**Poetry Flash**	"The Work of Morning"
1995	**Chelsea**	"The Greatest Show...," "Why I Forgive...," "Golden Gate," "Flamenco Guitar," "Hayward Shoreline," "Because Summer"
	N.W. Poets & Artists Calendar	"Late Summer"
1994	**Chelsea**	"The City at Sunset"
	Southern California Anthology	"AIDS Education: 7th Grade"
	Artful Dodge	"Scene with Pelicans," "Letter from Anywhere"
1993	**Parnassus: Poetry in Review**	"History"
	Provincetown Arts	"And the light"
	Americas Review	"The City," "In Guatemala" (reprints)
	Southwest	"The Offering," "Late Monologue for a Traveler"
1992	**Zone Three**	"After the Killed Bird"
	Sow's Ear	"Almolonga"
	San Francisco Bay Guardian	"The City"
	New Letters	"In Guatemala," "Possible," "Near Us, a New House"
1991	**Yellow Silk**	"Homecoming," "Fear of Sex"
	Visions, International	"Mother and Child"
	Primavera	"How We Might"
	Nimrod	"Poems of the Body" (six-poem sequence)
	Outlook	"The Same Moon"
	Confrontations	"Life in the Forest"
1990	**Birmingham Poetry Review**	"Future Tense"
	S.F. Bay Guardian	"It is National Poetry Week and Navy Fleet Week ..."
	Madison Review	"When They Know"
	Taos Review	"Here Among Mountains Without You," "By Asking"
	Pudding Magazine	"At Eight"
	American Writing	"The Snake," "The Juggler...," "September...," "17 Aliens"
1989	**Hayden's Ferry Review**	"Father, After the Divorce"
	South Coast Poetry Journal	"The Burglars"
	Moving Out	"The Seamstress"
1988	**Evergreen Chronicles**	"Making it Last"
1987	**Berkeley Poetry Review**	"A Neighbor Remembers Invention"
	South Coast Poetry Journal	"The Secret"
	Evergreen Chronicles	"Taking Leave," "Grapefruit Ice"
	San Francisco Sentinel	"The Surface Break," "Next Time"
1985	**Widener Review**	"Choices"
	Blue Ox Review	"Contours"

- continued -

Ruth L. Schwartz
Page Four

Creative Non-Fiction Publications

Anthologies:
1996	**Anchor Press -** <u>The Wild Good</u>	*from* "The Kidney Transplant Chronicles"
1996	**Dutton Press -** <u>Sisters, Sexperts, Queers</u>	"New Alliances: Lesbians, Gay Men & AIDS"
1988	**Cleis Press -** <u>AIDS: The Women</u>	"Many a Long Month"

Journals:
1998	**The Sun**	"Acts of Love"
	Utne Reader	"My Fat Lover" (reprint)
1997	**The Sun**	"Pills," "Roommates," "My Fat Lover"
1996	**The Sun**	"We Don't Know What It Is"

Work In Progress

<u>Survival</u>, a second book of poems
(Finalist in numerous 1998 competitions, including the 1998 National Poetry Series)

<u>Edgewater Park</u>, a third book of poems

<u>Death in Reverse</u>, a prose memoir

Teaching Experience

Assistant Professor of Creative Writing, Cleveland State University, Cleveland, OH, 1998-present
Co-Director, Poetry Center, Cleveland State University, Cleveland, OH, 1998-present
- Develop and teach courses in Poetry Writing, Creative Writing, Sexuality in Literature, and other writing- and literature-related subjects, for both undergraduate and graduate students.
- Advise M.A. students on creative and scholarly thesis projects.
- Participate in planning and development of Cleveland State's M.F.A. Creative Writing Program.
- Facilitate community Poetry Forum, participate in judging literary contests, including the Poetry Center's annual book competition, and co-coordinate reading series.
- Play key role in editing and translation of Spanish-language manuscripts published by the Poetry Center.

Poetry Instructor, Antioch Writer's Workshop, Yellow Springs, OH, 1999, 1998
- Delivered craft-related lectures to large audiences, facilitating stimulating, productive discussions among participant writers at all levels of expertise; provided individual conferences on student work.
- Led week-long "Poetry Intensive," combining reading, writing and craft exercises.

- continued –

Ruth L. Schwartz
Page Five

Teaching Experience *(continued)*

Poetry Instructor, Oklahoma Summer Arts Institute, Tahlequah, OK, 1998, 1997
- Conceived and taught two intensive poetry courses, combining a variety of activities -- including craft lectures, free-writing, and writer's-eye-view analysis of contemporary poetry -- to provide the academic equivalent of a semester-long college seminar over two weeks of all-day classes.

Guest Poet/Workshop Leader, *Nimrod Magazine* **Writing Seminar,** Tulsa, OK, 1991

Graduate Teaching Assistant, University of Michigan, Ann Arbor, MI, 1983-85

Teaching Assistant, Wesleyan University, Middletown, CT, 1980-81, 1982-83

Recent Readings & Presentations

Featured Reader & Presenter, Wright State University, Dayton, OH, 1999

Featured Presenter, *WRITE ON! Cleveland*, Cleveland, OH, 1999

Featured Reader & Panel Discussion Member, Antioch Writer's Workshop, Yellow Springs, OH, 1998
- Participated in *Getting Naked on the Page,* a reading/panel discussion on writing about sex and sexuality.

Featured Reader, Cody's Books, Berkeley, CA, 1998, 1997, 1995

Featured Reader & Presenter, Oklahoma Summer Arts Institute, Norman, OK, 1998, 1997

Featured Reader, San Francisco State University, San Francisco, CA, 1997

Featured Reader, A Different Light Bookstore, San Francisco, CA, 1997

Featured Reader, Alexander Book Company, San Francisco, CA, 1996

Editorial Experience

Lead Editorial Committee Member, Cleveland State University Poetry Center, 1998-present
- Lead four-member Editorial Committee through the process of screening the approximately 1000 book-length poetry manuscripts submitted each year for C.S.U.P.C.'s annual contest, identifying ten finalists to be sent on to contest's final judge.

Poetry Reader (Editorial Committee), *FEMSPEC* **Journal,** Cleveland, OH, 1999-present

Editorial / Administrative Volunteer, *Poetry Flash,* Berkeley, CA, 1997-98

Screening Judge, *The Loft* **Annual Poetry Contest,** 1996

- continued -

Ruth L. Schwartz
Page Six

Editorial Experience *(continued)*

Screening Judge, *San Francisco Bay Guardian* **Poetry Contest,** 1996

Co-Editor, *Five Fingers Review,* San Francisco, CA, 1989-91
* Initiated chapbook contest, co-edited and produced nationally-renowned literary magazine

Editor, *AIDS Poetry Anthology Project,* 1989-92

Associate Editor, *Art and Understanding,* 1990-93

Additional Work Experience

Professional Writer / Editor, Oakland, CA, 1990-present
* Write and edit a wide variety of documents, including health education materials, brochures, résumés and marketing copy, both independently and as an associate in Susan Ireland's Résumé Service.

Health Educator, San Francisco, San Mateo and Union City, CA, 1986-97
* Coordinated AIDS education programs in schools (San Mateo County AIDS Program, 1992-94), the Northern CA AIDS Hotline and AIDS Speaker's Bureau (San Francisco AIDS Foundation, 1986-92).
* Served as overseas AIDS education consultant, helping to establish AIDS Hotlines in St. Lucia, West Indies and Swaziland, Africa (AIDSCOM/U.S.A.I.D., 1989-92).
* Provided detailed medical information, advocacy, counseling and referrals to callers to a federally-funded Cancer Information Service (1994-97).
* Counseled and translated for Spanish-speaking clients of San Francisco General Hospital's Genetic Counseling Program (1996).

Languages

Verbal and written fluency in Spanish, with special interest in literary translation.

Sample Comments from Recent Student Evaluations
(Original evaluations available upon request)

* *"Professor's attitude was very helpful to novice writers."*
* *"She knew her content, and made the course fun by having structured and enriching classes."*
* *"The course was inspiring and constructive."*
* *"(She was) able to be honest and candid in her comments and instruction, while remaining respectful."*
* *"Gave good constructive criticism... very personable, easy to talk to, and open to suggestions."*
* *"(The course) definitely improved my writing... and the instructor successfully interested me in poetry reading and writing."*

Ruth Schwartz's curriculum vitae.

The Least You Need to Know

➤ Curriculum vitae is the term used in academic and scientific communities for resume.

➤ CVs are usually longer than two pages (and may be as long as 20 pages) and frequently don't include a Job Objective section.

➤ You can use either a chronological, functional, achievement, chronological hybrid, or functional hybrid format, but keep it conservative in presentation and language for most uses.

➤ A large part of your CV should be laundry-list sections such as Publications, Awards and Honors, and Presentations.

➤ Be sure to number all pages and include "Continued" at the bottom of all but the last page.

Part 4

Letters That Work

With the exception of junk mail, a letter is welcomed by almost everyone, and your prospective employer is no exception. In fact, your cover and thank-you letters might be the elements of your application that send the message that you're the one for the job. Whether it's the way you sell yourself in writing or the personality that comes through in your words, your letter holds the power to make a personal connection between you and the manager.

"Easy for you to say," you mumble. "You're a writer. I freeze at the thought of putting my pen to paper." Relax! Part 4 gives some easy-to-follow advice that will make your fingers fly across your keyboard to create letters that work.

You've Got Style

Your writing technique says a lot about whether your letter is a winner that will get you the result you want or a loser that will get tossed into the wastebasket. Now don't wince at the word *technique*. I'm not suggesting you pull out your old high school textbooks to study dangling modifiers and past participles. I'm talking about down-to-earth, easy communication.

This chapter explains how to use a writing style that sounds like you, not some old grammar book buried in a library basement. I'll show you how to write in an engaging, confident style that will make the reader sit up straight and listen to what you have to say.

Writing with Style

There's nothing mysterious about good letter-writing style. The biggest mistake most people make is that they try too hard. In an effort to make their letter sound just right, they use extraordinarily long sentences, dense paragraphs, tons of multisyllable words, and overly formal language. If there's a longer, more complicated way to say something, they'll do it in a sincere but often useless effort to impress the reader.

My advice is to relax and just be yourself on paper. Let the words flow out of your pen or onto your computer screen as if you were talking with a friend or someone you would like to know. After all, you're hoping that your letter will spark a relationship that could last for years. So think of your letter as one part of a conversation, not a lengthy, detailed dissertation.

Use these techniques to keep your writing style casual yet on the ball:

➤ Don't use overly formal language.

➤ Let your personality shine through your words and phrases.

➤ Choose words that demonstrate confidence and sincerity.

➤ Use action verbs instead of passive verbs whenever possible.

➤ Check that your grammar, spelling, and punctuation are correct.

Let's see how each of these points can give your letter zing!

Bonus Check

Learning how to write effective job-search letters is a good investment of time. Persuasive letter writing is a skill you're bound to use on the job for proposals, requests, and other business correspondence.

Job-Hunt Hint

After you've composed your job-search letter, read it out loud to a friend and ask her, "Does this sound like me?" If her answer is "No," your letter probably has some stilted language that needs to be made more conversational.

Dump the Stilted Stuff

A good rule of thumb for knowing what's appropriate language for your job-search letter is to write as you would speak in a friendly business conversation. That way your letter will sound like you—someone the reader will want to chat with—not like some stuffed shirt who's completely boring.

Stilted language is deadly in job-search letters, yet it's commonplace because most job seekers make the mistake of thinking they should be formal in their correspondence. The good news is that because most job seekers use stilted language, your letter's going to really stand out when you follow the advice in this chapter.

Are you wondering what I mean by stilted language? Here are some examples:

"Enclosed, please find my resume for … " (Way too formal for a letter that's meant to be an ice-breaker.)

"Pursuant of our conversation, I would like to apply for … " (Reads like a legal document, hardly like a message to someone you'd like to know better.)

"In response to your advertisement in the *Gazette*, I am enclosing … " (That's way too stuffy for a letter intended to increase rapport.)

Were you surprised to read that I disapprove of these commonly used phrases? I thought so. The main problem with these stilted sentences is that they lack personality, and personality is a key element in a winning letter. Read on to learn good alternatives to stilted phrases and how to make your letter reflect your winning personality.

Yours Truly

You have a set of skills and personal characteristics to offer a lucky employer. Start demonstrating them early on in your job-application process by infusing your letter with your

Job-Hunt Hint

To write in a friendly tone, write by ear. Jot down sentences the way you would speak them. Then go over them to see whether you need to correct the punctuation or phrasing.

➤ Ability to engage in conversation. With a dynamite first sentence, you can grab the reader's attention.

➤ Talent for making someone feel at ease with you. You can achieve this by having a friendly first paragraph.

➤ Skill at presenting ideas concisely. In the middle of your letter, use short paragraphs, bullet points, or columns to organize your thoughts.

➤ Understanding of the reader's goals. Speak directly to the employer's situation in your sentences.

➤ Finesse at initiating the next move. In your last paragraph, state that you'd like to meet with the employer or whatever it is you'd like to have happen next.

➤ Gratitude for the employer's attention. End your letter on a note of thanks.

Bonus Check

One way to relax your writing style is to use contractions instead of two words, for example, "It's been three years since ..." instead of "It has been three years since ...." But don't overdo it and make everything a contraction. Read the letter out loud and insert a contraction where it sounds natural.

After perusing a letter that contains these attributes, your potential employer will think, "I feel like I'm getting to know this person, and I like her!" That's the response you want.

Showing Your Gold

Confidence and sincerity are two qualities that are always valued by hiring managers. Let's talk about how your letter can reflect these two characteristics.

Career Casualty

Don't use multisyllable words as a gimmick to impress the reader when a shorter word will work. For instance, write *use* instead of *utilize.*

Job-Hunt Hint

Although exclamation marks can be effective in giving your writing dynamism, use them sparingly in your letter! One or two per letter is plenty! Too many are distracting and create an overly excited tone! (See what I mean?)

Confidently Spoken

You might be surprised at how your choice of words can imply either confidence or insecurity. Many folks confuse politeness with insecurity. They write words such as *if, might, could,* and *maybe* in an effort to be polite when those words often ring of insecurity. Instead, choose words that send signals of confidence: *when, will, would,* and *certainly.* It's important that employers get the sense from your letter that you believe in yourself. After all, if you don't, why should they?

The following examples contrast insecure and confident writing styles:

Insecure: If I don't hear from you, I'll call to see if we can meet.

Confident: I'll call you next week to see when we can meet.

Insecure: I hope that you will find my qualifications suitable for the job.

Confident: I'm confident that I can do the job.

Insecure: I might be a good candidate for the job.

Confident: I'm the one for the job.

Insecure: Hopefully we can get together to talk.

Confident: Let's get together to talk.

Insecure: Perhaps I might meet with you.

Confident: I'd like to meet with you.

Insecure: Maybe sometime next week we could find time to meet.

Confident: Next week is a good time for me to meet with you.

Insecure: I was wondering if you have any job openings in sales.

Confident: I understand that you need a good salesperson.

Get the point? If you're tempted to write a word or phrase that rings of insecurity, resist and opt for the confident approach.

Most Sincerely

Showing sincerity can be a tricky thing. You want to use words and phrases that imply sincerity without your letter sounding contrived. These seven tips will help you express sincerity in your letter:

1. It's okay to start a few sentences of your letter with I, but don't overdo it. A letter that becomes too I-focused (especially by having I at the beginning of each paragraph), is apt to draw a response like, "I, I, I! Doesn't this guy ever think of anyone except himself?"

2. Use concrete terminology in your letter. Refer to specifics you've learned from your research or can present from your own experience. Whenever appropriate, use exact numbers, names, and places instead of generalities. For example, "I can envision a 10 percent growth in sales in each of your 25 branches" is much better than "I can envision sales growth in your various offices."

3. Speak specifically to the employer's goals, challenges, mission statement, or anything that's relevant to your work for the company. For example, "I'd like to be a part of opening your four new plants in Illinois."

4. Weave the employer's name into the text of your letter so it's clear this letter is truly for her. For instance, "Ms. Reinhardt, we met at the last U.S. Shipping Convention in Miami."

5. If your letter has a humorous tone throughout, break that tone from time to time with a comment such as "Seriously, I know I can …" or "Joking aside, there are several issues …."

6. Use an *assertive* (but not *aggressive*) tone in your closing paragraph that lets the employer know you're sincere about wanting the job. For example, "I'll contact you next week to follow up on this proposal."

7. Say thank you in a simple and honest way toward the end of your letter. Let your potential employer know that you appreciate her attention. For ideas for an appropriate thanks, refer to Chapter 17, "The Cover Letter Connection," and Chapter 18, "Thanks Very Much," depending on what type of letter you're writing.

Job-Hunt Hint

Research is key to writing a good letter. The more you know about an employer's goals, problems, and culture, the better you can address his concerns in your letter.

Terms of Employment

Aggressive means combative, which is not a quality to exhibit to an employer in your letter. **Assertive** means boldly positive, which is a good quality to demonstrate in your letter.

Your Most Persuasive Voice

To make your writing really come alive, use an active voice instead of a passive voice. The easiest way to do that is to use action verbs instead of passive verbs whenever possible.

A letter loaded with *action verbs* will imply that you're a go-getter, someone who produces results. On the other hand, a letter filled with *passive verbs* tells the reader that you're the one who watches things happen and occasionally they affect you. Which message do you think is a more persuasive one to send a prospective employer? You got it—the first one!

Following are some examples of active and passive sentences:

> **Passive:** I was assigned the task of shipping out the inventory quickly in order to compensate for a missed production deadline.

> **Active:** I shipped the inventory in record time and thereby compensated for a missed production deadline.

Terms of Employment

An **action verb** is one that says that someone did something. For example, "I earned a raise." A **passive verb** tells what happened to someone or something. For example, "I received a raise," or "A raise was given to me.")

Passive: I was awarded a special distinction that led to the start of an employee contest called "Hero of the Month."

Active: After I earned a special distinction for my achievement, I started a new company-wide contest called "Hero of the Month."

Bonus Check

To come up with appropriately friendly language for your letter, imagine that you're having an easy chat with your prospective boss. What things would you talk to him about? How would you phrase your sentences in that conversation? The answers to these questions will tell you how to write your letter.

Looking Smart with Good Grammar

This section highlights a few grammar rules that are important to letter writing. For a more complete list of grammar and writing guidelines, refer to my other book, *The Complete Idiot's Guide to the Perfect Cover Letter* (Macmillan USA, 1997).

Consistency

Be sure that the subject and verb of each sentence agree, even in tricky situations like this one: "The issue of falling profits is very serious." Because the subject (issue) is singular, the verb (is) must be singular.

Consistency is the most important rule in composition. Once you've chosen a punctuation style (such as periods at the end of bullet-point phrases or commas before the and at the end of a string of items), follow that style throughout your entire letter.

Periods

A period is optional at the end of each phrase in a list. Either of the following examples would be acceptable:

For starters, let's look at my experience in writing:

➤ Three published books.

➤ A multimedia package with nationwide distribution.

➤ Editorial work for the *New York Times*.

Periods are also optional after the initials of academic degrees, so either B.A. or BA would be fine to use.

Commas

Commas should separate elements of a date. However, no comma is needed when just the month and year are stated. The following examples demonstrate this rule:

➤ I am available starting on Wednesday, June 23, 1999.

➤ During June 1999, I oversaw the opening of four new stores.

Insert a comma between a person's name and an abbreviation that follows his name, except when the abbreviation is Jr. or Sr.:

Maria Twang, M.D.

George Grossman Sr.

Place a comma after the salutation in an informal letter. If the letter is of a more formal nature, a semicolon or colon may be used instead of a comma in the salutation:

Dear Mr. Corazon,

Dear Mr. Corazon;

Dear Mr. Corazon:

Bonus Check

To be sure you haven't used too many commas in your sentences (a common writing mistake), do this simple trick: Remove all the commas from a sentence. Then replace a comma only if you need it to have correct grammar or to clarify the meaning of the sentence.

Numbers

Don't use an apostrophe to indicate the plural form of a number. The following example shows the correct method:

The job market had some lows in the 1990s.

Bonus Check

Capitalizing a job title in the text of your letter is optional. If you want to give it importance or emphasis, capitalize it. If you capitalize one title, you must capitalize all other titles in your letter. When referring to the official name of a department, the name should be capitalized. For example, "I sent my resume to the Human Resources department." Don't capitalize the name if you're referring to it as a function. For example, "I've worked in human resources for 10 years."

Job-Hunt Hint

For clarity when referring to a range of figures, repeat the word *thousand, million,* or whatever increment you're speaking of each time you mention a number. For example, write, "20 million to 40 million," not "20 to 40 million."

Spell out numbers from 1 to 10. Use numerals for numbers 10 and greater. The number 10 may be either spelled or numerated:

Our department oversees the work of eight engineers and five technical writers. When all 13 employees are in high gear, things cook!

If two or more numbers appear within a sentence, their written form should be consistent (either spelled out or numerated):

➤ We hired 12 waiters and 3 chefs.

➤ We hired twelve waiters and three chefs.

You can state large amounts of money in all numbers, all words, or a combination of numbers and words or numbers and letters. All of the following examples are correct:

$50,000,000 (insert commas in large numbers to make the quantity easy to identify quickly)

fifty million dollars

$50 million

$50M

Career Casualty

Avoid short, choppy writing (short consecutive sentences) in your letter. In some cases, you can combine two shorties with a semicolon to create one comprehensive sentence.

A Few Good Words

Among the many frequently confused words, I've selected the ones most commonly misused in job-search letters. The following information can keep you out of trouble when it comes to using these tricky words:

➤ **Anxious and eager.** Use anxious to mean "fearful or concerned." Use eager to mean "desirous or willing." For example, I'm eager to work for this company, but I'm anxious about the repercussions of quitting my current job.

➤ **Assure, ensure, and insure.** *Assure* means "to give someone confidence." *Ensure* means "to make certain." *Insure* means "to protect against loss." Here are some examples:

I assure you that I will be there Monday morning.

I have taken every measure to ensure that the sale will go through.

I will insure the house for every cent it's worth.

➤ **Its and it's.** *Its* is the possessive form of *it*. *It's* is a contraction that means *it is*. The difference between the two is shown in the following examples:

Please place the resume back in its file.

It's been a long time since I updated my resume.

➤ **Who and Whom.** *Who* is never used as the object of a preposition. *Whom* is always the object of a preposition. Here are some examples:

Who is the person in charge?

My interview is with whom?

Job-Hunt Hint

If you think your reader doesn't know the translation for an acronym you've used, spell it out and put the acronym in parentheses. Thereafter in your letter, you can use the acronym alone.

To find the answer to other sticky-word questions, consult a dictionary. Then you can be sure to write the right word in the right place.

Back to the Source

You don't have to be a grammar know-it-all to be a good writer. Just keep the following resources nearby so you can look up anything you're unsure of:

➤ Dictionary

➤ Thesaurus

➤ Writing manual for grammar and writing style (such as *The Chicago Manual of Style*)

In addition to good books, your computer can help you with grammar and writing style. Microsoft Word and other word-processing programs have excellent grammar, dictionary, spelling, and thesaurus tools. But be careful: There's no substitute for reading it yourself. Computer spell checkers can't catch everything; they won't flag incorrect usage of *its* and *it's*, for example.

Your letter is often the first contact an employer has with you. Make sure it sends a positive impression! Don't embarrass yourself by having a grammatical error in your letter. Ask a knowledgeable friend, turn to a grammar book, or search online for the answer to your question. And always proofread your letter carefully before sending it out! A well-written, polished letter that showcases your personality can open the door to further contact.

Bonus Check

If you have writer's block, try my "crazy draft" technique: On a blank computer screen or piece of paper, write a very quick draft of a cover letter. Exaggerate your attitude to the point of being silly, maybe something like "Hey buddy, I really need that job you're offering and I'm going to give you three good reasons why I should have it." Don't worry about grammar or spelling; just write anything that comes to mind. After writing your crazy draft, go back and polish it: "Dear Mr. Black, I've learned that you need a technical writer for the WidgetMaster program you're about to launch. Here are three reasons I'd be a great member of your writing team."

The Least You Need to Know

➤ Avoid overly formal language in your letter. Aim for a friendly, yet respectful style that initiates rapport with your reader.

➤ Convey confidence, sincerity, and other positive attributes in the way you phrase your sentences.

➤ Use action verbs instead of passive verbs to tell the reader that you're someone who gets things done.

➤ Refer to books and online resources to ensure that your grammar, spelling, and writing style are correct.

Chapter 17

The Cover Letter Connection

In This Chapter

➤ Your secret weapon: a cover letter that lets your personality shine through

➤ The issue of including salary on your cover letter

➤ An effective cover letter, part by part

➤ Four easy steps to creating multiple cover letters

You have a great-looking resume, and you're eager to send it off to Mr. or Ms. Employer. But wait! You need one more thing: a cover letter. And not just any old cover letter—you want a terrific letter that makes a great first impression. In this chapter, you'll learn how to write a cover letter that's quick and easy to compose, sounds personable, and gets you the results you want!

The Secret to Success

Here's my secret for writing an outstanding cover letter: Think of your letter as the basis of the ideal script for the job interview you'll have with the person to whom you're writing. Let your letter indicate the following things to the reader:

➤ What topic could break the ice at the beginning of the interview

➤ What kind of personality you have

➤ What types of things you have to talk about in your meeting

➤ What you hope to get from the interview

If your cover letter can say these four things, it will make an employer start imagining that you and she are having a conversation. When she does that, she'll be more apt to read your resume and then reach for the phone to call you for an interview!

Career Casualty

Don't be afraid to let your personality shine through in your cover letter. If the employer doesn't like who you are, you probably won't like working for her.

Career Casualty

It's a known poker theory that the first player to show his hand is at a disadvantage. The same applies to salary negotiations. Avoid stating your salary expectations until after hearing what range the employer is offering.

Terms of Employment

Don't confuse salary with compensation. **Salary** is the amount of money you bring home in paychecks in one year. **Compensation** is your salary, benefits (such as insurance and retirement plan), and perks (such as travel and time off).

Salary Small Talk

You may run into a job posting that asks for your *salary* expectations. Most job seekers don't feel comfortable talking about these details before the interview. If, however, you feel compelled to do so in your cover letter (maybe you worry that you'll be disqualified if you don't comply with the ad's request), do so gingerly.

I suggest that you first find out what the position typically pays. You can do this by asking a job counselor or employment agency, by reading ads for similar jobs in the newspaper, or by going online to some of the salary information sites I recommend in Appendix C, "Other Cool Resources." Then do one of the following:

➤ Mention your salary expectations in your cover letter, using language that gives you room for negotiations, such as, "I am looking for a position in the $X to $Y salary range."

➤ Indicate that you would prefer to discuss salary during the interview.

In either case, you've addressed the issue, and you'll likely stand a chance at winning an interview where you can discuss the full *compensation* package, not just the take-home pay (which is what a salary range implies).

The Template of Zoom

Here's how to zoom through your letter-writing process: As I go through each step of writing a cover letter, follow the template in this chapter. That will help you understand what goes where.

You can choose from any of the following format types for your cover letter:

➤ Block

➤ Semi-block

➤ Full-block

➤ Simplified

Because the semi-block format is widely accepted in both personal and professional realms, I used it for the following template. If you're interested in learning about the other formats, consult a writing manual such as *The Chicago Manual of Style*. Check out the following sample generic cover letter; it should teach you what you need to know about the format—as well as the contents—of a cover letter.

Your Name
Street address
City, state, and zip
Contact number(s)
E-mail address (optional)

Today's date

Your addressee's name
Professional title
Organization name
Mailing address
City, state, and zip

Dear Mr. (or Ms.) last name,

Start your letter with a grabber — a statement that establishes a connection with your reader, a probing question or a quotable quote. Briefly name the job you are applying for.

The mid-section of your letter should be one or two short paragraphs that make relevant points about your qualifications. You should <u>not</u> summarize your resume! You may incorporate a column or bullet point format here.

Your last paragraph should initiate action by explaining what <u>you</u> will do next (e.g., call the employer), or asking the reader to take a specific step (e.g., contact you to set up an interview). This is also a good place to thank the reader for his or her attention.

Sincerely yours,

Your name (signed)

Your name (typed)

Enclosure: resume

Cover letter template.

Career Casualty

Use bold and italics sparingly in your letter. An overdose of these features can make your letter hard to read.

Job-Hunt Hint

With all the good networking you'll be doing during your job search, you're bound to have a friend suggest you send your resume and cover letter to a friend of his. When writing a cover letter to that person, ask your friend whether you should use the person's first name or her surname in the salutation (for instance, "Dear Mary" or "Dear Ms. Kramer"). The answer will probably depend on how well your friend knows the person he's referring.

A Head Start

Your heading should contain the same info as the one on your resume.

➤ Name

➤ Address

➤ Telephone number(s)

➤ E-mail address (optional)

➤ Fax number (optional)

For help figuring out how to create a tasteful heading, see Chapter 6, "Step One: Heading Your Way." In fact, you could just duplicate the heading from your resume and use it for your cover letter letterhead.

Set the Date and the Place

Immediately under the heading, place the date and inside address. The inside address is your recipient's name and mailing address. (There's no need to include the recipient's phone, e-mail, or fax numbers.)

Hello, Hello!

The salutation is very simple: Dear so-and-so. Hopefully you know the person's name and can use it in the salutation. If not, a quick call to the company's Human Resources department can give you that information. If you know the person on a first-name basis, use just her first name (for example, Dear Jane). If you've never met her or you have a formal rapport with her, use her last name (for example, Dear Ms. Graham).

If you don't know the manager's name and have no way of finding it out, start your letter with a job title that makes sense for your letter, as shown in the following examples:

➤ Dear Manager

➤ Dear Director

➤ Dear Recruiter

Jumping In

The opening line is one of the most important parts of your letter. It has to be a good one, or you could lose the employer before you even begin. Think of a grabber that will make the employer want to keep reading. (See the sample letters later in this chapter for ideas.)

Bonus Check

Be creative in how you start your letter. Avoid openings with ho-hum phrases so many job seekers use, such as

Enclosed please find my resume for ...

I'm responding to your ad in the ...

I'm applying for the position as ...

These overused openers are boring and show no personality or originality. They sound like a form letter, which is the very thing you want to avoid.

The Meat of the Matter

The middle of your letter is your opportunity to paint the picture of what you'll be able to contribute to the interview. Use this section to point out

➤ Topics you want to discuss that relate to the organization's issues.

➤ Your understanding of what it takes to fill the specific position and be a good employee.

➤ That you've done your homework and therefore have a hunch as to what the company's up to and how you would fit in.

Getting What You Want

Near the end of your letter, do two things:

1. Ask for what you want (probably a job interview).

2. Thank the person.

Try to keep the ball in your court by saying something to the effect of "I'll call you to see when we can meet" instead of a more passive approach such as "I hope to hear from you."

If you don't have contact information for the employer and therefore can't call her, or if the ad specifies no phone calls, try an assertive close that nudges the employer to call you for an interview, such as the following:

➤ I'll be interviewing in Florida during the last week of this month. Please call me to schedule an appointment.

Career Casualty

Don't write "To whom it may concern" or "Dear Sir or Madam" as a salutation in your cover letter. It's far too formal and impersonal. Instead, use one of the suggestions in this section.

Job-Hunt Hint

Think of your letter as the bridge between your resume (which is a monologue) and your interview (which is a dialogue).

249

> ➤ With the end of the second quarter approaching, you may need to do some catch-up in sales. The sooner I get to work, the more I can contribute to reaching your annual goals. Let's talk!

You can thank the employer very simply:

> ➤ Thank you for reviewing this resume in advance of our meeting.

> ➤ I appreciate the time you've spent considering my request.

> ➤ I'm looking forward to our meeting. Thank you.

Bonus Check

Don't be afraid to use demonstrative language in your letter—after all, you really want a job from this employer, don't you? As long as your phrases are natural and appropriate, say them with confidence.

Terms of Employment

Complimentary close is the term for the word or short phrase just above your signature. "Sincerely yours" is perhaps the most commonly used complimentary close for job-search correspondence.

What would you say in person to thank a prospective employer for considering you for a job? What you would say verbally is a hint as to what to write at the end of your cover letter.

Ten-Four

It's time to sign off with a *complimentary close* such as the following:

> ➤ Sincerely,

> ➤ Sincerely yours,

> ➤ Very sincerely,

> ➤ With regards,

> ➤ Regards,

> ➤ Thank you!

Skip a few lines after your complimentary close, and type your name. After you've printed out your letter, sign the letter in the space between your close and your typed name.

Flush left on the next line, type "Enclosure: resume." This way, the recipient of your package knows that you've included your resume, without your having to take up valuable space in your letter saying so.

By Example

Following are three sample cover letters that demonstrate the points I've been talking about. They should give you some ideas for formulating your one-of-a-kind cover letter.

Bonus Check

Mentioning the employer's friend or colleague in the first paragraph is a great way to grab the employer's attention. The person you name is likely someone whose opinion the employer trusts. And by referring to his buddy, you increase the chance that your letter and resume will be read because the employer knows his colleague might ask him about your application.

Name Dropping

A great way to start your letter is with the name of someone both you and your reader know. This person could be any of the following:

➤ A mutual friend ("Your cousin Larry suggested I contact you about …")

➤ A respected professional associate ("When Linda Standall mentioned your name at the dental convention …")

➤ A well-known person, even if neither of you knows him personally ("In the words of our industry's guru, Bill Gates …")

A familiar name is apt to make the employer sit up and take notice. It'll also make the employer realize that you already have something in common and that a conversation with you will feel natural. Check out Bill Steinberger's introductory sentence in his cover letter (following). See how it grabs you and draws you into the rest of the letter?

Bonus Check

Your first sentence is critical for nabbing the employer's attention. Here are some ideas for how you could kick off your letter:

➤ Begin with a question that piques the reader's interest.

➤ Lead in with the name of someone you both know.

➤ Start out with a quote that applies to the type of business the employer is involved with.

➤ Explain how you learned about the job opening you're applying for.

For details on each of these ideas and lots of sample letters that use these techniques, refer to my other book: *The Complete Idiot's Guide to the Perfect Cover Letter* (Macmillan USA, 1997).

Bill Steinberger

01 Terrace Street
El Sobrante, CA 94657
123-123-1234

January 3, 2000

Mr. Ron Gratchet, Owner
Tools, Etc.
123 Greystone Road
Portland, OR 12345

Dear Mr. Gratchet,

Linda Zeffer has often spoken highly of you, usually in reference to the likelihood of our meeting someday.

In fact, that's what this letter and resume are about. I'd like to speak with you about the opening for General Manager at Tools, Etc.

I grew up in the hardware business — my parents owned and ran an Ace Hardware store in a small town for 25 years before they sold it to me. As much as I love managing the store, it's time to move on to bigger things... such as Tools, Etc.

Could we talk soon? I'd like to be the first candidate you consider. I'll call your office to see when you are free to meet. Thank you!

Sincerely,

Bill Steinberger

Enclosure: resume

Bill Steinberger's cover letter.

Getting Personal

Your cover letter should not summarize your resume. After all, you worked hard to write about your qualifications in concise statements on your resume. Why would you do it again in the cover letter? Instead, the cover letter should add a personal message that your resume doesn't convey.

In the following letter, Lorri Rainey introduces the fact that she has multiple sclerosis, a point that will help her identify with the employer's clients. Although such a personal statement did not appear in her resume, it's perfectly appropriate in her cover letter.

Take My Hint, Please!

Sometimes it pays to give an idea away. By proposing a solution to the manager, you take the risk of having it stolen, but more than likely you'll be perceived as a bright individual the employer wants on his team.

In her cover letter, notice how Carla Smith hints at what she thinks is a great idea for her prospective employer's Marketing department. Without giving away the details of her program, she indicates that she knows what she's talking about and can pull it off—to the employer's benefit!

Getting the Hang of It

If you need to write cover letters to more than one potential employer, follow these steps:

1. Make a list of all the cover letters you need to write.
2. Prioritize the list so that your most preferred potential employer is first, second most preferred is second, and so on.
3. Write your first letter, concentrating on your number-one employer.
4. When your first letter is completed, make a copy of it on your computer to use as a guide to create cover letters to your other prospects.

This technique for writing several letters will bring some magical results. By starting with your number-one choice, you'll bring the most juice to your creative process of writing. And by concentrating on just one employer at a time, your letter will be customized for your recipient and therefore won't sound like a form letter. That's an important aspect of good cover letter writing: Your letter must sound personalized to the specific employer.

Job-Hunt Hint

Make sure your cover letter looks quick and easy to read. Avoid a bulky midsection by keeping paragraphs short, using bullet-point statements, or using columns to present your thoughts.

Career Casualty

In the grand scheme of corporate paper shuffling, your resume and cover letter may get separated. Be sure to include "Enclosure: resume" at the bottom of your letter so the manager will know to look for your resume.

Lorri Rainey

123 Alameny Ave.
Sheridan, WY 12345
(123) 123-1234

December 10, 1999

Ms. Alice Foremost
Director of Job Placement
Agency for the Disabled
1234 Congress Rd.
Sheridan, WY 12345

Dear Ms. Foremost;

Do you believe in fate? I didn't until I opened the *Sheridan Bee* this morning and saw your ad for Job Placement Officer. It sounded like the job I've been searching for.

In a flash, you'll see from my resume that my qualifications line up perfectly with your announcement. But here's how I <u>really</u> fit into your agency: I have a deep commitment to working with people with disabilities.

As a person with MS, I have a solid comprehension of the American Disabilities Act, as well as a full understanding of career development issues experienced by your job candidates.

I would very much like to speak with you in person. I'm eager to learn more about the agency and, specifically, the job placement position. I'll call you in a few days to see when we can talk.

In the meantime, thank you for reviewing my application.

Sincerely,

Lorri Rainey

Enclosure: resume

Lorri Rainey's letter.

Carla Smith
Marketing Professional
123 Halstead Rd.
Rochester, NY 12345
123-123-1234

November 3, 1999

Mr. James Callahan
General Manager
Household Paints, Inc.
123 Grand Blvd.
White Plains, NY 12345

Dear Mr. Callahan:

Research shows that women have a greater sensitivity to color than do men. For that reason, I propose that I create a marketing program for Household Paints that targets women.

As your Marketing Director, I can design programs that keep down production costs by generating "umbrella" collateral to be used for multiple niches. My enclosed resume demonstrates how I've used this technique to save thousands of dollars and bring in significant revenue for former employers.

Let's talk in person about your new "Colors for Women" program. I'll call you in a few days to arrange an appointment.

Thank you!

Carla Smith

Enclosure: resume

Carla Smith's letter.

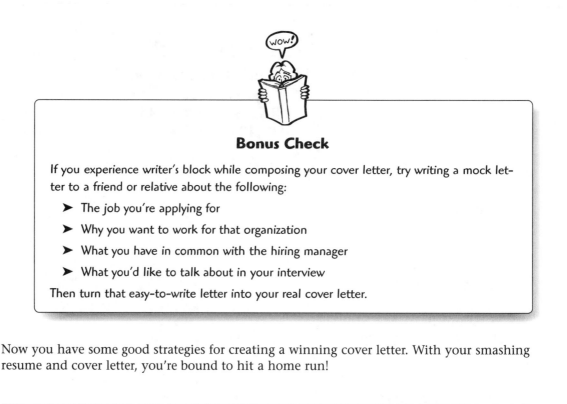

Bonus Check

If you experience writer's block while composing your cover letter, try writing a mock letter to a friend or relative about the following:

➤ The job you're applying for

➤ Why you want to work for that organization

➤ What you have in common with the hiring manager

➤ What you'd like to talk about in your interview

Then turn that easy-to-write letter into your real cover letter.

Now you have some good strategies for creating a winning cover letter. With your smashing resume and cover letter, you're bound to hit a home run!

The Least You Need to Know

➤ Make your cover letter personable and targeted to the employer. Don't let it sound like a form letter.

➤ Create an opening sentence that grabs your potential employer's attention.

➤ Paint the picture of you and the employer conversing about the company through the body of your letter.

➤ End your letter with a word of thanks and a request for an interview.

➤ After you've written a strong cover letter for your number-one choice of employment, tailor it toward other employers.

Chapter 18

Thanks Very Much

In This Chapter

➤ Why it's important to thank an employer after each interaction

➤ How to write an effective thank-you note for an interview

➤ How to acknowledge your job acceptance with a thank-you

➤ What to say if you get rejected

➤ How to thank all your buddies with a cool job announcement

We all know how good it feels when someone says, "Thank you," even if it's for a small thing we've done. Likewise, you'll make a favorable impression on an employer if you send a thank-you letter whenever appropriate in your job search. In this chapter, you'll learn all the reasons to send a word of thanks. I'll also explain how to keep your thank-you letter short and meaningful.

Think Thanks

Some situations require a thank-you letter. Yes, a thank-you letter, not a phone call or the statement "Thanks a lot" as you walk away from someone. The following are certain times when you need to sit down and express your thanks on paper:

➤ When you've had a great interview

➤ After you've had an interview that you wished had gone better

➤ After you've accepted a job offer

➤ When you get a job rejection

There's another type of thank-you note that isn't a must, but it sure is nice: a note to your supportive friends and colleagues who helped you in your job search.

Let's look at each of these situations and how to create a thank-you note that fits the bill.

The Terrific Job Interview

As soon as you walk away from a good job interview, ask yourself how it went.

➤ Were you pleased with your performance?

➤ What things in particular did you appreciate about the way the manager conducted the interview?

➤ What did you learn about the company that especially interested you?

➤ What thoughts have come to mind about your conversation that you'd like to share with the employer?

The answers to these questions are grist for the mill for your thank-you letter. Your letter should be short, to the point, and essentially say "thank you." This letter is also your opportunity to continue the conversation from your interview with one or two follow-up thoughts.

In the following letter, Jane Harbinger thanked Ms. Gomez for her interview and added a hint of things to come at their next meeting. Jane's letter showed that she was very interested in this job.

Not One to Write Home About

You know that icky feeling when you walk away from a situation and you know you could have done better? We've all experienced it at one time or another, and you may get that uneasy feeling after one of your job interviews. If so, don't throw in the towel! Try this simple fix-it: Write a thank-you letter that fills in the holes and repairs your performance.

Before writing your note, ask yourself these questions:

➤ What do I think went wrong in the interview?

➤ Did I say something that might have been misunderstood?

➤ Was I nervous and therefore didn't project a sense of self-confidence?

➤ Did I miss an opportunity in the conversation to state an idea or mention an achievement that would have impressed the interviewer?

Career Casualty

Don't worry that sending a thank-you letter will pester the employer. Keep your note short and to the point. It will take her just a minute to read and will send the right message: You sincerely want the job.

Job-Hunt Hint

Get in the habit of saying "Thank you" in person, on the phone, and in writing. That could mean thanking not only the manager, but also the receptionist when you leave your job interview; it could also mean being appreciative of someone who took the trouble to give you a job lead.

Career Casualty

Never misspell the employer's name. Check and double-check that it's spelled correctly before sealing your envelope.

Jane Harbinger
123 Coolidge Lane
Cranston, NY 12345
123-123-1234

March 23, 2000

Ms. Francine Gomez
President and CEO
Highcrest Divisions Management Group
123 23rd Ave.
Albany, NY 12340

Dear Ms. Gomez;

My interview with you this morning was all that I had hoped for and more. Not only are we on the same page regarding consumer education, we share a similar view on management training. I agree that distance learning is a must if we're to keep our management abreast of our industry's trends.

I plan to research the points we discussed and bring you more concrete ideas at our next meeting on Monday.

Thank you for a truly exhilarating meeting.

Sincerely,

Jane Harbinger

Jane Harbinger's letter.

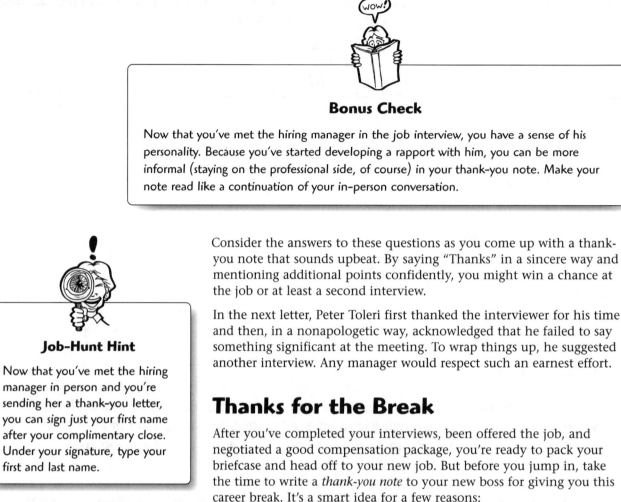

Bonus Check

Now that you've met the hiring manager in the job interview, you have a sense of his personality. Because you've started developing a rapport with him, you can be more informal (staying on the professional side, of course) in your thank-you note. Make your note read like a continuation of your in-person conversation.

Job-Hunt Hint

Now that you've met the hiring manager in person and you're sending her a thank-you letter, you can sign just your first name after your complimentary close. Under your signature, type your first and last name.

Terms of Employment

A **thank-you note** is a short letter of appreciation. A thank-you note sent to a friend for a job-search favor can be handwritten or typed on any size sheet of paper or note card. When sent to an employer, your letter should be typed on an $8\frac{1}{2}" \times 11"$ sheet of paper.

Consider the answers to these questions as you come up with a thank-you note that sounds upbeat. By saying "Thanks" in a sincere way and mentioning additional points confidently, you might win a chance at the job or at least a second interview.

In the next letter, Peter Toleri first thanked the interviewer for his time and then, in a nonapologetic way, acknowledged that he failed to say something significant at the meeting. To wrap things up, he suggested another interview. Any manager would respect such an earnest effort.

Thanks for the Break

After you've completed your interviews, been offered the job, and negotiated a good compensation package, you're ready to pack your briefcase and head off to your new job. But before you jump in, take the time to write a *thank-you note* to your new boss for giving you this career break. It's a smart idea for a few reasons:

➤ The boss stuck her neck out for you, and you want to assure her that she made the right decision.

➤ That extra gesture of thanks sets an even friendlier stage for your first day of work.

➤ You are appreciative of your job acceptance, and it's appropriate to say so.

In her letter, Doreen Mathers showed her appreciation to the hiring manager for making her next career step possible. Without being sentimental, she expressed enthusiasm for her upcoming first day.

Peter Toleri

123 Shore Road
Lyme, NH 12345
123-123-1234

March 4, 2000

Mr. Richard Lee
Director of Customer Service
Pearson & Lansing Manufacturers
Salem, NH 12345

Dear Mr. Lee,

Thank you for an insightful interview yesterday. I enjoyed meeting both you and your office staff.

After leaving your office, I realized there was a point I'd like to add to our conversation: I believe a peer-assessment program would be an effective way of improving the customer service issues you mentioned.

I'd like to draw up my ideas for how to put together such an assessment program that would ensure a positive approach to the problem.

I'll follow up on this idea in a few days by phone. Again, thank you for the interview.

Sincerely yours,

Peter Toleri

Peter Toleri's letter.

Doreen Mathers
12 Manchester Drive
Willmington, VA 12345
(123) 123-1234

February 28, 2000

Ms. Rachel Samson
Director of Public Relations
Rightsworth Printing, Inc.
123 Howard's Pt.
Wilmington, VA 12340

Dear Rachel,

Thank you for selecting me as your new Public Relations Representative. I feel honored to have you as my supervisor and mentor at such an early point in my career.

I plan to direct every ounce of energy to demonstrating that you made the right hiring decision.

With my briefcase in hand, I will be in your office at 8:00, Monday morning.

Thank you!

Doreen Mathers

Doreen Mathers's letter.

Thanks a Lot for the Bad News

Nobody likes hearing the bad news that they weren't accepted for the job, but it happens to the best of us. So after you've had some time to pull up your chin, consider writing a letter of thanks to the manager who rejected you. Before putting your fingers to the keyboard, ask yourself these questions:

➤ Did I get the feeling that I was close to getting the job?

➤ Is there any chance I could still get the job if the chosen applicant doesn't work out?

➤ Are there other job opportunities at the company I'd like to be considered for?

➤ Might the manager have hiring contacts within or outside his organization that he could share with me?

Job-Hunt Hint

Your thank-you letter should be brief, no more than one page, and centered on the page, with lots of white space incorporated into its layout so that it's easy to read.

Armed with answers to these questions, you're ready to write a thoughtful thank-you note that could keep your job application alive. In the next letter, Lynette Fields acknowledged her rejection, thanked the employer for his time, and asked for consideration for other job openings.

Bonus Check

Even if your thank-you note after a job rejection doesn't turn into another opportunity, you'll have the satisfaction of knowing that you handled a difficult situation with dignity. That's the mark of a true professional.

Good-News Letter to the Gang

You've got the new job, and you know you didn't do it all on your own; the members of your support team helped you win it. So now's the time to thank each of them.

A cool way to develop your good-news thank-you letters is to print out a bunch of general announcements, and then personalize each one with a handwritten message. The computer-generated good-news letter by Carolyn Maxer worked for her whole network. The added note on the bottom acknowledged exactly how Carolyn's friend George helped her out.

Career Casualty

Don't be a sourpuss! Look beyond your rejection notice to see what hidden opportunities might lie there. Even if none are evident, a kind thank-you note to the employer could open doors you didn't know existed.

Lynette Fields

12 Ferndale Dr.
Santa Rosa, CA 12345
(123) 123-1234

June 19, 1999

Mr. Malcolm Johnson
Director of Human Resources
Fairchild & Associates
Santa Rosa, CA 95721

Dear Mr. Johnson,

Thank you for updating me on your selection for human resources clerk. Although I was not chosen, I want to thank you for your generosity of time.

You mentioned that your wife works in human resources at Gravestone's. May I call you in a few days to get her contact information?

I look forward to speaking with you then.

Thank you!

Lynette Fields

Lynette Fields's letter.

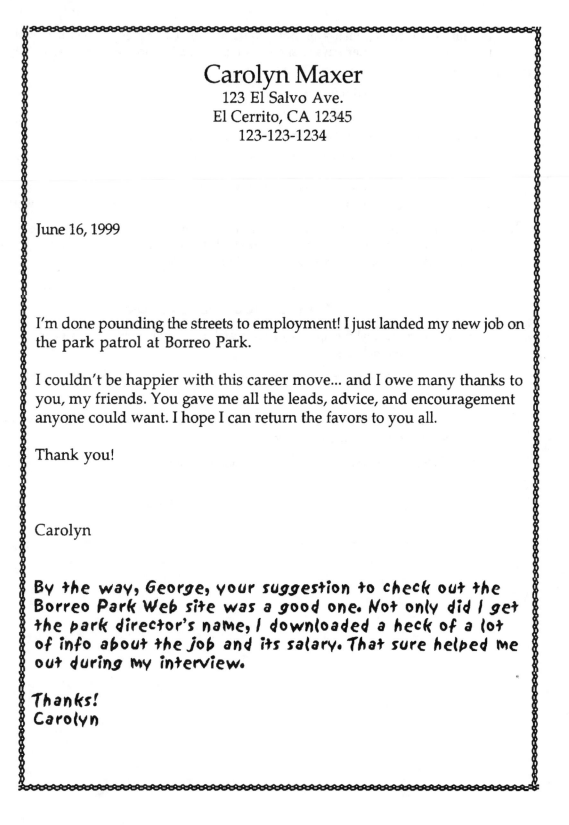

Carolyn Maxer
123 El Salvo Ave.
El Cerrito, CA 12345
123-123-1234

June 16, 1999

I'm done pounding the streets to employment! I just landed my new job on the park patrol at Borreo Park.

I couldn't be happier with this career move... and I owe many thanks to you, my friends. You gave me all the leads, advice, and encouragement anyone could want. I hope I can return the favors to you all.

Thank you!

Carolyn

By the way, George, your suggestion to check out the Borreo Park Web site was a good one. Not only did I get the park director's name, I downloaded a heck of a lot of info about the job and its salary. That sure helped me out during my interview.

Thanks!
Carolyn

Carolyn Maxer's letter.

In addition to sending thank-you notes to friends and colleagues for their help with your job search, think of other ways to show your gratitude for those who were especially kind or generous:

➤ Take them out to dinner.

➤ Send flowers or other meaningful gifts.

➤ Offer to help them with their career advancement.

➤ Think of something special they love to do and make that activity possible for them.

Networks are built on mutual goodwill and two-way favors. When thanking the members of your network, be sure to ask if there are ways you can help with projects they're working on.

Each thank-you note you write during your job search will undoubtedly increase the rapport with that member of your network. I'll bet you'll thank yourself later for having taken the extra effort to show your appreciation.

The Least You Need to Know

➤ Thanking those who help in your job search is not only polite, but it's also smart for building your network.

➤ Write a short thank-you letter after an interview to increase your chances of winning the job.

➤ Send a thank-you letter to acknowledge your job acceptance and assure the manager that she made a good choice.

➤ Thank an employer who has rejected your job application; it may keep the doors open.

➤ Remember your supportive friends and colleagues by sending them thank-you notes after you land your new job.

Part 5

The Electronic Job Search

E-mail. The World Wide Web. Cyberspace. If you haven't had personal experience with the Internet, you may worry that it's too complicated for you to use, that you're not techno-savvy enough to learn it, or that somehow you might endanger the world if you click that little mouse on the wrong icon.

The surprising thing is how easy it is. Once you're hooked up, conducting an online job search is, without a doubt, simpler than programming your VCR. So sit down at your computer and let your cyberfingers do the walking through the career sections of online directories.

In Part 5, you'll learn how to prepare a resume for your cyberspace job search. You'll also learn about the scanning technology that your resume may encounter once it reaches the employer's desk.

Ready? Set? Click!

Chapter 19

Getting Hooked on the Internet

In This Chapter

➤ What you need to know about an Internet job hunt

➤ How to choose the hardware and online services that are right for you

➤ How to navigate the World Wide Web

➤ Where to go online for juicy job-hunt info

What could be more magical than job hunting in front of a colorful screen filled with cool pictures, graphics, and animation? That's what an Internet job hunt can be like. The Internet has become a remarkably fun and efficient job-searching tool. In just minutes you can learn the latest job-market trends, research specific companies, and do a myriad of other nifty things that otherwise could take weeks, even months, of running around to libraries and waiting for the U.S. Postal Service to deliver responses.

This chapter tells you how to get up and going online and how to find lots of job-search goodies when you're in cyberspace. Before long, you'll be performing online job-hunt magic. (If you're an experienced computer and Internet user, skip to "The Online Job Hunt" section of this chapter.)

Joining the Online World

In case you're new to computers and the online world, here are the basic steps for getting up and going:

1. Get a computer.

2. Hook up a modem.

3. Sign up with an Internet service provider (ISP).

Let's break down these three steps so you can get online right away.

Career Casualty

If technophobia has kept you from your online job search, hire someone to hook up your computer components and give you an online tour.

Career Casualty

Many first-time computer buyers think they have to buy the most expensive computer available just to get up and running. Beware of this faulty logic. You may find the perfect computer for your needs at a fraction of the top price through used or discount computer channels (retail outlets, online stores, or catalogs).

Job-Hunt Hint

If you travel a lot, sign up with an ISP that has local access numbers in all of your normal destinations.

The Powerful Gray Box

If you don't have a computer yet, take a deep breath and consider taking the plunge. Why?

➤ It can greatly expand the range of your job search.

➤ It can help you organize that search.

➤ It can help you write, revise, and print a world-class resume.

➤ It lets you do all these things in your pajamas!

Once you get the hang of using your computer, you'll wonder how you ever lived without one. And the getting-the-hang-of-it part has become increasingly easy over the years as technology has become more user-friendly. These days, you can buy a computer for under a thousand bucks and get started in a matter of hours.

When selecting which computer to buy, consider the following questions:

➤ What tasks would you like to perform on your computer? (Do you want to do word processing, graphic design, online explorations, Web-site development?)

➤ How portable do you want your computer setup to be? (Maybe you need a laptop instead of a desktop computer.)

➤ How expandable do you need it to be? (In other words, if you decide later you want to link to three printers, is there a way to do that easily?)

➤ How much can you afford to spend? (That's one of the first things a salesperson will ask you.)

➤ What kind of technical support is available to you through the store or manufacturer? (There's bound to be at least one question you'll want a pro to answer.)

➤ How convenient will it be to get repairs done on the brand you're considering? (Where's the nearest authorized repair shop?)

➤ What compassionate and knowledgeable friend will hold your hand as you become accustomed to your new computer? (That friend needs to be familiar with the type of computer you buy.)

When you've answered these questions, you'll be ready to purchase your computer. By the way, don't forget to get a monitor (the thing that looks sort of like a television) with your computer. Without one, you won't be able to see any of the cool pictures or words.

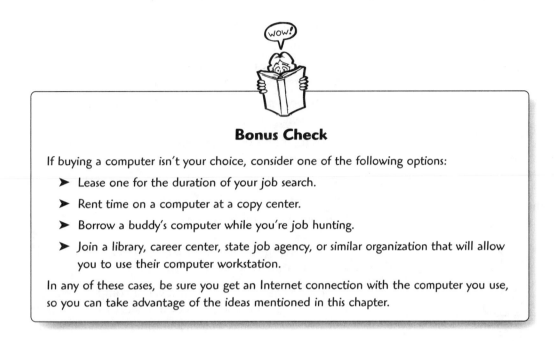

Bonus Check

If buying a computer isn't your choice, consider one of the following options:

➤ Lease one for the duration of your job search.

➤ Rent time on a computer at a copy center.

➤ Borrow a buddy's computer while you're job hunting.

➤ Join a library, career center, state job agency, or similar organization that will allow you to use their computer workstation.

In any of these cases, be sure you get an Internet connection with the computer you use, so you can take advantage of the ideas mentioned in this chapter.

Modern Modems

The *modem* is a device that connects your computer to the vast network that is the Internet. You can buy a computer that has an internal modem, meaning there's no manual hook-up required except to the phone line. If your computer doesn't have an internal modem, it's no big deal; just get an external modem that plugs into your computer, the phone line, and a power source. In either case, the process is very simple; just follow the instructions that come with the modem or the computer, and you shouldn't have any problems.

One thing you'll notice about modems is that they're upgraded almost every time you turn around, meaning that the speed at which they transmit data gets faster and faster. These days, 56.6K modems are fairly standard. For most of us, that's fast enough and reasonable for our pocketbooks, too.

Terms of Employment

A **modem** is a piece of hardware that allows your computer to connect to the telephone system in order to access the Internet or to fax documents.

In Search of an ISP

An Internet service provider (ISP) is a company that offers accounts to users (for a subscription price) so they can access the Internet. Using a modem, the ISP member dials a local telephone number (called a local access number) that connects the user's computer to the ISP, which acts as a gateway to the Internet.

Here's what most ISPs offer each of their customers:

Terms of Employment

A **browser** is software, such as Netscape Navigator or Internet Explorer, that allows you to navigate the World Wide Web.

Job-Hunt Hint

For a low monthly rate (about $20 a month), you can get a good ISP that provides the structure and support needed for your online job search. If you're a college student, you can probably get free online access through your school.

➤ An e-mail address, where you can send and receive your electronic mail

➤ One or more search engines to scour the Web and give you the Web addresses on topics you choose

➤ A Web *browser* (such as Netscape Navigator or Internet Explorer) that takes you to Web sites you specify

➤ Access to chat rooms, newsgroups, and channels of local and national news

➤ Links to specific Web sites (I'll explain what these are in a minute)

➤ Help building simple Web pages

You can choose from hundreds of ISPs. Here are some thoughts on how to pick the best one for you:

➤ Choose an ISP that suits your level of computer competency. If you're a beginner, you may want to start with one of the user-friendly ones such as America Online, CompuServe, or Prodigy.

➤ Select an ISP that fits your price range. Most have a variety of monthly rate schedules; and a few ISPs, such as America Online, offer a flat rate for unlimited time online and a lower rate with a per-minute charge.

➤ Confirm where the ISP's local access telephone numbers are. You don't want to be surprised by long-distance calls on your phone bill for accessing your ISP.

➤ Get recommendations from friends to see which ISPs they like and why.

Bonus Check

If you're into speed, there are some deluxe ways to connect to the Internet that are superfast (they're also a little pricey for most individual users):

➤ Your cable TV company may offer an Internet cable modem.

➤ You can get a direct Internet connection called ISDN (Integrated Switched Digital Network) or DSL (Digital Subscriber Line).

If you're interested, check out these alternative services and consider how much time you'll be spending online to determine which route is most cost-effective for you.

With a little research, you're bound to find a suitable ISP that will provide you with the software and instructions for getting online through its system.

Caught in the Web

A few words about the World Wide Web and its terminology: The World Wide Web (called the Web for short) is a system of Internet sites that are owned by individuals, companies, organizations, governments, and just about any entity you can think of. Each site can connect to other sites through *links*, which appear as underlined words in the text on the site. Because thousands and thousands of sites are connected directly or indirectly, the entire system has been characterized as a web. And because this web is global, it's called the World Wide Web. Individual Web sites are identified by Web addresses (also called *URLs*).

To understand what a Web site looks like, check out the following snapshot of part of my site (Resumes That Work). The underlined words in the text are links; when you click on them with your mouse, they take you to a different Web site.

Terms of Employment

URL (Universal Resource Locator), also known as a Web address, is a word or string of words, most often starting with www. and ending with .com (or .org, .net., .gov), that you type into the browser in order to access (or "go to") a particular Web site.

Snapshot of Links That Work Web page.

273

Job-Hunt Hint

Don't be intimidated by technical jargon. Most hardware, software, and online services have tech-support staff people who are skilled at answering questions of every kind. Just ask!

Job-Hunt Hint

If you're new to computers and the Internet, check your local college, adult education center, or career center for classes on these topics.

The Online Job Hunt

You don't have to master the whole Internet to be a savvy online job hunter; you need to know only enough to conduct your job search. Most of what you need to understand is right here in this chapter. You'll discover how to do the following:

➤ Find master indices of career-related Web sites.

➤ Get the inside scoop on organizations you might want to work for.

➤ Learn about company executives and hiring managers.

➤ Investigate salary surveys.

➤ Check out lists of job openings.

➤ Discover ways to distribute your resume.

That's quite a list of things to pull out of a little gray box, isn't it? Think of how much time and money you're going to save by not having to shuffle through pages and pages of bibliographic material or make tons of phone calls to uncover important job-market trends.

Mastering the Sites

The online job-search community is very well organized. Not only are there plenty of excellent sites with credible information, there are also some time-saving master index sites to help you find your way through the many options. These master sites categorize, recommend, summarize, and link to hundreds of job-related Web sites. I suggest visiting these sites first so you can get a feel for the lay of the cyberland:

➤ Riley Guide (http://www.dbm.com/jobguide)

➤ Career Resource Center (http://www.careers.org)

➤ Yahoo! Jobs (http://www.yahoo.com/Business_and_Economy/Employment)

➤ My site (http://www.susanireland.com)

These master sites can save you tons of time and give you the assurance that you're in the know about the best job-search Web sites.

Company Insider Scoop

You'd be surprised how much you can learn about a particular company. By conducting a simple online search, you can dig up information about the organization's

➤ Annual profits and losses.

➤ Products and services.

➤ Internal culture.

➤ Mission statement.

➤ Industry standing.

➤ Consumer ratings.

➤ Long- and short-term goals.

➤ Competition.

➤ Size and rate of growth.

➤ Customer base.

➤ Headquarters and branch locations.

➤ Job-application process.

Bonus Check

To get your computer to display a particular Web site, follow these steps:

1. Open your browser.

2. Type the desired URL in the Go To box near the top of the screen.

3. Push Return or Enter on your keyboard.

In a few moments, the Web site you want should appear on your screen.

Bonus Check

Because the Internet seems to be expanding faster than the speed of light, it would be impossible to list all the relevant Web sites available (such a list would inevitably be outdated by the time you read this book). Instead, use the search engines available to you through your ISP. Look up keywords such as *career, employment, jobs,* and *resumes.* You're bound to come up with a plethora of opportunities to explore!

So how do you get the inside scoop? Some Web sites specialize in this research, and much of the information is available for free. Visit the following sites and start snooping:

➤ Vault Reports (http://www.vaultreports.com)

➤ Hoover's Online (http://www.hoovers.com)

Job-Hunt Hint

When researching your prospective employer, look for unbiased information. Going to the company's Web site is helpful, but because the company writes the content for the site, you're sure to only get a positive view. By going to an outside source such as one listed in this section, you'll get the dirt on the company along with the jewels.

Career Casualty

If a Web site address listed in this chapter is no longer in service, go to my Web site (http://www.susanireland.com), where I have up-to-date links to most of the sites mentioned here.

➤ Wet Feet Press (http://www.wetfeet.com)

➤ The Securities Exchange Commission (http://www.sec.gov)

In addition to these suggestions, go to the Web site for the specific company you're interested in. There's apt to be some tidbits of info that will come in handy for your job-search needs.

Executive Investigation

Think of the psychological advantage you would have if you knew the personality, management style, salary, goals, and personal interests of your interviewer before you wrote your cover letter, went for your interview, and negotiated your paycheck. With a little effort, you just might get your hands on information like that. I'm not talking about doing anything illegal or unethical. I'm suggesting you check out some Web sites to see what there is to see.

➤ Using your search engine, type in the manager's name and see what comes up. You may find articles the manager has written, media coverage that mentions her, or even her personal Web site if she has one.

➤ Go to the company's Web site, look for an "About Us" or "Our Staff" link, and see whether there's any info about the manager there.

There's no guarantee that you'll find anything on your subject, but it's worth a try. Even one piece of information could help you get your foot in the door for an interview and help build rapport with your prospective boss.

Salary Stats

Knowing your market value before going into negotiations is extremely important to advancing your income. You can gather data on these sites to help figure out your market worth:

➤ Occupational Outlook Handbook (http://stats.bls.gov/ocohome.htm)

➤ JobSmart Web site (http://jobsmart.com)

➤ Your state labor department Web site

➤ Web sites for your profession's trade journals

Armed with the information you'll find on these sites, you'll be far ahead of the game when you walk into the salary bargaining room.

Job Lists Galore

A great way to learn about local, national, and international job openings is to check out the following Web sites. These sites list thousands of career opportunities:

➤ America's Job Bank (http://www.ajb.dni.us/index.html)

➤ CareerCity (http://www.careercity.com)

➤ CareerPath (http://www.careerpath.com)

➤ Headhunter.Net (http://www.headhunter.net)

➤ America's Employers (http://www.americasemployers.com)

➤ Classifieds2000/Employment (http://www.classifieds2000.com), click on "Employment"

➤ Net-Temps (http://www.net-temps.com)

➤ JobSafari (http://www.jobsafari.com)

➤ HotJobs (http://www.hotjobs.com)

➤ MonsterBoard (http://www.monster.com)

➤ CareerMosaic (http://www.careermosiac.com)

➤ career.com (http://www.career.com)

➤ CareerSite.com (http://www.careersite.com)

➤ The Career Builder Network (http://www.careerbuilder.com)

Job-Hunt Hint

If searching online seems like a chore, hire an information researcher to get the dope on your prospective employer. All the researcher services I recommend in the "Go Hire Yourself a Pro" section of Appendix C, "Other Cool Resources," are skilled at online research.

Also, check your local TV news channels and newspaper Web sites. Many have career sections that list available jobs, as well as interesting articles about job-market issues.

If you find a site that you want to visit regularly, you can bookmark the site, which means you tell your online software to hold that site's URL in its memory so you can go to it directly without typing the URL into your browser. Refer to your ISP's instructions (or your browser's Help menu) to learn how to bookmark a site.

You're raring to go! Now you just need to prepare your resume for online job applications. I'll cover that issue in the next chapters.

Bonus Check

While you're online checking out the salary statistics for your line of work, do the same type of search to see what salary ranges are typical for someone in your hiring manager's position. Doing so will give you an idea of the manager's perspective on earned income.

The Least You Need to Know

➤ You can go online if you have a computer, a modem, and an Internet service provider.

➤ Save tons of time by using master-index Web sites that can link you to recommended job-search sites.

➤ Use your search engine to explore other Web sites such as those for specific organizations, people, professions, and industries.

➤ Prepare for interviews and salary negotiations by reading about salary surveys and labor studies on federal and state government sites.

➤ Discover Web sites that list local, national, and international job openings.

Chapter 20

The ABC's of E-Resumes

In This Chapter

➤ What an e-resume is

➤ How resume databases work

➤ What it means to have your resume searched

➤ How to get your resume into a resume bank

Electronic resumes are no longer just a thing of the future: they're here now, and they're here to stay. They come in a variety of formats, and employers can process them in different ways. The challenge is to keep up with the techniques and opportunities in the quickly changing world of e-resumes. In this chapter, you'll learn what's behind the e-resume trend and how this technology can benefit your job search.

What Is an Electronic Resume?

An *electronic resume* is a nonpaper resume, meaning it's a computer document that can be

➤ Viewed on a screen.

➤ Stored on a hard drive or floppy disk.

➤ Sent over the Internet.

➤ Searched for keywords.

➤ Manipulated into other types of documents.

➤ Printed out for review on hard copy.

E-resumes are used for e-mailing, depositing into Internet resume banks, posting on personal Web sites, and sending through scanners to be entered into resume banks.

Terms of Employment

E-resume stands for electronic resume, which is the computerized form of a resume. E-resumes are used for e-mail, online posting, and other forms of electronic transfer.

The E-Resume Appeal

Who benefits from e-resumes? Everyone: you, employers, and recruiting agencies. That's because e-resumes make the job-hunt/hiring process more efficient for all concerned.

Here are the three major benefits to employers:

1. **Money.** Employers can save tremendous amounts in recruiting costs through the use of e-resumes.

2. **Speed.** E-resumes can be processed much faster than hard-copy resumes.

3. **Organization.** Resume databases can store, sort, and search thousands of e-resumes according to a variety of criteria.

Bonus Check

The content of your electronic resume should employ the same marketing principles used in your hard-copy resume:

➤ Write about experiences that support your job objective.

➤ List achievements, not job descriptions.

➤ Disclose only information that promotes you as a qualified job candidate.

➤ Avoid mentioning things you don't want to do again.

➤ Tell the truth; don't exaggerate or lie.

The three major benefits to you, the job seeker, are as follows:

1. **Money.** Aside from saving money in postage, an electronic job search can help you get a job sooner (which means you'll be collecting a paycheck sooner) because it's usually more efficient than the nonelectronic job search.

2. **Speed.** An e-resume's capability to get in front of a hiring manager quickly could give you an edge over your competition.

3. **Organization.** E-resumes are easy for you to keep organized on your computer, and you can rest assured that your resume is in good hands once it's in the employer's computer system.

Sounds like a win-win situation, doesn't it? At the bottom of these winning points is the electronic backbone of the e-resume system: the database. Let's look at why a resume database can be a hiring manager's best friend and how it can take you to the top of the candidate lineup.

Data in the Database

Resume databases (also referred to as *resume banks*) are systems for storing information about inquiring job seekers. Resume databases vary in their complexity. A high-end system will hold the following information:

➤ A Summary of Qualifications form for each applicant; this information is extracted from the job seeker's resume and placed in a database file according to predetermined fields such as education, work history, or job objective.

➤ A list of each job seeker's keywords (see the "Key Placement" section later in this chapter for a sample list) compiled by the database's search engine.

➤ Each job seeker's resume, either the electronic version or an image of the paper resume if it was scanned into the system. (See Chapter 21, "It's All a Scan: Scannable Resumes," to learn more about the scanning process.)

Low-end systems have an abbreviated version of the preceding information, or they have the same set of information but require manual inputting, which inevitably increases the chance of errors.

The value in a resume database lies in its ability to store, search, and display resumes in a matter of minutes. Let's look at how this process works.

The Inner Workings

When your resume is in a database, it can be accessed in a few ways. A manager or human resources clerk might

➤ Browse through resumes at random.

➤ Sort resumes so they can be seen in groups according to job objective, industry, or other logical categories.

➤ Conduct keyword searches to select and prioritize resumes by how many of those words appear in the resumes.

The beauty of this system is that even if your resume doesn't make the cut for one hiring manager's search, it remains in the database for others to consider. With this collective storage system, your resume is potentially visible to anyone who has access to the database.

Job-Hunt Hint

It's important to be an e-resume pro in today's job market as more and more employers are relying on electronic processing of resumes to meet their recruiting needs.

Terms of Employment

A **resume bank** is a database that holds lots of resumes. Most resume banks have search capabilities to select resumes according to job objective, resume headline (which you'll read about in Chapter 23, "Banking on Success: Online Resume Banking"), and keywords specified by the employer or headhunter.

Bonus Check

Unlike a filing system for hardcopy documents (the standard filing cabinet), a resume database allows several people to access the same resume at the same time. For example, three managers in three different locations could each pull up your resume for review at the same time. In the old-fashioned filing cabinet, only one manager at a time could access the resume.

Keyword: Search

Most searches rely on two things: a search engine and keywords for the engine to search for. The search engine is built into the system (and works similarly to the engine you use when you search the Internet for a topic). The keywords are usually subjective, because they're created by the person who is operating the search engine. For that reason, there may be no set list of keywords for your profession because it depends entirely on who is generating the list on the hiring side.

A keyword search might examine each resume for up to 60 keywords. Keywords could indicate the following information:

➤ Technical expertise

➤ Management skills

➤ Industry knowledge

➤ Education

➤ Geographic location

➤ Employment history

After the keywords are entered into the search engine, the engine goes through its database, matches resumes with the designated keywords, and even ranks the selected candidates against each other according to how many keywords appear in each resume. The most sophisticated systems have synonym-search capabilities that find not only the exact word listed for the search (such as *management*), but also related words (such as *supervision, administration,* and *leadership*).

Bonus Check

Despite all your research, you probably won't be able to find out exactly what keywords are being programmed into the computer by the hiring manager in his search for the perfect job candidate. To come up with a sure-fire list, put yourself in the hiring manager's shoes and write down 20 to 60 keywords you would use to define the ideal job applicant.

The E-Creation

An e-resume isn't all that different from your hard-copy resume. With just a few alterations to that hard-copy version, your resume will sail through scanners, e-mail systems, online resume banks, and the World Wide Web.

Terms of Employment

Keywords are the terms an employer enters into the database search engine to scour the database for the *ideal job candidate*.

Here are some guidelines:

➤ Use formatting that's acceptable for the type of e-resume you're creating. In addition to the general principles for e-resumes in this chapter, see details for specific types in Chapters 21, 22, and 23.

➤ Include *keywords* in your resume that an employer would use to search for a top candidate in your field.

➤ When listing dates for your college degree, put only the year you completed each of your degrees.

Let's go over some tips for good e-resume construction.

Electronic Headings

Your name should be the only thing that appears on the first line at the top of your resume. Here's why: The search engine interprets the first line (no matter what is written on the first line) as your name and will input it into the resume database as such. By the way, everything in the first line is interpreted as your name, so be sure you put your professional title (if you include it in your heading) on the second line.

Also, place each piece of your contact information on a separate line, as in this example:

Kerrie Oslow
Medical Technologist
123 Perkins Cove Lane
Brentwood, CA 12345
123-123-1234
OslowK@thenet.net

For your e-mailable resume, it makes sense to include your e-mail address in your heading because it's a tool the employer is likely to use to contact you.

Bonus Check

Consider signing up with Hotmail ™ (http://www.hotmail.com), an e-mail service provided by Microsoft. Your personal Hotmail™ account can be accessed from anywhere in the world as long as you are at a computer that's hooked up to the Internet. This type of e-mail service is ideal if you travel a lot or if your access to the Internet doesn't offer you a personal e-mail account (for instance, if you use your company's ISP account, it would be inappropriate for you to use it to send and receive personal e-mail). And to top it off, Hotmail™ is free!

Job-Hunt Hint

Most managers look for nouns, so list nouns in your Keyword section. In other words, list *Management*, not *Manage*. Adjectives may accompany those nouns, for instance, *Personnel management*.

Key Placement

There are two ways to get keywords into your resume so that they'll get spotted whether your document is read by a human being or searched while in a computer database. You can do one of two things:

1. Place a Keyword section near the beginning of your e-resume.
2. Sprinkle keywords throughout your document.

A Keyword section makes sense in any e-resume because the e-resume may be subjected to a resume database search. If, however, you don't want to have a Keyword section, it's acceptable to submit a resume without one. In that case, be sure to include the essential keywords in the content of your resume.

Create a Keyword section near the top of page one (right above your Summary of Qualifications section) by following these steps:

1. Make a list of 20 to 60 keywords you think the hiring manager will use to search for the position mentioned in your Job Objective. Keywords can be technical, such as *MIS analysis*, or nontechnical, such as *Conflict resolution*.

2. Compile your keywords in paragraph format, starting each term with a capital letter and placing a period at the end of each term.

3. Title the section "Keywords."

For example, a resume for an accountant might have a Keyword section that looks like the following:

Keywords

C.P.A. CPA. Certified Public Accountant. Accounting. Controller. Great Plains. MAS 90. Peachtree. QuickBooks. Excel. Lotus. Quattro Pro. Microsoft Word. MS Word. Conversion. Internal accounting system. Job costing. Strategic planning. Supervision. Management. Cost control. Audit. Compliance. Policies. Procedures. Administration. Communication. Team relations.

Years of Completion

Resume search engines have a tendency to interpret dates in the Education section in a rather peculiar way: If there are two dates given for a degree (for example: B.A., 1994–1998), the computer will assume that you did not receive your degree. To make sure you get credit for your degree accomplishment, put only the year of completion (for example: B.A., 1998), and the computer will recognize that you have your degree.

Breaking into the Banks

By now, you're dying to get your resume into a resume database, right? It's a simple task. Basically, there are three ways to do it:

1. Send your hard-copy resume to an employer who uses resume scanning.

2. Submit your resume to a company via e-mail.

3. Post your resume on an online resume bank.

To get the lowdown on how to prepare and deliver your resume for each of these methods, turn to the following three chapters. You'll find out that it's all within a few clicks of your mouse!

Electronic to Paper

A manager may print out an electronic resume so that he can read it in its hard-copy form. Here's what might happen:

➤ After receiving your resume as an e-mail, the manager may print it out to read before sending the electronic version to the company's resume database.

➤ The manager could print out your e-mailed resume and then have the hard copy of your e-mail scanned into the company's resume bank.

➤ The manager might download your resume from an online resume bank and print it out to review.

You see, your e-resume could be read by a human being after all. So as you go through the following chapters, pay attention to tips on how to make your resume look good as well as be technically sound.

Career Casualty

Don't be misled by the resume section heading Keywords—not all of your entries have to be one word each. In addition to listing individual words that an employer might key into a search engine, include terms made up of two or more words (such as *Marketing Communications*) and acronyms (such as *DSL*).

Career Casualty

It's very easy for a poorly created e-resume to fall through the cracks. If an employer can't open or read the version you submit, she can delete it with a click of her mouse. For that reason, it's well worth your time to learn the technical aspects of creating the particular type of e-resume you plan to use.

Bonus Check

If you list an acronym (such as CPA) in your Keyword section, also list the acronym's spelled-out version (Certified Public Accountant). You want the term to be noticed whether the hiring manager keys in the acronym or the spelled-out term of that job qualification.

Also, if a keyword has different forms (such as "accountant" and "accounting"), list both forms in your Keyword section so you're sure to match the exact word the manager enters into the search engine.

The Least You Need to Know

➤ An e-resume can be e-mailed, posted online in resume banks, and sent to employers to be scanned into their resume databases.

➤ Electronic resumes may be printed out by an employer or entered into a resume database for automated candidate selection.

➤ Keywords are essential in order for a resume to be spotted by a resume database search engine.

➤ E-resumes have different formatting requirements depending on how they will be used (e-mailed, posted to an online database, or scanned).

Chapter 21

It's all a Scan: Scannable Resumes

In This Chapter

➤ What resume scanning is

➤ Which organizations electronically scan resumes

➤ What the employer's side of scanning technology is like

➤ What the pros and cons of resume scanning are

➤ How to create your own scannable resume

You may be assuming that a person will read your hard-copy resume when it arrives at a potential employer's address. Instead, your resume could encounter a nonhuman "reader": the resume scanner.

Resume scanning, although not widespread, is something you might run into, in which case you'll need to know how to create a resume that passes the scanning test. This chapter will tell you when and how to submit a resume that's specially prepared for the almighty scanner.

Where Did Everyone Go?

A resume-scanning system is a computerized tool used by some human resources departments and agencies to manage the floods of resumes. Resume-scanning software does the following:

1. It creates an electronic image of the resume.

2. It uses *Optical Character Recognition (OCR)* software to turn the image into an electronic text file.

Bonus Check

The electronic image file that a resume scanner makes is similar to a photograph produced by a camera. Once the photo is taken, the shapes and positions of the people or things in the picture cannot be changed. Likewise, in an electronic image of your resume, the words on your document cannot be manipulated. Not until the OCR software converts it to a text file can the words on your resume be extracted and transformed into other forms such as the employer's database file.

Terms of Employment

Scanning is the process of turning a hard-copy document into an electronic image. **Optical Character Recognition** software (**OCR**) is the computer's tool for converting an electronic image into electronic text, which can then be searched for keywords and manipulated into new formats such as database files.

Here's how it works on the employer's end: When your resume arrives in the mail, it won't be read by human eyes. Instead, it'll be placed face-down in a scanner (which looks sort of like a photocopier). The scanner creates an electronic image of your document (sort of the way a camera snaps a picture of a person). The OCR software then goes through the image file to recognize characters and convert the file into a text document.

From there, the text of the document is stored in a database system. (In sophisticated systems, the snapshot of the original resume is also stored in the database so that the hiring manager can view that as well.) Once in the database, the information from your resume is accessible to hiring managers who use search words (keywords) to select qualified job candidates (as discussed in Chapter 20, "The ABC's of E-Resumes").

Wait a minute, what happened to the humans in the human resources departments? Have computers taken over and made people obsolete? No, there are still people working in those departments, just not as many as before the introduction of resume scanning and electronic resume databases. But don't worry, no matter how automated the resume-review process becomes, human beings (hiring managers) will always conduct the interviews and make the hiring decisions.

Get with the Program

How can you know for sure if you need to adjust your resume for a scanning encounter? Call the Human Resources department of the company where you'd like to work and ask whether it uses resume scanning. If the answer is "no" the paper resume you've created using Parts 1, 2, and 3 of this book is all you need. If the answer is "yes," ask if the department can mail, fax, or e-mail you a set of guidelines so you can create your resume for their system.

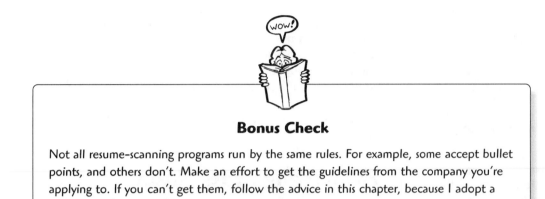

Bonus Check

Not all resume-scanning programs run by the same rules. For example, some accept bullet points, and others don't. Make an effort to get the guidelines from the company you're applying to. If you can't get them, follow the advice in this chapter, because I adopt a better-safe-than-sorry approach that should work for all scanning systems.

The Pros and Cons of Scanning

Your mind is probably racing ahead to the pros and cons of your resume going through a scanning system. That's good, because understanding the advantages and disadvantages of scanning will help you produce the most effective resume for the scanning process.

Thumbs Up

Here are reasons why resume scanning could be a plus for your job search:

➤ Resume scanning ensures that all resumes are evaluated consistently. Some human resources personnel have so many resumes to review that not all get careful consideration. Using the scanner helps to ensure that each resume is evaluated impartially.

➤ Longer resumes (up to three pages) are acceptable. Having more pages lets you include as much information as possible to catch the search engine's attention.

➤ Scanning programs are also used to read cover letters, so you can still use that real estate to market yourself.

You have to admit that some of these reasons are pretty darn good, and they just might get you in the employer's electronic door for an interview.

Thumbs Down

No matter how hard you try to create the perfect scannable resume (I'm going to explain how to do that in the next section), there are no guarantees that it will be read accurately by the scanner. OCR

Job-Hunt Hint

Before crafting a scannable resume, read Chapter 20 to understand the ins and outs of electronic resumes. After all, the purpose of resume scanning is to transform a paper resume into an e-resume.

Career Casualty

Don't print your resume on two sides of the same piece of paper. If you do, it's very likely that the second page won't get scanned into the computer because the scanner operator probably won't notice the second side.

software isn't perfect. It has a rate of error that almost guarantees that there will be a few mistakes in the way it interprets the print on your resume. For this reason, companies are moving away from scanning and encouraging job seekers to submit their resumes electronically (via e-mail or through resume banks) in order to avoid the scanning process all together. But many companies still have their scanners at work deciphering resumes, and you may need to produce one for such a system.

Formatting at Its Finest

If you find you need to create a scannable resume, first follow the instructions in Parts 2 and 3 of this book for developing a chronological, functional, achievement, chronological hybrid, or functional hybrid resume. Then make the following changes to adjust your resume for resume scanning:

➤ Put your name, address, and contact information on separate lines.

➤ Create a Keyword section near the top.

➤ Use scannable fonts.

➤ Don't use fancy formatting.

➤ List only one date for each of your degrees.

➤ Print your resume on white paper.

Let's take a look at each of these points.

Going Solo

Make sure that each element of your Heading (your name, address, and contact information) appears on a separate line, as explained in Chapter 20. On your scannable resume, don't use parentheses around the digits of your area code because the OCR software may have difficulty identifying them as part of your phone number.

Career Casualty

Don't delay your job search because you don't have a scannable resume. Follow the instructions in this chapter, attend a class in preparing your resume for scanning, or hire a professional resume writer to get the job done.

Job-Hunt Hint

Put "continued" at the bottoms of the first and second pages of your hard-copy scannable resume and list your name and appropriate page numbers at the tops of pages two and three. This will help the Human Resources clerk keep track of your pages while entering them into the scanning system.

Bonus Check

Here's a great way to get the hang of how search engines work: Use the Find function in MS Word to search for a particular word in your resume. Notice that unless you use correct spelling, hyphenation, and spacing, the software won't find your word.

Keywords for Key Candidates

One of the most noticeable features of a scannable resume is the Keyword section near the top of page one. To learn how to create a Keyword section or to incorporate them into the text of your resume, read Chapter 20. Also, check out the following two examples of scannable resumes.

The Skinny on Scannable Fonts

An important factor in passing a resume-scanning test is to make sure the OCR can read your text. The following guidelines will help you produce a resume an OCR will love:

1. Stick to scanner-friendly fonts such as Palatino, Helvetica, and the other fonts listed in Chapter 11, "Step Six: The Big Production."

2. Don't use italics.

3. Don't underline words.

4. Limit the size of your text to no smaller than 10 point and no larger than 14 point.

5. Don't use bold unless you know that the scanner you're sending your resume to accepts bold.

If you think your resume might also be read by a human being, you could use all caps to emphasize a word that you would otherwise have italicized, underlined, made bold, or put in extra-large type.

Nothing Fancy-Schmancy

Keep the formatting of your resume simple and straightforward. Follow these tips:

➤ Don't incorporate horizontal or vertical lines into your layout.

➤ Don't use shaded bars.

➤ Change bullet points to dashes, asterisks, or plus signs, because some scanners can't read bullets.

Rest assured that indents, columns, and centered text are perfectly fine, so use those techniques if you wish.

Career Casualty

Avoid resume scanning if possible. If an employer says "E-mail your resume or send a paper resume for scanning," take the first option. That way you'll bypass the error-ridden scanner and go directly into the resume database.

Career Casualty

Don't underline words on your electronic resume. A scanner can't interpret a word if any letter in that word intersects a line. For example, in "profit," notice how the letter *p* touches the line that underlines the word. If that happens on your resume, you lose because the computer won't decipher the *p* character and therefore won't acknowledge your profit.

Bonus Check

Thanks to today's excellent personal computers, word-processing programs, and printing capabilities, it's easy to produce a high-quality resume that passes the scrutiny of both the resume scanner and the human eye.

Job-Hunt Hint

In a nutshell, a good Keyword section says who you are and what you have to offer. Even to a human reader of your resume, the Keyword section tells the whole story.

Career Casualty

Never use a condensed font for your scannable resume. Condensed fonts squeeze together the characters, and the scanner may have trouble distinguishing where one letter ends and another starts.

The Final Years

As I mentioned in Chapter 20, to make sure you get credit for your degree accomplishment, you need to list it in language that the computer will understand. That means that instead of listing a range (example: B.A., 1994–1998), you should list just the year of completion (example: B.A., 1998).

Black on White Is Right

High contrast between the type and background is the name of the game when it comes to easy scanning. Follow these two guidelines for achieving the highest contrast possible:

➤ Use black ink.

➤ Print on white paper—I mean real white, not gray or buff.

By printing black ink on white paper you should have no problem passing the OCR test.

Into the Database

Once the scanning and character recognition process is completed, the applicant's files are entered into the resume database. As mentioned in Chapter 20, depending on the sophistication of the system, the entry may include database files of candidate information, a text file of the resume that's ready for a keyword search by any hiring manager in the organization, and/or an electronic image file of the original resume.

Looking Scannable

Philip Baker was applying for a high-tech position and felt certain the employer would use a scanner to process his resume. He created the following resume with these features:

> ➤ His name is the only item on the top line.

> ➤ He created an extensive Keyword section that included technical and business terms, as well as words that describe his personal attributes.

> ➤ His simple formatting includes Palatino type, which can be read easily by a scanning system.

> ➤ Two pages of material captured all the data he thought a hiring manager might search for.

Notice that Philip's resume has very bland formatting—something the OCR software will appreciate.

Ever Ready

Douglas Cruikshank thought it was unlikely that his prospective employer used resume scanning, but he didn't know for sure. So he produced a resume (following) that was pleasing to the human eye and would also pass through a scanner and keyword search successfully:

> ➤ On a separate sheet of paper, he jotted down the following list of keywords that he assumed the employer would program into the database search engine.

> ➤ He incorporated those words appropriately into his resume.

Here's the list of keywords he came up with:

Management

Safety

Employee relations

Health education

Health-risk assessment

Employee communications

Assessment

Job-Hunt Hint

In order to create a sense of separation between two sections on your scannable resume, insert an extra space instead of a solid line and shaded bar. OCRs interpret white spaces as dividers between blocks of material.

Career Casualty

When printing your scannable resume, never use colored ink or colored paper because they make it harder for the scanning system to pick up text.

Job-Hunt Hint

When applying to an organization that uses resume scanning, avoid sending your resume via fax. Faxes sometimes blur the print, which could gum up the works when the OCR goes to read the resume.

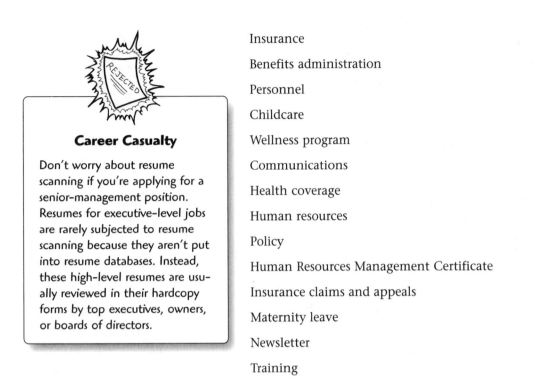

Insurance

Benefits administration

Personnel

Childcare

Wellness program

Communications

Health coverage

Human resources

Policy

Human Resources Management Certificate

Insurance claims and appeals

Maternity leave

Newsletter

Training

Having an official Keyword section near the top of your resume is useful, but it's also optional. Even without it, the search engine will scour your document for relevant words. Can you find each of these words in his resume, as a search engine would?

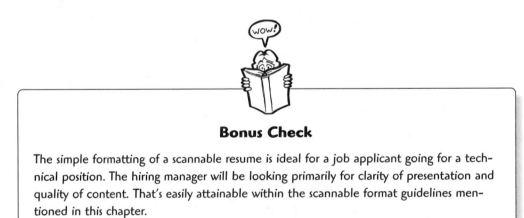

Bonus Check

The simple formatting of a scannable resume is ideal for a job applicant going for a technical position. The hiring manager will be looking primarily for clarity of presentation and quality of content. That's easily attainable within the scannable format guidelines mentioned in this chapter.

Philip Baker
123 Hillside Street, Apt. 5C
Boston, MA 12345
123-123-1234
pbaker@thenet.net

Business Development Professional
for High Speed Online Services and Solutions

KEYWORDS

ISDN. Integrated Switched Digital Network. Regional Bell Operating Company. Internet. Mosaic. World Wide Web. Adobe Acrobat. Multimedia. Interactive. DDAP. Digital Delivery of Advertising to Publishers. Online Delivery. Online Subscription. BBS. Bulletin Board Service. Client Server. Groupware. Integration. LAN. Local Area Network. WAN. Wide Area Network. Japanese. Japan Working Visa. International. Sales. Solutions. Installation. Training. Development. Strategic business agreements. Press relations. Public relations. Product rollouts. Marketing. Trade shows. Promotions. Contract negotiations. Tenacious. Competitive. Adaptable. Creative. Self management. Ability to plan. Problem solving. Accurate. Detail minded. Initiative. Supportive. Ethical. Follow through. Communication skills. Multitasking.

SUMMARY OF QUALIFICATIONS

+ Expertise in the creation and marketing of ISDN fulfillment services including hardware, software, and support service packages.

Innovator of product solutions to fill the public demand for:
- Conducting private business via Switched Digital Services
- High-speed Internet access
- Accessing other stand alone online services

+ Interested in developing information provider services to be accessed by the public via Internet, BBS, or other means.

+ Recent success in business development for U.S. and Japanese online service companies.

+ Conversant in Japanese language, business customs, and culture. Japan working visa.

PROFESSIONAL EXPERIENCE

1996-present   Telebiz Inc., Boston, MA
                      VICE PRESIDENT, BUSINESS DEVELOPMENT
+ Collaborated with president in building sales 500% through development of new ISDN integration business unit that creates and markets solutions for companies wanting to connect LANs at high speeds. ISDN solutions include:
- High-speed digital delivery of advertising to newspapers (DDAP). Clients: Boston Free Press, McMillan Advertising.
- Distribution of syndicated news materials. Clients: Telenews and Chicago Times Syndicate.
- Implementation of national pre-press networks. Clients: Graphics Central, Smith-Jones Inc., Bananas Press.

+ Integrated hardware and software from Adtran, Transware, 4-Site, and SoftArc into one package to facilitate wide area network connections and file management.

- continued -

295

Philip Baker, page two

+ Deemed Authorized ISDN Sales Agent for MABELL and SNYX.

+ Managed client ISDN projects including workflow evaluation, installation, training, and development of support packages for hardware and software.

+ Advised president regarding strategic business agreements including a co-marketing contract with Califia Corporation.

+ Managed company endorsement of Graphgo 1.0 and 2.0 for viewing and sending documents over ISDN. Handled press relations and participated in product rollouts.

+ Planned and executed marketing tools, trade shows, and promotional events.

1992-96   Yamamoto Products, Toyama, Japan
                 MANAGER, BUSINESS DEVELOPMENT, Graphics Division, 1994-96
+ Served as advisor to the Vice President of Corporate Planning of this company with $50M in annual sales.

+ Expanded sales 200% by researching and initiating dialogues with American software manufacturers for localization and resale of products in Japan.

+ Developed Japanese and Foreign Information Providers photography and graphic packages sold via TaggartMark network.

+ Established links between Tokyo and New York for producing The Journal of Economics in Japan in Japanese. This was the first time magazine pages were transmitted from Mac to Mac over ISDN in Japan.

+ Represented Japanese company in contract negotiations with American firms, bridging cultural and language barriers to ensure strong business relations.

+ Planned and developed first ever Japanese stock photography CD-rom products, a line that has since expanded 325%.

+ As project leader, organized multimedia presentations, exhibitions, and marketing materials.

CREATIVE DIRECTOR, Newcomb Publishing, 1992-94
+ Principally involved in the start up of this desktop publishing unit which in one year reduced production expenses 25%. Reported to Vice President of Corporate Planning.

+ As leader of team comprised of Japanese nationals and Americans, directed the Infini-D software localization project which re-designed the original packaging to appeal to Japanese market.

+ Conceived, designed, and produced $175,000 theme booths for participation in Computer World Tokyo. Utilized bi-cultural skills to introduce new products to a foreign market.

+ Directed creative teams in the production of print and interactive presentations.

EDUCATION

College of Arts and Letters, 1991, Wesleyan University, Middletown, CT

AFFILIATIONS

Certified SoftArc Consultant
Member, Picture Agency Council of America
Member, Newspaper Association of America

Phillip Baker's resume.

Douglas T. Cruikshank

123 Peavy Road
Dallas, Texas 12345
(123) 123-1234
d_cruikshank@range.net

JOB OBJECTIVE: A position in Human Resources with a focus on Benefits Administration.

SUMMARY OF QUALIFICATIONS

- Eight years experience in human resources-related positions.
- Two years in benefits administration.
- Designer and director of highly successful corporate wellness program.
- Currently enrolled in UTD Human Resources Management Certificate Program.

PROFESSIONAL ACCOMPLISHMENTS

EMPLOYEE BENEFITS

Brown & Brown
- Produced firm-wide Wellness Program including a 20-vendor Health Fair, health education newsletters, and health risk assessments. Chaired 15-member Wellness Committee.
- Played key role in restructuring insurance benefits, as member of Insurance Advisory Committee. Co-developed employee communications regarding program changes.
- Wrote and produced quarterly benefits newsletter, which increased employee awareness of preventive medicine and cost-effective utilization of health coverage.
- Analyzed childcare needs and presented findings that led to firm's pilot childcare program.

Singer Services
- Successfully handled complex insurance claims and appeals.

PERSONNEL ADMINISTRATION

Brown & Brown
- Co-developed new maternity leave policy and introduced options through large staff presentations and written communications.
- Served on Quality Progress Committee and developed telephone skills training series.
- Assisted in organizing safety awareness programs and staff CPR/First Aid training.

Singer Services, Orwell Associates, and The Teachers School
- Supervised teams of 30+, involving performance evaluations and employee relations.

WORK HISTORY

1992-present Wellness Program Administrator/Legal Secretary, Brown & Brown, Newberg, TX
1990-1992   Staffing and Insurance Claims Manager, Singer Services, Houston, TX
1988-1989   Executive Secretary, National Oil, Austin, TX
1984-1988   Personnel and Sales Manager, Orwell Associates, Austin, TX

EDUCATION AND AFFILIATION

B.A., Sociology, 1980, University of Texas at Austin
Human Resources Management Certificate Program, University of Texas at Dallas
Member, Texas Human Resources Council

Douglas Cruikshank's resume.

The Least You Need to Know

➤ Before assuming you need a scannable resume, call your potential employer's Human Resources department to ask whether they use resume scanning in their applicant-review process.

➤ If the company uses resume scanning, ask what its guidelines are so that you can produce a resume for the company's particular system.

➤ You can create a resume that is both scannable and pleasing to the human eye.

➤ Never use italics, underlines, or fancy fonts on your scannable resume.

➤ Employ simple formatting in your scannable resume; do not include vertical or horizontal lines.

➤ Use black ink on white paper; it's the easiest combination for the scanner to read.

Chapter 22

E-mail Express

> **In This Chapter**
>
> ➤ Learning the advantages of e-mailing your resume to an employer
>
> ➤ Understanding why you shouldn't send your resume as an attached file
>
> ➤ Preparing your document for its trip through cyberspace
>
> ➤ Launching your cover letter and resume

"Please e-mail me your resume." If an employer or headhunter hasn't already said that to you, one probably will in the near future. E-mail resume submission is becoming more prevalent by the minute; it's expanding to more industries and professions even as you read this book. It's important for you to know how to e-mail your resume successfully so that when you get an e-mail request, you'll respond with a confident "Yes!"

In this chapter, I'll explain the details of how to transform your hard-copy resume into an e-mailable one. Then I'll tell you how to launch it into cyberspace so that it'll land in an employer's electronic inbox in terrific shape.

Easy E-mail Resumes

E-mailing your resume isn't complicated at all. With an understanding of the process, you'll be zipping your resume through cyberspace in minutes. In a nutshell, here's what to do:

1. Go online, open a new e-mail message, and address it to your prospective employer.
2. Copy and paste your cover letter and resume into the e-mail document.
3. Click Send.

Bonus Check

You can access your ISP's e-mail software by clicking on a self-evident icon or underlined word on the ISP's main page or by selecting a Mail option in the ISP toolbar.

Job-Hunt Hint

If speed is critical to winning a job, e-mailing your resume could be the way to go.

Terms of Employment

PDF (Portable Document Format) is a very reliable format for sending and receiving documents as attached files. PDFs are known for their ability to maintain the fonts, graphics, and layout specifications of an e-mailed document. To create a PDF you must have Adobe Acrobat™ software. And for the employer to receive an attached PDF, she must also have Adobe Acrobat™.

In order to do these three simple steps, you need a computer that has a connection to the Internet, e-mail software (both of these are discussed in Chapter 19, "Getting Hooked on the Internet"), and a version of your resume specially prepared for e-mail transmission. Let's look at how to create your e-mailable resume so you can send it on its way quickly.

Staying Out of Trouble

Now that you have your e-mail system up and running (see Chapter 19), you're ready to send your resume electronically to an employer. You can e-mail it in one of two ways:

1. Send it as an attached file. This is not recommended unless the employer tells you specifically what type of file (such as MS Word for Windows or *Portable Document Format*) your resume should be.

2. Insert it directly into the e-mail message (recommended).

Here are my thoughts on these two options.

Getting Attached to Files

You may be tempted to send your resume as an *attached file*, thinking that the employer will then receive your nicely formatted document. But here's why you shouldn't do that:

➤ The employer may be operating under different ISP (Internet service provider) standards. It's possible that the employer's e-mail system won't be compatible with yours and will refuse to open the attachment.

➤ You and the employer may be using different computer platforms. If you and the employer aren't both using the same computer system (whether Windows, UNIX, or Macintosh), the employer's system might not be able to accept your attachment.

➤ You and the employer might have different word-processing applications. Your resume might have been prepared in an application or version that the employer can't read.

If any of these are the case, your resume will not be read unless the recipient jumps through some technical hoops to convert it. Trust me, most employers won't bother; they'll just throw it away.

Direct Message

Sending your resume in the body of an e-mail message (rather than sending it as an attached file) is a much surer way of delivering it to the employer. Granted, it's not going to look like a fancy document, but that's okay because the employer won't expect it to. Besides, I'm going to show you how to make it look pretty darn good, considering the layout limitations of e-mail.

Getting the Job Done

Prepare your cover letter and resume as one e-mailable document. Here are the steps for doing that:

1. Put your cover letter and resume into one MS Word document.

2. Save that document as Text Only.

3. Use all caps for words that need special emphasis.

4. Replace each bullet point with a standard keyboard symbol (such as a dash, plus sign, or asterisk).

5. Make sure to use straight ("stupid") quotes in place of curly ("smart") quotes. (I'll show you the difference a little later in this chapter.)

6. Limit line lengths to 65 characters and spaces.

7. Save the document again, this time as Text Only with Line Breaks.

8. If your document exceeds three pages, whittle it down to three pages or less by adjusting the spacing or editing the text.

Read on to find out more about these steps.

Doubling Up

Ultimately you'll want both your cover letter and resume to appear in your e-mail message to the employer. Because there are a few steps to preparing MS Word documents for e-mailing, it makes

Terms of Employment

An **attached file** is a document that accompanies an e-mail message. (When you have your e-mail window open, you'll notice an option for attaching a file.)

Job-Hunt Hint

If a job posting specifically says to send your resume as an attached file, rest assured it's OK to do so. The ad's request indicates that the employer has what it takes to open your attached document.

Career Casualty

When following the step-by-step instructions in this chapter, don't be dismayed if your version of MS Word uses slightly different terminology for its commands than what I've listed here. If the translation is hard to figure out, consult your MS Word manual or the Help menu near the top of your screen.

301

sense to combine your letter and resume into one MS Word document so that you can make the adjustments to both at the same time. That should cut your work in about half.

Follow these steps for an efficient way to combine your cover letter and resume:

1. Open the document that contains the cover letter you've composed for your prospective employer.

2. Go to the File menu in your toolbar and select Save As. Create a logical name for your new document (such as "letter and resume" or the name of the company you're applying to). Choose where on your computer you want your new document to reside. Click Save or OK.

3. Delete the heading, date, and inside address of the cover letter in your new document.

4. Close the gap between the complimentary close and your name.

5. Replace "Enclosure: resume" with "RESUME".

6. Open the MS Word document containing the resume you want to send to this employer.

7. Copy and paste your resume into your new "letter and resume" document so that your resume follows your cover letter immediately after "RESUME".

8. Make sure that each element of your resume heading (your name, address, and contact information) appears on a separate line (See Chapter 20, "The ABC's of E-Resumes," for an example of how your Heading should look.)

9. Add a Keyword section if you think your resume will be put into a resume database. (See Chapter 20.)

10. If your resume is more than one page, eliminate "Continued" at the bottom of page one and your name and "page two" at the top of page two. You won't need these once your resume is in an e-mail message.

11. In your Education section, be sure that there is only one date for each college degree completed (as explained in Chapter 20).

12. Review your resume to make sure you've followed each of these steps.

Job-Hunt Hint

Stay up to date on new versions of your e-mail software. File transfers are bound to keep improving and a day will come when e-mailing your resume as an attached file will be as reliable as Mom's apple pie. Until then, follow the step-by-step instructions in this section for a safe e-mail resume transfer.

Take a look at the original cover letter and resume for Carter Wood (the following two examples) and then check out how they looked when combined into one MS Word document (the third example).

Don't worry if the formatting of your resume alters when you combine the two documents; you'll be adjusting that.

Bonus Check

Here's a crash course in how to cut and paste in MS Word:

1. Using your cursor, highlight the text of the document that you want to copy and place elsewhere (either within that document or in a different one).

2. Go to "Edit" in your toolbar and select "Copy." (The text is now in your computer's memory.)

3. Place your cursor where you would like to place the text you just copied.

4. Go to Edit in the toolbar and select Paste.

You did it!

Better Save Than Sorry

Now it's time to adjust the formatting of your cover letter and resume document so that it'll slip into your e-mail message easily. Brace yourself: This two-step process will transform your handsome cover letter and resume into a very blandly formatted document. Here's how to do it:

1. Open the MS Word document that contains both your cover letter and resume (the "letter and resume" document you just created).

2. Go to File in the toolbar and select Save As.

3. When you have the Save As window open, rename your document using a name that will identify it accurately (like "resume in Text Only").

4. Still within the Save As window, go to the pull-down menu for Save As Type and select Text Only.

5. Click Save or OK.

6. Close the document (no need to exit MS Word).

7. From within MS Word, reopen the document you just closed, which you've named "resume in Text Only." (Warning! If you reopen the file by clicking the icon, it will become a Notepad document, which is not what you want. Instead, go to File in the toolbar and select Open, find the file named "resume in Text Only.txt," and open it.) There's your document, completely stripped of fancy formatting!

You've now converted your document into *Text Only,* and you're ready to make just a few more adjustments before sending it off to the employer.

Terms of Employment

Text Only is very simple formatting (no bold, indents, italics, or varied type sizes) and is ideal for e-mailing and online distribution.

303

(Cover Letter in MS Word)

Carter Wood

001 Morningside Drive • Freetown, ME 12345 • (123) 123-1234

July 6, 1999

Ms. Beth Rainstree
Production Coordinator
A thru Z Dry Goods
Portland, CA 94115

Dear Ms. Rainstree,

Time is my friend. Why? My longevity in the dry goods industry has handed me just about every crisis you can imagine. What astounds my colleagues is the poise I exhibit throughout the inevitable ups and downs of sales work.

As I submit my resume to you for Inside Sales Director, I can honestly say that I'm one of the best in this business. I'd like a chance to prove that to you.

I will call your office to see when you are starting to interview candidates. I would like to be one of the first.

Thank you!

Carter Wood

Enclosure: resume

Carter Wood's cover letter.

(Resume in MS Word)

Carter Wood

001 Morningside Drive • Freetown, ME 12345 • (123) 123-1234

JOB OBJECTIVE: Inside Sales Director

SUMMARY OF QUALIFICATIONS

- More than 10 years as a Sales Manager who consistently takes sales forces to the top.
- Risk-smart sales professional who knows how to improve and promote product lines.
- Highly motivated self-starter and problem solver.
- Increased sales up to 200% through excellent customer relations.
- Featured in *Maine Business Today* and a national sales magazine for creating an exceptional sales program.

SALES ACCOMPLISHMENTS

- Consistently ranked top sales person within first month of employment at every company; went on to train sales forces in winning techniques.
- Broke records in initial, referral, and repeat sales through exceptional customer service.
- Drove local and regional sales groups to the top of division by improving sales dollars per purchase, sales per hour, items per purchase, and referrals.
- Trained and supervised an average of 15 employees a year over a 10-year period in sales and customer service. Resolved employee-management conflicts to keep focus on sales.
- Designed and implemented a door-to-door sales program that increased sales, productivity, and profit while reducing turnover of personnel.
- Planned and directed marketing strategies, including advertising, promotions, and tradeshows.

WORK HISTORY

Telemarketing and Inside Sales Manager	Northeast Dry Goods, Portland, ME, 1993-pres.
Sales/Business Manager	Gardens & More, Greenville, VT, 1986-1993
Sales Associate	Vision Shack, White River, VT, 1984-1986

EDUCATION

B.A., Economics, minor in Psychology, University of MA, Amherst, MA, 1984

Carter Wood's resume.

(Resume and Cover Letter in MS Word)

Dear Ms. Rainstree,

Time is my friend. Why? My longevity in the dry goods industry has handed me just about every crisis you can imagine. What astounds my colleagues is the poise I exhibit throughout the inevitable ups and downs of sales work.

As I submit my resume to you for Inside Sales Director, I can honestly say that I'm one of the best in this business. I'd like a chance to prove that to you.

I will call your office to see when you are starting to interview candidates. I would like to be one of the first.

Thank you!
Carter Wood

RESUME

Carter Wood

001 Morningside Drive
Freetown, ME 12345
(123) 123-1234

JOB OBJECTIVE: Inside Sales Director

KEYWORDS

Dry Goods. Sales. Director. Manager. Inside Sales. Problem solving. Customer relations. Customer service. Training. Sales program. Supervision. Conflict resolution. Employee retention. Marketing strategy. Advertising. Promotions. Tradeshows. Telemarketing. Management. College degree. B.A. BA. Bachelor's degree.

SUMMARY OF QUALIFICATIONS

- More than 10 years as a Sales Manager who consistently takes sales forces to the top.
- Risk-smart sales professional who knows how to improve and promote product lines.
- Highly motivated self-starter and problem solver.
- Increased sales up to 200% through excellent customer relations.
- Featured in *Maine Business Today* and a national sales magazine for creating an exceptional sales program.

SALES ACCOMPLISHMENTS

- Consistently ranked top sales person within first month of employment at every company; went on to train sales forces in winning techniques.
- Broke records in initial, referral, and repeat sales through exceptional customer service.
- Drove local and regional sales groups to the top of division by improving sales dollars per purchase, sales per hour, items per purchase, and referrals.
- Trained and supervised an average of 15 employees a year over a 10-year period in sales and customer service. Resolved employee-management conflicts to keep focus on sales.
- Designed and implemented a door-to-door sales program that increased sales, productivity, and profit while reducing turnover of personnel.
- Planned and directed marketing strategies, including advertising, promotions, and tradeshows.

WORK HISTORY

Telemarketing and Inside Sales Manager   Northeast Dry Goods, Portland, ME, 1993-pres.
Sales/Business Manager   Gardens & More, Greenville, VT, 1986-1993
Sales Associate   Vision Shack, White River, VT, 1984-1986

EDUCATION

B.A., Economics, minor in Psychology, University of MA, Amherst, MA, 1984

Carter Wood's cover letter and resume.

Saving your document as a Text Only file removes all the formatting, which is perfect for e-mailing. Text Only documents are by nature no-frills: no italics, bolds, underlines, tabs, or tables. And typically the font size of all text will be the same. Here's what happened to the letter and resume of Carter Wood when he converted his document into Text Only (see preceding example to make a comparison).

Capitalizing on Headings

In your hard-copy resume, you may have used bold, underline, and italics to highlight particular words. If you've used a lot of bold, italics, and underlines in your resume, you may be floored when you save it as Text Only because those extras will disappear. Because Text Only stripped your document of those special effects, use all caps for those words that were previously emphasized on your original. That'll draw attention to important words, and it's perfect for e-mailing! Rest assured, your resume is still going to make a good impression if you compensate with the limited e-mail formatting mentioned in this section.

Job-Hunt Hint

An easy way to make overall changes in your document (such as changing all bullets to dashes) is to use the Search and Replace function in your word-processing program.

Bite the Bullet

Bullet points in your original resume were used to break your text into bite-sized pieces. But because some e-mail applications won't allow bullet points in their e-mail messages, you need to come up with an alternative that will transfer well. To make sure your e-mail resume still has the punch of your original, replace bullet points with one of the following:

➤ Dashes (-)

➤ Plus symbols (+)

➤ Asterisks (*)

Use the space bar to place a single space immediately after the symbol and before the first word of the statement. (Don't use a tab as you would in creating a hard-copy resume.)

Straight Quotes

There are two types of quotation marks: straight and curly.

➤ Curly quotes look like "this" and are known as *smart quotes*.

➤ Straight quotes look like "this" and are called *straight quotes*.

Your e-mail resume must use straight quotes, because some e-mail programs can't read smart quotes.

Job-Hunt Hint

If you have an old version of MS Word (pre-Windows 98), you may not have a "Characters (with spaces)" option in your toolbar. In that case, add the number from Character Count with the number from Word Count. (Because there's one space between each word in a line, the number of words will tell you how many spaces there are in that line.)

(Text-Only Document)

Dear Ms. Rainstree,

Time is my friend. Why? My longevity in the dry goods industry has handed me just about every crisis you can imagine. What astounds my colleagues is the poise I exhibit throughout the inevitable ups and downs of sales work.

As I submit my resume to you for Inside Sales Director, I can honestly say that I'm one of the best in this business. I'd like a chance to prove that to you.

I will call your office to see when you are starting to interview candidates. I would like to be one of the first.

Thank you!
Carter Wood

RESUME

Carter Wood
001 Morningside Drive
Freetown, ME 12345
123-123-1234

JOB OBJECTIVE: Inside Sales Director

KEYWORDS
Dry Goods. Sales. Director. Manager. Inside Sales. Problem solving. Customer relations. Customer service. Training. Sales program. Supervision. Conflict resolution. Employee retention. Marketing strategy. Advertising. Promotions. Tradeshows. Telemarketing. Management. College degree. B.A. BA. Bachelor's degree.

SUMMARY OF QUALIFICATIONS
• More than 10 years as a Sales Manager who consistently takes sales forces to the top.

• Risk-smart sales professional who knows how to improve and promote product lines.

• Highly motivated self-starter and problem solver.

• Increased sales up to 200% through excellent customer relations.

• Featured in Maine Business Today and a national sales magazine for creating an exceptional sales program.

SALES ACCOMPLISHMENTS
• Consistently ranked top sales person within first month of employment at every company; went on to train sales forces in winning techniques.

• Broke records in initial, referral, and repeat sales through exceptional customer service.

• Drove local and regional sales groups to the top of division by improving sales dollars per purchase, sales per hour, items per purchase, and referrals.

• Trained and supervised an average of 15 employees a year over a 10-year period in sales and customer service. Resolved employee-management conflicts to keep focus on sales.

• Designed and implemented a door-to-door sales program that increased sales, productivity, and profit while reducing turnover of personnel.

• Planned and directed marketing strategies, including advertising, promotions, and tradeshows.

WORK HISTORY
Telemarketing and Inside Sales Manager   Northeast Dry Goods, Portland, ME, 1993-pres.
Sales/Business Manager   Gardens & More, Greenville, VT, 1986-1993
Sales Associate   Vision Shack, White River, VT, 1984-1986

EDUCATION
B.A., Economics, minor in Psychology, University of MA, Amherst, MA, 1984

Carter Wood's Text Only resume.

Characters That Count

Most e-mail messages have a limit to the number of characters and spaces they will allow per line. This limit is determined by the particular e-mail software being used. The tricky part is that the recipient's e-mail software may have a different character-per-line limit than your e-mail software. If the receiving e-mail software allows fewer characters and spaces per line than your e-mail software, your recipient may see some illogical line wraps when he or she opens your e-mail message. It might look something like the following figure.

It's best to cut this problem off at the pass by using very conservative line lengths in your message. My rule of thumb is to limit line lengths to no more than 65 characters and spaces. Here's how:

1. Use the Word Count function in MS Word (highlight the longest line in your document, and go to the Tools menu and select Word Count) to check the number of characters and spaces.

2. Adjust the margins of your document so that no line is more than 65 characters and spaces long.

Career Casualty

Don't use curly quotes in an e-mail message because they sometimes translate as un-readable symbols (shaded rectangles) on the recipient's end.

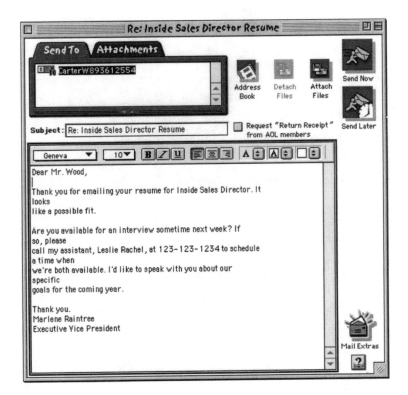

Sample of weird e-mail line wraps.

After setting the margins, you may want to do a little adjusting of the text to make sure things look right. For instance, delete extra line spaces that may have inadvertently been created in the conversion or insert commas into the Work History where tabs once divided information.

Give Me a Break

You need to save your MS Word document one more time in order to preserve the short line lengths you created in the previous section. Here's how:

1. Follow the same steps you did to save the document as Text Only, only this time save it as Text Only with Line Breaks.

2. Close your document and then open it again from within MS Word (just as you did for your Text Only version).

Here's what Carter Wood's resume and cover letter document looked like in his Text-Only-with-Line-Breaks version.

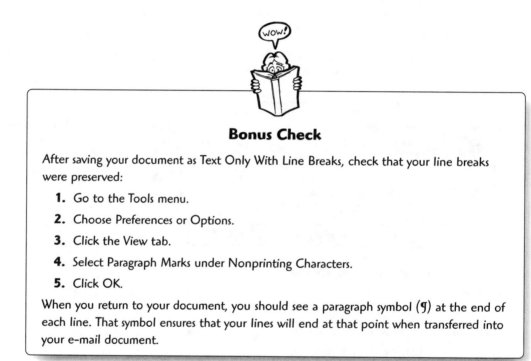

Bonus Check

After saving your document as Text Only With Line Breaks, check that your line breaks were preserved:

1. Go to the Tools menu.

2. Choose Preferences or Options.

3. Click the View tab.

4. Select Paragraph Marks under Nonprinting Characters.

5. Click OK.

When you return to your document, you should see a paragraph symbol (¶) at the end of each line. That symbol ensures that your lines will end at that point when transferred into your e-mail document.

You're doing great—you're just a few tortilla chips away from the big enchilada! Let's keep going.

Setting Limits

Don't let your resume and cover letter extend past three pages while they're in your "Text Only with Line Breaks" document. If necessary, edit your resume or consider a shorter cover note.

(Text-Only-With-Line-Breaks Document)

Dear Ms. Rainstree,

Time is my friend. Why? My longevity in the dry goods industry
has handed me just about every crisis you can imagine. What
astounds my colleagues is the poise I exhibit throughout the
inevitable ups and downs of sales work.

As I submit my resume to you for Inside Sales Director, I can
honestly say that I'm one of the best in this business. I'd like
a chance to prove that to you.

I will call your office to see when you are starting to
interview candidates. I would like to be one of the first.

Thank you!
Carter Wood

RESUME

Carter Wood
001 Morningside Drive
Freetown, ME 12345
123-123-1234

JOB OBJECTIVE: Inside Sales Director

KEYWORDS
Dry Goods. Sales. Director. Manager. Inside Sales. Problem
solving. Customer relations. Customer service. Training. Sales
program. Supervision. Conflict resolution. Employee retention.
Marketing strategy. Advertising. Promotions. Tradeshows.
Telemarketing. Management. College degree. B.A. BA. Bachelor's
degree.

SUMMARY OF QUALIFICATIONS
+ More than 10 years as a Sales Manager who consistently takes
sales forces to the top.

+ Risk-smart sales professional who knows how to improve and
promote product lines.

+ Highly motivated self-starter and problem solver.

+ Increased sales up to 200% through excellent customer
relations.

+ Featured in "Maine Business Today" and a national sales magazine
for creating an exceptional sales program.

SALES ACCOMPLISHMENTS
+ Consistently ranked top sales person within first month of
employment at every company; went on to train sales forces in
winning techniques.

+ Broke records in initial, referral, and repeat sales through exceptional customer service.

+ Drove local and regional sales groups to the top of division by improving sales dollars per purchase, sales per hour, items per purchase, and referrals.

+ Trained and supervised an average of 15 employees a year over a 10-year period in sales and customer service. Resolved employee-management conflicts to keep focus on sales.

+ Designed and implemented a door-to-door sales program that increased sales, productivity, and profit while reducing turnover of personnel.

+ Planned and directed marketing strategies, including advertising, promotions, and tradeshows.

WORK HISTORY
Telemarketing and Inside Sales Manager
Northeast Dry Goods, Portland, ME, 1993-pres.

Sales/Business Manager
Gardens & More, Greenville, VT, 1986-1993

Sales Associate
Vision Shack, White River, VT, 1984-1986

EDUCATION
B.A., Economics, minor in Psychology,
University of MA, Amherst, MA, 1984

Carter Wood's Text-Only-with-Line-Breaks version.

Testing, Testing

Almost all of us get discouraged when we have technical difficulties. If you run into obstacles trying to e-mail your resume, don't give up! Get help from a friend, refer to your ISP manual, call tech support, or take a break and come back to your project later when you feel refreshed.

Even though you've followed the instructions in this chapter to the letter, conduct an e-mail test-run: E-mail your resume to yourself first to make sure it transfers accurately (using the directions following, minus addressing it to the employer!). If that works, try sending it to a friend who uses a different ISP or who works at a company with its own e-mail system. When you hear that your friend received your e-mailed resume with success, you're ready to send it to your prospective employer.

Career Casualty

Keeping organized as you make multiple versions of your resume can be a challenge. Develop a plan to name your files logically and place them in folders that keep things straight.

3-2-1, Take Off!

You've done a great job of preparing your cover letter and resume in one word-processing document. Now you're ready to drop it into an e-mail message and send it on its way. The following steps will get the job done:

1. Open a window to write a new e-mail message.

2. Fill in the e-mail address in the Send To box by typing the recipient's e-mail address exactly as you see it, right down to the capital and lowercase letters. (Some addresses are not case-sensitive, but this accuracy may be important to the employer's e-mail system.)

3. Put a title in the Subject line, and make it a good one like "Resume: Marketing Position".

4. Without closing your e-mail message, open the MS Word document (Text-Only-with-Line-Breaks version) that contains your cover letter and resume.

5. Copy the entire text of your cover letter and resume and paste it into the e-mail window, where the body of the message goes.

6. Now that your cover letter and resume are in the e-mail message window, check that they look the way you want the employer to see them.

7. Take a deep breath and click Send.

Bonus Check

Give yourself the three-word test when it comes to writing a good subject line for your e-mail. Because most e-mail systems show only a few words of a subject line, make the first three words of your headline strong enough to make the employer open your e-mail.

Take a peek at the following e-mail message that contains Carter Wood's letter and resume to his prospective employer.

Snapshot of e-mail message with Carter Wood's resume in it.

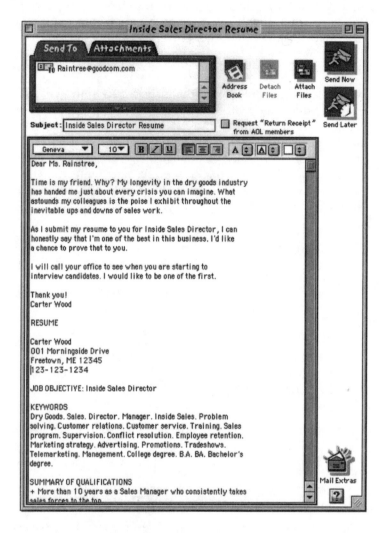

Congratulations! You're now an e-mail resume pro.

The Least You Need to Know

➤ When delivering your resume and cover letter via e-mail, insert them both into the e-mail message window instead of sending them as attached files.

➤ Use all caps instead of bold, underline, or italics to give emphasis to important words.

➤ Don't exceed three pages once your cover letter and resume are combined into one e-mailable document.

➤ Run an e-mail test by sending your resume to yourself and to a friend who uses a different ISP, type of computer, or word-processing program.

Chapter 23

Banking on Success: Online Resume Banking

In This Chapter

➤ What online resume banking is

➤ Who benefits from online resume databases

➤ What industries use online recruiting sources

➤ Where to find the best resume banks for you

➤ What to watch out for when posting online

➤ How to deposit your resume into an online bank

Now that you've mastered the e-mail resume, you're ready to take advantage of one of the handiest developments since employment centers discovered the 3 × 5 card and push pin: online resume banks. By posting your resume in an online database, your qualifications can be seen by thousands of employers and headhunters—think of the potential that holds! In this chapter, you'll learn how to find online resume banks, how to post your resume on one, and how to steer clear of pitfalls.

Resumes in a Bank?

Online resume banks appear on job search Web sites. They're sort of like regular banks, only resume banks deal in their own currency: resumes. Job seekers deposit (*upload*) their resumes into online databases, and employers withdraw (*download*) them from the databases.

Terms of Employment

To **upload** a document means to transfer it from your computer to a remote computer or to an Internet site. To **download** a document means to transfer it from a remote computer or Internet site onto your computer.

Job-Hunt Hint

Before posting your resume online, make sure you know what charges might apply (and what benefits you'll get for those charges).

Who Pays the Bill

Make no mistake about it, there's money being saved and earned through recruitment Web sites. Most of the commercial resume-bank Web sites offer their services free to job seekers and charge employers and headhunters to access the resumes in their databases. A few sites charge the job seeker and give free access to employers and recruiters. Still others charge all parties involved. Then again, there are nonprofit and government employment sites that are free to job seekers and employers.

Let's look at why employers and recruiters like using online resume banking to find job applicants.

The Employer's Dream

As you can imagine, employers are happy to use online resume banks because they can

➤ Greatly augment the talent pool available to them.

➤ Cut in-house recruiting costs by outsourcing the initial screening process to the online service

➤ Eliminate the need to contract a headhunter, potentially saving significant amounts in commission fees

It's no wonder that many employers love this efficient system for discovering terrific job candidates.

Headhunting on the Web

Headhunters find resume banks an efficient way to search through hundreds of job seekers' qualifications by just a click of the mouse. This system, of course, cuts their time dramatically because they don't have to make a zillion phone calls to find likely candidates for jobs they're trying to fill. And they can do their scouting any time of the day or night.

Who's Looking for Whom?

When online resume banks first came on the scene, they were used primarily by high-tech companies to find technical applicants. Gradually, the range of industries that use online resume banks for recruiting has grown. Today almost all industries use online recruiting to fill most levels and types of employment. It's very likely that your profession is represented somewhere online—your job is to track down where.

Bonus Check

Most headhunters will contact you by phone or e-mail if they consider you a marketable candidate. During that initial contact with the recruiter, pay attention to his ability to

➤ Ask you good questions to determine whether you're a good match for the job he has in mind for you.

➤ Address your concerns and questions about the job.

➤ Be honest in his dealings with both you and the employer. (You may have to follow your gut feeling on this one.)

If he's not even up for such a discussion, you probably don't want to do business with him.

Resume banks can fall under one or more of the following categories. They may

➤ Specialize strictly in your industry (such as high-tech or health care).

➤ Focus on a particular profession (such as human resources or sales).

➤ Provide recruiting services to special-interest groups (such as women, the disabled, or other minorities).

➤ Cater to a geographic region (such as a state or metropolitan area).

➤ Cover a wide range of industries and professions so applicants are considered for lots of job titles.

Job-Hunt Hint

For a list of job-search Web sites that I recommend, turn to the Caught in the Web section of Appendix C, "Other Cool Resources."

Let's look at how to find resume banks in these categories.

The Professional Approach

Many Web sites specialize according to industry, profession, or both. Here are ways to learn of those that apply to your job search:

➤ Use your search engine (see Chapter 20, "The ABC's of E-Resumes"), inserting keywords that indicate your area of expertise or industry (such as *jobs, e-commerce,* and *marketing* for a marketing position in online business).

➤ Read professional magazines in your field or visit their Web sites to see what online recruiting services they suggest.

➤ Ask your colleagues what resume banks they recommend (assuming you can speak freely with them about your job search).

You could also do a search for specific companies in your field and go to their Web sites, where you might be able to submit your resume.

Specializing in Special Interests

Many resume Web sites focus on special interests, such as a social cause or an ethnic population. These sites have a couple of advantages over the large generic sites in that they may

➤ Offer current employment information that's specific to that interest group.

➤ Provide job-search support through articles, chat rooms, and member profiles to enable individual networking.

Good ways to find your special-interest Web sites include asking friends in your special-interest group, using your search engine, and looking for Web site addresses in literature from your interest group.

Career Casualty

Don't be shy about following up on an electronic resume submission. After you've uploaded your resume onto a company recruitment Web site, call or e-mail a few days later to ask whether they received it and whether it's been routed into their system.

Bonus Check

Special-interest Web sites are one of the best types of sites for networking. These sites frequently have chat rooms and e-mail options which make it easy to contact others with the same interests.

It's a Regional Thing

A Web site that represents regional recruiting efforts is highly valuable, whether you live in that geographic area or are planning to relocate to it. Such sites are often sponsored by the following organizations:

➤ Career centers

➤ Local media (TV, radio, or newspapers)

➤ Special-interest groups for the area

➤ Recruiting agencies

➤ Specific companies

In addition to supplying their resume databases to local employers, the sites frequently announce (and sometimes sponsor) career fairs, lectures, workshops, and other networking events that you might attend online or in person.

Job-Hunt Hint

If you're planning to relocate for your next job, find job search Web sites through organizations in the area where you plan to live. You might meet your next employer online!

The Big Guys

You've probably heard of online career sites such as The Monster Board (http://www.monster.com), Career Builder (http://www.careerbuilder.com), and others advertised on the radio, TV, and in print. This type of megasite is well-managed and usually features a resume bank that offers the following:

➤ A large client base of employers

➤ A wide range of industry job categories

➤ National and international job openings

➤ A job agent (a service that e-mails you job listings that fit your criteria)

➤ Online job-search advice (for instance, how to write a resume)

➤ E-newsletters sent to you via e-mail

➤ The option to keep your resume anonymous to all or particular employers

➤ The ability to update your resume after it's been posted

Job-Hunt Hint

If your resume is in an employer's resume bank you could be considered for a fantastic job you didn't know you were qualified for. The search engine might select your resume based on the keywords an employer has used to find the perfect candidate for a job you haven't even thought of.

These large resume sites have a high volume of companies and headhunters that search their databases regularly. This means that you could get a response within hours of submitting your resume.

Bonus Check

Although resume bank sites may fall into the categories listed here, many of them belong to more than one category. For instance, you might find a site that serves women of color (a special interest), in broadcasting (a profession), in the Boston area (a region) by typing "jobs, women of color, broadcasting, Boston" into your search engine's window.

The Downside of Uploading

Not surprisingly, there are some possible down sides to posting your resume online. Here are some of them:

➤ Your current employer could find out about your job search.

➤ You could be shopped around by several recruiters without your knowledge.

➤ Your personal and professional information becomes public knowledge.

Job-Hunt Hint

The online job market is bound to have some new twists and turns as it continues to develop. Read your newspaper's career section regularly to get the latest on Internet job-search tips and warnings.

Career Casualty

If confidentiality is a major concern for you, don't post your resume online. There's no guarantee that your employer won't hear about your job search from another employer in your field or from a headhunter who picks up your resume and tries to sell you to your current boss.

These points are worth examining, because they'll help you weigh the pros and cons of posting online.

The Invisible Job Seeker

Your employer may be using an online database to search for future employees, and she could run across your resume in the process. Yikes! The cat would be out of the bag about your job search.

To spare you from such an embarrassing and potentially job-threatening situation, many of the banks have one or more "anonymous" options:

➤ You can have your resume made invisible to employers you specify.

➤ You can have your name, address, and even the companies you've worked for blocked out on your resume so that no employers can see that info.

In the last option, the job bank site's system acts as your agent, notifying you of each employer's request for information about you. Then you can decide which opportunities to pursue.

Headhunter Overkill

Because resume banks are accessed by lots of headhunters, your resume could easily be picked up by several recruiters and shopped around in your field. Here's why that's not to your advantage: Many headhunters work on a commission basis with employers. If more than one recruiter presents the same candidate, the employer may disregard the candidate rather than have to sort out which recruiter wins the commission, should the candidate accept the job offer.

This multiple-submission problem can be eliminated by carefully selecting which resume banks you use. For instance, some sites are run by reputable recruiting agencies (such as Korn/Ferry International at http://www.futurestep.com) that maintain strict confidentiality and carry exclusive job openings. Posting on such a site essentially gives you many of the advantages of working personally with a recruiter who has a huge database of employment opportunities.

Bonus Check

Reputable headhunters get a job seeker's permission each time he sends that job seeker's resume to an employer.

Telemarketing Alert

In most situations, once your resume is deposited into a resume bank, your personal and professional information may no longer be kept confidential. With little effort, a telemarketer, direct-mail solicitor, or scam artist can access the files and download your info.

Here's how data such as your name, contact info, place of employment, and salary history could be misused: Someone could pose as an employer or headhunter, access the database, discover your resume, and use it for their own purposes. For instance, a stockbroker could find your resume, speculate that you're a good client prospect for the type of investments he brokers, and contact you to solicit his services. If the resume Web site's managers aren't screening their clients for your protection, almost anyone could get access to your files.

Job-Hunt Hint

Ask fellow job seekers which resume banks they respect. You can get recommendations from career centers and your professional colleagues and through job-search seminars.

Go to the Bank and Fill Out the Forms

Online resume banks are constantly changing the layouts of their Web sites and fine tuning their procedures as they become more sophisticated.

At most resume banks, you'll be presented with a two-step process:

1. Fill in the blanks at the top of an online form (also called an e-form).
2. Copy and paste the body of your resume into a large window.

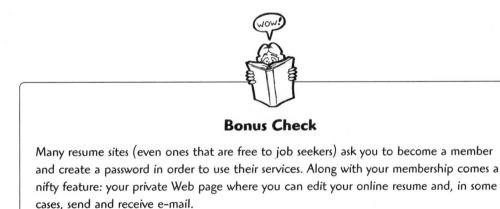

Bonus Check

Many resume sites (even ones that are free to job seekers) ask you to become a member and create a password in order to use their services. Along with your membership comes a nifty feature: your private Web page where you can edit your online resume and, in some cases, send and receive e-mail.

Both steps are straightforward, but let's look at a few tricks that will ensure your success.

Blankety-Blank

Here are the items you will most probably be asked to type in:

➤ Your name, address, phone/fax, and e-mail address

➤ The location where you'd like to work

➤ Your job objective or professional title (sometimes referred to as the "Headline")

Filling in your name and contact information should be no problem. (If you have questions, read Chapter 6, "Step One: Heading Your Way," for advice on what to put in the Heading section of your resume. The same concepts apply to the e-form.) Selecting the geographic area where you'd like to find employment is usually done through a pull-down menu where you choose from what's listed.

The headline is a very important part of your e-form. It's likely to be the first thing the employer sees, so this isn't the place for that story about your fishing trip. Keep it simple: Tell the employer something about yourself as concisely as possible, with the most important words at the beginning of the line, as in the following examples:

➤ Sports-Industry Marketer

➤ Energetic Sales Trainee

➤ Resume: Medical Librarian

What three words describe who you are and what job you're looking for?

The Heart of the Matter

The next step is to fill in the "Body of Your Resume" section. The directions on the site will tell you what type of text format that particular e-form accepts. Usually it will ask for a Text Only document.

To convert your hard-copy resume into Text Only, follow the instructions in Chapter 22 for creating your Text Only resume. When you paste your Text Only resume into the e-form window, pay attention to where you might need to insert a forced return (by pushing Enter or Return" on your keyboard) in order to keep all the text visible inside the window.

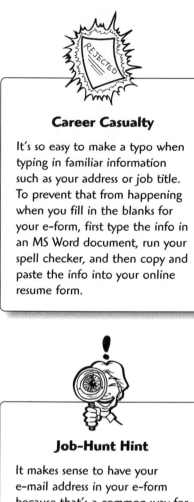

Career Casualty

It's so easy to make a typo when typing in familiar information such as your address or job title. To prevent that from happening when you fill in the blanks for your e-form, first type the info in an MS Word document, run your spell checker, and then copy and paste the info into your online resume form.

Job-Hunt Hint

It makes sense to have your e-mail address in your e-form because that's a common way for employers and headhunters to contact an e-resume savvy person like you!

Bonus Check

Remember the three-word test for writing the subject line of your e-mail message that I explained in Chapter 22, "E-mail Express"? The same principle applies to creating the headline of your e-form.

By the way, because you've already entered the info from your Heading in the e-form on your screen, you can delete that from the material you paste into the Body of Your Resume window. That's right, you only need to insert the body of your resume into that window; there's no need for the Heading.

Keeping Up to Date

Most online resume banks offer you the capability to edit your resume. This is an important feature for several reasons:

➤ You can keep the info on your document up-to-date.

➤ You can improve your resume if it's not drawing the response you want.

➤ You can correct typos should you detect them after submitting your resume.

➤ You can extend the life of your resume in the bank if you need to. Most banks will list your resume for a limited number of days (typically 60 to 90). By editing your resume, you essentially reset the clock.

➤ In some systems, new resumes are listed at the top of the entire list of resumes or may be categorized under a section such as "New Listings," which employers are apt to look at first. By editing your document, you can re-enter the New Listings category.

Update your online resume by following the instructions on the resume Web site. If your edits are extensive (let's say you want to rewrite your Summary of Qualifications section), compose your points in MS Word, run your spell checker, and proofread carefully. Then copy and paste it into your online resume. Aside from these reasons, it's a good idea to occasionally review your resume to make sure it's marketing you in the best way possible.

Job-Hunt Hint

For your online "postable" e-resume, you don't need to save the document as Text Only With Line Breaks (as you did for your e-mailable resume) because there is no standard line length for e-forms.

Bonus Check

Some resume bank e-forms will ask for your salary expectations. Before inputting an amount, think carefully about whether you want to disclose that figure online. You may choose to leave that box blank for two reasons:

➤ You don't want your financial information floating around in cyberspace.

➤ You want to wait until an in-person interview to discuss the whole compensation package with your potential employer.

Remember, you don't have to answer all the questions on an e-form unless the program specifically requires you to do so.

Getting Out While You're Ahead

As soon as you land a job, be sure to delete your resume from the resume banks where you've posted it (check with the site for instructions). You don't want your resume in circulation once you're happily employed (unless you do contract work, in which case you may always want to have your resume on the market). After all, you don't want your new boss to find your resume floating around in the job market and think that you're already looking elsewhere.

The Least You Need to Know

➤ Online resume banks can be a very efficient way for you to find a fulfilling job and for employers to recruit great job candidates.

➤ Some resume banks specialize according to profession, industry, special interest, or location. Others offer a wide range of criteria that can be narrowed to fit your search.

➤ You can find online resume databases by using your search engine; reading the Caught in the Web section of Appendix C, "Other Cool Resources;" asking friends for recommendations; reading professional journals; and going to my Web site: http://www.susanireland.com.

➤ To post your resume online, fill out an e-form, which includes pasting the body of your resume into the form.

➤ Before uploading your resume onto a site, understand what charges you may be responsible for and what risks are involved in placing your information on the site.

Terms of Employment Glossary

achievement resume   A resume format that lists five or six strong, relevant achievements under a main heading such as Professional Accomplishments or Selected Achievements.

action verb   A verb that says that someone did something. For example, "I *earned* a raise."

age discrimination   The illegal practice of prejudice against a person because of his or her age. In this form of discrimination, an employer may eliminate job candidates because she's too old or too young.

attached file   A document that accompanies an e-mail message.

bottom line   A term that means different things to different people. In for-profit organizations, the bottom line is measured by revenue, savings, and profit. In nonprofit organizations, the bottom line may be program effectiveness, enrollment, or budget growth. The key to writing effective achievement statements on your resume is to understand the reader's bottom line.

browser   Software, such as Netscape Navigator or Internet Explorer, that allows you to navigate the World Wide Web.

bullet point   A graphic symbol (➤) used to highlight a statement.

career coach   Someone who helps a client develop his job-search strategy and motivates him through the process.

career counselor   Someone who helps a client assess his qualifications and decide what career move to make.

chronological hybrid   A chronological resume with skill subheadings (similar to the skill headings in a functional resume) incorporated into the Professional Experience section.

chronological resume   A resume format that organizes the job seeker's achievements according to his work history.

compensation   The combination of salary, benefits, and perks to pay an employee for work.

complimentary close In a letter, the word or short phrase just above your signature. "Sincerely yours" is perhaps the most commonly used complimentary close for job-search correspondence.

consultant A temporary worker (someone who's not on a payroll) who is used in fields such as business management and technology development.

contractor A temporary worker (someone who's not on a payroll) who is used in fields such as construction, administration, and business management.

curriculum vitae Also referred to as a vita or CV, this term is used by the academic and scientific communities to mean resume.

download a document To transfer the document from a remote computer or an Internet site onto your computer.

e-mail Short for electronic mail, this is mail sent electronically over the Internet.

Employment History A section on a resume that lists your paid work.

e-resume Short for electronic resume, this is the computerized form of a resume. E-resumes are used for e-mailing, posting online, and transferring by other electronic means.

fax Memos and documents delivered over a facsimile machine.

fonts Typefaces, which come in two styles: serif (with the little feet on the characters) and sans serif (without the feet).

freelance Working on an independent basis. A **freelancer** is someone who works under his own direction, finds his own work, and often (but not always) works at home. Fields such as graphic design and interior decorating often employ freelancers.

functional hybrid A functional resume with company subheadings included in the Relevant Achievement section to indicate where the achievements took place.

functional resume A resume format that organizes the job seeker's achievements according to his transferable skills.

Heading The section at the top of a resume, composed of the job seeker's name, address, and contact information (phone, fax, and e-mail).

horizontal career move Taking a new job that is of equal status to the one the person currently holds within a given field.

ISP (Internet Service Provider) A company that offers dial-up Internet access.

job agent A service provided by some online resume banks that sorts through job listings and then e-mails the job seeker only those listings that match his job-search criteria.

Job Objective A brief statement near the top of a resume that states the job seeker's goal. This section can also be called Objective, Career Objective, or Career Goal, whichever fits the individual's situation.

keywords The terms an employer enters into a resume database search engine to scour the database for the ideal job candidate. A job seeker places these terms near the top of his e-resume in a Keyword section or distributes them throughout his resume so that the search engine will identify him for certain job openings.

leading The space between lines of text. You can adjust the leading of individual lines to accent headings and increase ease of reading.

modem   A piece of hardware that allows a computer to connect to the telephone system in order to access the Internet or to fax documents.

network   A carefully crafted web of people that has you in the center. Made of invisible threads that extend from you to all the people you know, to the people they know, and so on, your network is a conduit for information and favors.

networking card   A hybrid between a business card and a resume: a small card with the job seeker's name, contact info, and key professional qualifications.

nondisclosure   Not mentioning something. This is not the same as lying (telling something that isn't true). Nondisclosure is acceptable on a resume; lying is not!

Optical Character Recognition (OCR) software   A computer's tool for converting an electronic image into electronic text, which can then be searched for keywords and manipulated into new formats such as database files.

paragraph   In word-processing jargon, a paragraph is any text that begins after a hard return (pressing Return or Enter on your keyboard) and ends with the next hard return.

passive verb   A verb that tells what happened to someone or something. For example, "A raise *was given* to me."

point size   A measurement used by typographers to gauge the size of type. The larger the number of the point, the larger the letter, number, or symbol.

Portable Document Format (PDF)   A very reliable type of file used for sending and receiving documents through e-mail as attached files. PDFs are known for their ability to maintain fonts, graphics, and layout specifications. To create a PDF you must have Adobe Acrobat™ software. And the recipient of the PDF must have Adobe Acrobat™ in order to open and read the file.

post your resume online   To place an electronic version of your resume on the Internet for employers and recruiters to view.

Professional Experience   The midsection in the chronological resume that contains a job seeker's work history and achievement statements. That section may also be called Professional Accomplishments, Career Achievements, Achievements, Selected Accomplishments, or Experience.

professional title   This could be an official job title a person has held or simply the professional role she's qualified to fill. For instance, a resume writer could use any of the following professional titles at the top of her resume: Resume Writer, Resume Consultant, Career Counselor, or Career-Development Professional. The writer would chose her professional title based on how she was using her resume.

resume   A short account of one's professional experience and qualifications, typically used by a job applicant. Resumes are also used for projects that don't involve a job search, such as business plans, school applications, and consulting proposals.

resume bank   An electronic database that holds many resumes. Most resume banks have search capabilities to select resumes according to job objective, resume headline, and keywords specified by the employer or headhunter.

salary   The amount of money one brings home in paychecks in a year. Not be confused with *compensation*, which is one's salary, benefits (such as insurance and retirement plan), and perks (such as travel and time off).

scanning   The process of turning a hard-copy document into an electronic image.

search engine   A software tool that uses keywords to locate specific sites on the World Wide Web, particular files within a database, or specified words within a text document.

smart quotes   Quotation marks that curl around the words that they enclose. (Also called curly quotes.)

snail mail   A slang term for what the U.S. Postal Service delivers.

stupid quotes   Quotation marks that do not curl around the words that they enclose. (Also called straight quotes.)

Summary of Qualifications   A section on a resume that contains a brief set of points that say the job seeker is qualified for his job objective. This section can also be called Highlights of Qualifications, Qualifications, Highlights, Summary, or Profile.

template   A formatted guideline, not a boilerplate (a rigid form in which you simply fill in the blanks).

Text Only   Text without fancy formatting such as bold, indents, italics, or varied type sizes. This style of text is ideal for e-mailing your resume or distributing it online.

thank-you note   A short letter of appreciation. A thank-you note for a job-search favor sent to a friend can be handwritten or typed on any size sheet of paper or note card. When sent to an employer, your letter should be typed on an 8½" × 11" sheet of paper.

upload a document   To transfer a document from your computer to a remote computer or to an Internet site.

URL (Universal Resource Locator)   An address that you type into the browser in order to access (or go to) a particular Web site. It's also known as a Web address.

vertical career move   Making a transition to a higher job level within the same profession or industry.

vitae   The possessive form of *vita*, which means life. Therefore "life's course" is "curriculum vitae." Life is just plain *vita*. See also *curriculum vitae*.

voice mail   Messages left on someone's telephone answering machine or service.

Work History   A section on a resume that may include paid and unpaid work (because work is work, whether it's done for free or for hire).

Portfolio of Sample Resumes

In this appendix, you'll find examples of just about every kind of resume you could ever need. Take some time to examine all the different varieties and styles to find the ones that best suit your needs.

Joseph W. Leichter

123 Hawthorne Street, Apt. 1 • Cicero, Illinois 12345 • (123) 123-1234

JOB OBJECTIVE

Communications Manager/Writer/Editor

SUMMARY OF QUALIFICATIONS

- 10 years as a professional communications specialist, writer and editor for high-profile organizations and individuals.

- Experience in front-line positions requiring maturity and sound judgment to handle sensitive and volatile communications.

- Skilled at becoming an "expert" in complicated subjects and translating them into lay terms for the media, government bodies and the public.

- Proficient at:

Press releases	News reporting	Column writing
PR material	Speeches	Letters to the editor
Op-ed pieces	Legislation	Humor pieces
Editorials	Sports reporting	Reviews

PROFESSIONAL EXPERIENCE

1994-present **Media Specialist/Senior Account Executive**
KING & KIRBY COMMUNICATIONS, Chicago, IL
Assist clients in developing their messages and presenting them effectively to the media.

- Managed a Chicago department store campaign that won "Best Communications Package," an annual public relations award presented by the Chicago Publicity Club.

- Instigated a public demand for local representation on a regional governmental body. Wrote press releases that led to newspaper coverage and supporting editorials. Authored resolutions passed by three city councils.

- Played a significant role in managing a unique public relations program that saved the jobs of 600 workers facing termination. Wrote releases, arranged press conferences and served as media spokesperson.

- Edited material for Chicago's only successful pro-development election campaign in 1995.

- Help clients prepare for press conferences, governmental hearings, council meetings and other forums where effective presentation is crucial.

— Continued —

Joseph W. Leichter
Page 2

1992-1994   **Editor in Chief**
GREAT LAKES TEAMSTER NEWSPAPER, Chicago, IL
Produce a quality bi-monthly newspaper with circulation of 85,000.

- Manage the writing, photography, layout and on-time production of the publication in a highly-charged political environment.

- Upgraded quality by computerizing production and widening the scope of coverage.

- Serve as media spokesperson. Write news releases, speeches and PR pieces.

- Reported on first open election in the history of the Teamsters. Served as liaison among lawyers, election overseers and local unions in the publication of critical election notices.

1990-1992   **Assignment Editor/Reporter**
LAKE MICHIGAN NEWS SERVICE, Chicago, IL
Managed news reporting, editing and client relations for this regional wire service with 120 clients including top print and broadcast news outlets.

- Supervised staff of 15 reporters. Selected stories for assignment. Edited up to 50 stories a day.

- Scooped Chicago media with major developments in the case of serial murderer Leon Rosetti and the arrest of sport celebrity Dave Russo on sexual assualt charges.

1989-1990   **Administrative Aide to Councilman Fred Luna**
CITY OF CHICAGO, CITY COUNCIL
Managed this high-profile office under constant media scrutiny.

- Authored legislation, summarized Council agendas, and wrote news releases and letters on behalf of Councilman Luna.

- Represented the councilman before committees to present legislation.

EDUCATION

B.A., Journalism, 1988
Sigma Chi Scholars Club, Dean's List
Northwestern University, Chicago, IL

Juliette Lanier

12 Lanai Street • San Francisco, CA 12345 • (123) 123-1234

Creative Manager/Producer of award-winning media
for prominent national and local clients.

PROFESSIONAL EXPERIENCE

ACCOUNT MANAGER, National Media Promotions, Inc., San Francisco, CA, 1998-pres.
Producer of corporate communications: multimedia, film, and video. Clients include:

Intel	Levi Strauss
Apple Computer	Clorox Company
Foote, Cone & Belding	Nestle Beverage Company
Ketchum Communications	California Lottery

- Increased billings 200% and established company as one of the premiere local producers of progressive media by introducing an innovative production approach that appealed to a wider client base.
- Secured high volume of projects through the creative bidding process, making exciting and persuasive pitches.
- Increased production efficiency by managing multiple projects simultaneously including client relations, vendors, schedules, and deadlines.

ACCOUNT MANAGER, Music Productions, San Francisco, CA, 1995-1997
A theatrical and stage design company with budgets ranging from $20K to $1+M.
Productions included:

Rolling Stones Tour	San Francisco Black and White Ball
The Doors (movie set)	Corporate product launches

- Ensured smooth productions by supervising budgets, conceptual development, design, vendor coordination, and on-site event management of complicated projects.
- Maintained excellent client relations; attended to details, deadlines, and budgets.

ASSISTANT TO DIRECTOR, On Set Company, New York, NY, 1994
A film company created to produce a movie based on the novel *On Set.*

- As director's right hand, served as liaison to talent and department heads, and managed day-to-day details.
- Personally handled local bit and extra casting. Coordinated wardrobe, hairstyling, and makeup for extras.

ASSISTANT PRODUCTION MANAGER, You're On Film & Video, San Francisco, CA, 1993
Formerly the largest full-service film and video company in San Francisco.

- Scheduled and facilitated national commercial shoots. Booked freelance and in-house camera crews. Handled equipment and prop rentals.

EDUCATION: BA, Communication and Social Science, 1993, UC Berkeley

Bruce Malloy
1234 Barkley Blvd., Apt. #1, Philadelphia, PA 12345
(123) 123-1234, brucemalloy@thenet.net

ORGANIZATION DEVELOPMENT CONSULTANT
with more than 10 years in management. Expertise in:

- Program design and implementation
- Team development and facilitation
- Crisis management and prevention
- Communication planning (writing, speaking, and media relations)
- Customer needs assessment

EXPERIENCE

Present UNIVERSITY OF PENNSYLVANIA
M.A. Candidate, Human Resources and Organization Development

1988-99 AMERICAN MEDICAL CARE PROGRAM
Administrative Manager, National Office, Pittsburgh, 1995-99
Executive Assistant, Physician Liaison, National Office, Pittsburgh, 1992-95
Senior Public Affairs Representative, Northern Pennsylvania Region, 1990-92
Public Affairs Representative, Northern Pennsylvania Region, 1988-90

Selected Accomplishments

- Trained multidisciplinary teams throughout the U.S. to identify and correct management and systems problems, thereby reducing law suits, enhancing public image, and maintaining revenue growth.

- Designed communication programs to promote understanding of strategic change efforts to improve the cost structure of this $11 billion organization.

- Developed national assessment process to determine the largest driver of overall costs.

- Oversaw design and implementation of a management training and mentoring program which increased the quality of professionalism and administrative efficiency nationwide.

- Developed the $21 million Wright Memorial Fund to support research and innovation projects to improve service delivery.

1987-88 THE AIDS PROJECT, Philadelphia, PA
Executive Director

1981-87 THE WHITE HOUSE, Washington, D.C.
Director, First Lady's Correspondence Office, 1986-87
Correspondence Assistant, 1985-86
Senior Mail Analyst, 1981-85

EDUCATION

M.A. Candidate, Human Resources and Organization Development
University of Pennsylvania, Philadelphia, PA

B.S., 1982, Georgetown University, School of Foreign Service, Washington, D.C.

Consulting

333

HUGH R. DMITRI
123 Rudolph Street • San Francisco, CA 12345 • (123) 123-1234

AVIATION CONSULTANT

Strategic Partnerships   Negotiations   International Relations

CAREER SUMMARY

- 20 years experience in the international aviation industry, with a strong record of building consensus between labor and management through vision, creativity and a collaborative approach.
- An excellent and persuasive communicator, able to convey concepts with clarity and directness to diverse audiences at all organizational levels.

PROFESSIONAL EXPERIENCE

STRATEGIC PARTNERSHIPS
- Worked closely with other international union leaders within the Star Alliance to create a cohesive voice for nine flight attendant organizations.
- Developed a strong, ongoing partnership between flight attendants and senior management of Air Canada's Onboard Services through collaborative decision-making.
- Coordinated the work of 16 committees in addressing member concerns. Committees include: Safety & Health, Grievances, Insurance & Retirement, Hotel & Transportation, Schedules and Employee Assistance.

NEGOTIATIONS
- Chief negotiator for contracts between Air Canada and 8,000 flight attendants worldwide. Administered contracts via direct discussion, mediation and arbitration.
- Led the Association of Flight Attendants in controversial employee ownership negotiations with United Airlines.
- As primary liaison between flight attendants and Air Canada management, implemented interest-based bargaining in the 1997 contract negotiations process, resulting in a landmark, 10-year contract valued at over $1 billion.

—continued—

HUGH R. DMITRI
Page Two

COMMUNICATION & INTERNATIONAL RELATIONS

- Lobbied national and international governmental agencies on critical issues within the aviation industry, educating officials on matters including taxation, occupational health and safety, and global employee/government relations.
- Wrote proposals for contract bargaining, discussed final language with management, and delivered informative presentations to worldwide membership to explain contract terms, answer questions and prepare for ratification.
- Facilitated regular meetings in 20 international cities to discuss current issues and resolve concerns relevant to the staff at each location.
- As chief spokesperson of the Association of Flight Attendants, prepared and delivered interviews and remarks to media representatives, including print, television and radio.

Consulting

WORK HISTORY

| 1991-pres. | President (volunteer) | Air Canada Master Executive Council, Toronto, Canada |
| 1980-pres. | Flight Attendant | Air Canada, San Francisco, CA |

EDUCATION

B.S., Architecture, University of Michigan, Ann Arbor, MI
Negotiations Training, George Meany Center for Labor Studies, Silver Spring, MD

Patty Henderson

123 Toledo Street • Burlington, VT 12345 • Office: 123-123-1234
Home: 123-123-1234 • phenderson@thenet.net

JOB OBJECTIVE

Reengineering Consultant

HIGHLIGHTS OF QUALIFICATIONS

- Accomplished Reengineering Manager with proven ability to design and implement processes for organizational improvement.
- Eight years as an effective manager within the nonprofit and for-profit sectors.
- Recognized throughout career for initiating productive change.

PROFESSIONAL ACCOMPLISHMENTS

1996-pres.   **University of Vermont, Burlington**
REENGINEERING PROJECT MANAGER, Office of Residential Programs, 1999-pres.

- Manager of the reengineering process for a student services unit with 396 employees.
- Facilitated a reengineering training retreat for 21 managers.
- Collaborated with 10 managers to establish the unit's first vision and mission statements.
- Wrote project management guidelines and determined appropriate software to manage the implementation of the reengineering process.
- Gathered reengineering recommendations from internal and external customers by conducting focus groups and Internet forums.
- Currently creating a multi-media presentation to market the benefits of the reengineering project to executive managers and employees.

RESIDENTIAL LIFE COORDINATOR, 1996-1999

- Developed a two-year restructuring proposal to save $200,000 and improve customer service. Proposal resulted in my promotion to Reengineering Project Manager.
- Redesigned and streamlined a recruitment and selection process for 150 staff members.
- Analyzed services and reorganized a program serving 1100 students from 20 countries.
- Managed the overall operations of a complex that housed 1000 students.
- Supervised and evaluated 80 staff members via eight coordinators.

1995-1996   **University of Denver, CO**
COORDINATOR, Housing and Dining Services Department

- Managed the overall operation of a residential facility for 1300 students.
- Created and instructed a 16-week training seminar for 100 employees.
- Chaired a committee that implemented a selection process for 65 new staff members.
- Supervised 84 staff members via four assistant coordinators.

1993-1995   **Loyola University, Chicago, IL**
PROGRAM TRAINING COORDINATOR, State of Illinois Special Project, 1995

- Designed the first "train the trainer" course to teach 25 educators to train 700 employees.

FULL-TIME STUDENT, 1993-1995

— Continued —

Patty Henderson, Page Two

1989-1993   **Perniper's South Corporation, Carbondale, IL**
RESTAURANT MANAGER
- Managed a full-service restaurant and catering service that seated 300.
- Trained and supervised 32 employees and managed their payroll and benefits.
- Administered complex allocations of $600K in annual revenue.
- Evaluated costs, inventory, and service contracts.
- Oversaw preventive maintenance for the facility and equipment.

EDUCATION

Master of Arts, Education (Specialization: Higher Education), summa cum laude, **1995**

Loyola University, Chicago, IL
Coursework included: Recruitment and Evaluation   Research and Evaluation
Training Theories   Tests and Measurements

Bachelor of Arts, Psychology (Specialization: Industrial and Organizational), 1993
cum laude
Loyola University, Chicago, IL
Coursework included: Management   Industrial Psychology
Business Communications   Personnel Psychology
Organizational Behavior   Psychology of Leadership

Professional Training, 1996-1999

IMPAQ   Taking Advantage of Change
Pappas Consulting Group Inc.   Reengineering Higher Education
Price Waterhouse   Reengineering Human Resources
Fred Pryor Seminars   Project Management
Managing Multiple Priorities
Self Directed Work Teams
Developing a Budget
Empower Perspectives   Conflict In Organizations
UC Berkeley   Diversity Facilitator Training
Customer Survey Methods
Developing Budget Initiatives

Readings:
Reengineering the Corporation by James Champy and Michael Hammer
Reengineering Management by James Champy
Business Reengineering: The Survival Guide by Andrews & Stalick

RECOGNITIONS

National Association of Female Executives
Honorary Membership, 1999
University of Vermont, Burlington
Chancellor's Recognition for Diversity Education, 1996, 1997, 1998, 1999
Chancellor's Outstanding Staff Award Nominee, 1998
American College Personnel Association
Multicultural Program Award Nominee, 1998
Eastern Association of College Housing Officers
New Professional Award, 1998

Consulting

Jason Manriquez

001 Central Avenue, #1 • La Habra, California 12345 • (123) 123-1234

Elementary School Teacher

PROFILE

- Elementary School Teacher with experience working with culturally and linguistically diverse students.
- Expert at designing and implementing Whole Language programs.
- Fluent in Spanish.
- Currently applying for Language Development Specialist Certificate.

EDUCATION AND CREDENTIAL

California State Multiple Subject (Elementary) Teaching Credential, 1994

M.A., Educational Psychology, 1994
Developmental Teacher Education Program
CALIFORNIA STATE UNIVERSITY, Fullerton, CA

B.A., Cultural Anthropology, 1992
NEW COLLEGE OF CALIFORNIA, San Francisco, CA

TEACHING EXPERIENCE

1994-present **Elementary School Teacher,** EUCLID SCHOOL, Fullerton, CA

- Taught primary grade classes in this State Compensatory Education School with diverse student populations including: Latino   European American   Pacific Islander
  Filipino   African American   East Indian
- Designed and implemented developmental, student-centered, integrated curriculum covering all subject areas.
- Created and taught Whole Language program, including Writers' Workshop.
- Used Sheltered English and bilingual (Spanish) instructional techniques to help students of diverse linguistic backgrounds build content knowledge.
- Conducted parent conferences in both Spanish and English.
- Served as Master Teacher for five Fullerton State University student teachers.
- As a member of Euclid's Leadership Team, helped write four-year improvement plan and conducted staff inservices.
- Played active role in developing and writing Patterson's Achieving Schools proposal which was chosen one of fifteen in California for review in national competition.
- Planned and conducted staff in-service on teaching the concept of multiplication throughout the grade levels.

— Continued —

Jason Manriquez
Page 2

1993   **Student Teacher,** six mon., ARROWHEAD ELEMENTARY SCHOOL, Anaheim, CA
- Participated in an innovative university/public school liaison project.
- Worked extensively with Spanish and Cantonese speaking students, grades 1-6, using Sheltered English as an instructional technique.
- Implemented on-going dialogue journal writing for first grade Cantonese speaking students to increase English literacy.
- Conducted research and wrote Master's Project on the use of games to facilitate the development of emotional intelligence.

1992-1993   **Student Teacher,** six mon., BREA ELEMENTARY SCHOOL, Brea, CA

1992   **Student Teacher,** five mon., BALDWIN PARK ELEMENTARY SCHOOL, Baldwin Park, CA

1992   **Student Teacher,** two mon., GARDEN GROVE ELEMENTARY SCHOOL, Garden Grove, CA

1992   **Student Teacher,** two mon., ROWLAND ELEMENTARY SCHOOL, Rowland, CA

1990-1991   **Teacher,** ten mon., FULLERTON STATE UNIVERSITY CHILDREN'S SCHOOL, Fullerton, CA
- Participated in team instruction of children, ages six through eight.
- Planned and executed activities in the areas of language arts, math, science, computers, art, and dramatic play.
- Adapted and tested a language arts curriculum for children in the primary grades.

ADDITIONAL EXPERIENCE

1993   **Instructional Assistant,** ARTISTIC TALENT DEVELOPMENT PROGRAM, Los Angeles, CA
- Co-taught a poetry class for gifted and talented primary students.

1993   **Research Assistant,** CALIFORNIA STATE UNIVERSITY, Fullerton, CA
- Assisted in educational research by conducting experimental sessions and cleaning data.

1992   **Teaching Assistant,** CALIFORNIA STATE UNIVERSITY, Fullerton, CA
- Taught section of undergraduate cultural anthropology course. Supervised students and conducted review and study sessions.

Education

Charles Brunkley

123 Pennsylvania Street • Philadelphia, PA 12345 • (123) 123-1234

OBJECTIVE: Coach at Philadelphia High School

PROFILE

- Five years management experience combined with 20+ years experience in player and team development.
- Energetic coach with proven ability to build mental toughness in developing athletes.
- Skilled communicator; able to motivate diverse individuals to achieve group goals.
- Initiative, enthusiasm and uncompromising work ethic.
- Commitment to reestablishing the spirit and history in Philadelphia sports.

ACCOMPLISHMENTS

TEAM DEVELOPMENT
Philadelphia Youth Alternatives and the City of Philadelphia

- Patiently mentored young athletes, instilling:
  - Discipline, ownership and team spirit
  - Knowledge of the role and attitude of each position
  - Technique
  - Solid background in game and team history
- Developed winning teams by training players to work with each other's natural abilities.

Snowcap Designs

- Motivated top performance and reduced costly errors by maintaining clear written and verbal communications between management and front line staff.
- Trained and managed a staff of 12, setting a tone of teamwork, professionalism and respect.

MANAGEMENT
Snowcap Designs

- Directed all warehouse activities and operations for a 30,000 sq. ft. facility.
  - Coordinated priorities with other divisions to assure achievement of goals.
  - Negotiated with vendors to establish and maintain optimal rates and service relationships.
  - Oversaw inspections and ensured compliance with quality control measures.
  - Reorganized work areas and maintained facilities to maximize safety, security and efficiency.
- Managed an annual operating budget of $725,000.

Underground Railroad

- As liaison between staff and management, applied interpersonal skills and professionalism to improve communications around sensitive personnel issues.
- Entrusted by management to build an effective work team of up to 60 workers to complete large projects under deadline.

- continued -

Charles Brunkley
Page Two

WORK HISTORY

1994–99	Snowcap Designs, Philadelphia	WAREHOUSE MANAGER
1980–94	Underground Railroad, Liberty	WAREHOUSE SUPERVISOR (1987–94)
		WAREHOUSEMAN (1980–87)
1979	High-Five Distributions, Liberty	SHIPPING SUPERVISOR
		PACKER
1977–78	City of Philadelphia	RECREATION LEADER
1976	Philadelphia Youth Alternatives	COUNSELOR AIDE

VOLUNTEER COACHING

1999	Philadelphia Boys Club Basketball	COACH
1998	Liberty Little League	MANAGER
1996–97	Liberty Little League	COACH
1993–95	Liberty Adult Softball League	COACH
1982–84	Liberty High Girls Basketball	COACH
1981–82	Underground Railroad Basketball	COACH

EDUCATION

AA in Sociology, Liberty College, Liberty, PA
Diploma, Philadelphia High School, Philadelphia, PA

Education

ANTOINETTE REYNOLDS

1234 Smith Street • New York, NY 12345 • (123) 123-1234 • andireynolds@thenet.net

JOB OBJECTIVE

A Senior position in Operations for a regional insurance brokerage

SUMMARY OF QUALIFICATIONS

- More than 10 years experience as a Senior Operations Manager in the insurance industry, with emphasis on improving efficiency, productivity and organizational consistency.
- A skilled Human Resources manager, adept at matching top candidates with specific positions, and able to resolve concerns with sensitivity and objectivity.
- Known for resourcefulness in financial management and consolidation of functions, resulting in significant cost savings.

PROFESSIONAL EXPERIENCE

1989-pres. **BURNS INSURANCE OF NEW YORK,** New York, NY
Managing Director, New York Operations   1994-present
Division Director, Queens Operations   1989-94

Human Resources

- Oversaw recruitment of new brokers and support personnel via colleges, universities and job fairs. Developed internal standards and procedures for departmental hiring process.
- Worked closely with Training Manager to develop curriculum for training all new hires.
- Directed successful re-engineering efforts of all New York offices, maintaining respectful relations with staff and managing transition with clarity and grace.

Accounting / Financial Management

- Consolidated four accounting offices into one location, resulting in greater efficiency, streamlined operations and savings of over $500K in payroll alone.
- Conceived and developed customized financial reports for specific profit centers, based on in-depth knowledge of operations and the needs of divisional managers.

Legal

- Coordinated internal legal activity: errors and omissions, labor, regulatory and licensing issues.
- Acted as Security Coordinator to ensure compliance with regulatory agencies.
- Oversaw and managed agency, brokerage and vendor contracts.

Administrative & IT Support

- Initiated Help Desk for quick resolution of internal software/hardware problems by IT staff.
- Implemented new travel policy with effective controls, resulting in greater efficiency and consistency in travel planning and a $100K reduction in costs.
- Directed an exhaustive search for new office space, negotiated lease agreements and secured sub-tenants in two locations, resulting in savings of $2.5M.

Bonnie Sykes

123 Hamilton Place • Los Angeles, CA 12345 • (123) 123-1234

Logistics Executive

with expertise in:

Customer Relations	Distribution Systems
Strategic Planning	Operations Analysis
Retail Services	Team Leadership

SELECTED PROFESSIONAL ACHIEVEMENTS

1980-present GOTCHA SPORTSWEAR, Los Angeles, CA

Director, Retail Services, 1996-present	**Senior Distribution Analyst**, 1984-88
Manager, Customer Service, 1994-96	**Distribution Analyst**, 1982-84
Manager, Distribution and Services, 1992-94	**Financial Analyst**, 1981-82
Manager, Distribution Administration, 1988-92	**Manager of Training**, 1980-81

- Played executive role in the $10M, four-year re-engineering for Gotcha's U.S. $200M business.

- Managed closure of two distribution centers totaling 750K sq. ft. and started up two new distribution centers totaling 1.5M sq. ft. Planning and execution:

Inventory ($50M) and systems migration	Order processing and fulfillment
Physical product movement	Sales coordination

- Saved over $2M in logistics-related customer claims and increased retail product sell-through by introducing a new customer service concept that built liaisons between company logistics personnel and retail counterparts.

- Supervised direct staff of 10 and indirect reports of 40 who planned and managed the company's 1984 Olympics Host Program for over 500 retail executives and sweepstakes winners.

- Earned one team and two individual Gotcha Awards, the company's highest distinction for superlative professional achievement.

EDUCATION

M.S.W., California State University, San Francisco
B.A., California State University, Sacramento

PROFESSIONAL AFFILIATIONS

Featured speaker and member:	Council of Logistics Management
	National Retail Federation
	American Apparel Manufacturers Association
	International Customer Service Association
Featured speaker:	Strategic Research Institute
Member:	VICS (Voluntary Inter-industry Communications Standards) Committees

343

Randall Andrews

123 Easy Street • Nantucket, MA 12345 • cellphone (123) 123-1234

Automotive Service Manager/Director

SUMMARY OF QUALIFICATIONS

- Ten years automotive dealership service management experience building on 15 years as an automotive technician. Skills include:

Management	CSI	Training
Financials	Quality Control	Technical Support
Warranty and Policy	Team-building	Regulatory Compliance

RELEVANT ACCOMPLISHMENTS
JOHN QUINCY LEXUS DEALERSHIP

MANAGEMENT

- Recognized by the dealer principal for raising profitability through cost controls on supplies, outside service companies and vendors.
- Built repeat business and customer loyalty by:
    - Ensuring highest quality repair status.
    - Educating and problem-solving with customers on technical issues and vehicle operations.
- Improved customer satisfaction by implementing the Lexus-Argon service improvement program.
    - Worked with an Argon consultant to study workflow efficiency.
    - Instituted a program that streamlined service.
    - Implemented standardized written procedures.
- Strengthened the dealership reputation by providing expert technical explanations and resolving product disputes between customer, dealer and manufacturers.
- Succeeded at controlling company loss by favorably negotiating public liability disputes.
- One of 10 Lexus dealers selected out of more than 300 to participate in the NEARB Emission Parts Validation Study based on management of the program.

TEAM-BUILDING

- Promoted an above-average level of expertise among technical staff.
    - Maintained a standard of up-to-date O.E.M. training for all technicians.
    - Identified and corrected deficiencies in procedures and products.
    - Created and directed an "in-house" training and review program to develop new skills and "fixes."
- Cultivated an extraordinary level of technician loyalty, achieving a 10+ year tenure among 75% of employees over a 12-year period.
- Fostered teamwork that motivated employees to achieve their highest potential.

- continued -

Randall Andrews
Page Two

RELEVANT ACCOMPLISHMENTS (continued)

TECHNICAL
- Achieved a Master Auto Technician Certification through the Institute of Automotive Service Excellence (ASE).
- Served as Special Advisor to New England District Service Managers Advisory Committee Seminars.
- Special Advisor to the University of MA engineering students competing in Lexus Motor Company national invitational to develop a fuel efficient hybrid prototype.

WORK HISTORY

1994–present   CRAFTS IN WOOD, Nantucket, MA
           Operations Manager

1979–1994   JOHN QUINCY LEXUS DEALERSHIP, Quincy, MA
           Service Manager (1986–1994)
           Shop Foreman (1984–1986)
           Customer Service Advisor (1982–1984)

EDUCATION & TRAINING

Human Relations & Organizational Business program
University of MA—College of Professional Studies

Advanced Warranty and Policy, Lexus
Advanced Customer Satisfaction, Lexus

Human Relations & Management Training, Hoover Company
ADA • Family Leave Act • Employee and Company Rights

Business law coursework, Cape Cod Community College, Cape Cod, MA

345

Dave J. Ross

123 Newbury Street • Boston, Massachusetts 12345 • (123) 123-1234 • d_ross@thenet.net

JOB OBJECTIVE: Staff Accountant in a public accounting firm

SUMMARY OF QUALIFICATIONS

- Successfully completed **Uniform CPA Examination** in 1998.

- Four years experience in all levels of the accounting process, including:

A/R	Internal audits	Individual returns
A/P	Quality assurance	Partnership returns
Payroll	Inventory control	1120S
G/L	Budget management	C. Corporation

- Well-organized, focused and productive with proven ability to complete projects on time.

- Track record of developing strong client relationships, anticipating customer needs and providing timely, proactive service.

- Commitment to furthering the success of team members, as well as delivering quality individual performance in a high-pressure environment.

- Knowledgeable in the use of Excel and professional accounting software.

EDUCATION & CERTIFICATIONS

Certificate in Accountancy, Bentley College, Waltham, MA
BS in Accounting, Babson College, Wellesley, MA

RELEVANT ACCOMPLISHMENTS

ACCOUNTING

- Consistently met deadlines in preparing financial data for private clients, Ross Jewelers and Polaroid, including:

Payroll	Compilations	Tax returns
Reviews	Financial statements	

- Tracked inventory worth more than $4 million for Ross Jewelers.

- Reduced client tax obligation by effectively communicating with management and accounting departments.

BUSINESS DEVELOPMENT & MANAGEMENT

- Managed installation and conversion from manual ledgers to an in-house computerized accounting system at Ross Jewelers.
  - Researched and selected the system and software.
  - Communicated with software consultants to successfully resolve problems.
  - Trained staff and coordinated troubleshooting on the new automated system.

- Devised a marketing program for Ross Jewelers which expanded the customer base and increased profitability.

WORK HISTORY

1998–present	Accounting Consultant	
1997–1998	Medical Technologist	Massachussetts General Hospital, Boston, MA
1989–1997	Medical Technologist	Boston City Hospital, Boston, MA
1986–1989	Staff Accountant	Ross Jewelers, Boston, MA
1985–1986	Staff Accountant	Polaroid, Cambridge, MA

Pauline Yee

1234 14th Street • Boston, MA 12345 • (123) 123-1234 • PaulineYee@thenet.net

JOB OBJECTIVE: Accounting Manager

SUMMARY OF QUALIFICATIONS

- Seven years in finance management for organizations ranging from $30M-100M.
- Experienced supervisor with a management style that motivates staff productivity.
- Practical background in accounting.

PROFESSIONAL EXPERIENCE

1998-present **Accounting Manager and Human Resource Manager,** TNT, INC., Boston, MA

A hardware/software manufacturing concern that grew 38% each year during tenure.

- Created accounting control systems from manual system, enabling existing staff to support growth at no increase in costs.
- Drafted and enforced accounting policies and procedures in compliance with GAAP that provided the basis for all departmental budgeting.
- Prepared and guided company through its first external audit, allowing TNT to address other forms of working capitalization.

1995-1997 **Accounting Manager,** CATHOLIC CHARITIES OF BOSTON, Boston, MA

A non-profit corporation comprised of 36 agencies with an overall budget of $56M.

- Established separate accounting system to manage a $2M fund and oversaw its consolidation with agency financials.
- Streamlined AP/AR systems in compliance with federal and state fund restrictions.
- Helped division directors with budget drafts at RFP level.
- Ensured success of program funding by analyzing feasibility of program proposals.
- Identified agency's insurance needs and standardized coverage for all 11 divisions.

1993-1995 **A/R and Credit Manager,** PARADIGM TECHNOLOGIES, INC., Boston, MA

A hard drive manufacturer with $100M in annual sales.

- Cleaned up AR system and brought it within 90% of agreement, enabling company to borrow against that amount.
- Established credit and risk assessment policies.
- Assisted in accounting system conversion from manual to automated.

1988-1992 **Systems Analyst,** HERMAN, RIGHTLAND, FORM & MC MALLEY, Boston, MA

The 65th largest law firm in the U. S. with multiple locations worldwide.

- Served as troubleshooter for accounting department's computer conversion.
- Provided system training and support to three departments.

EDUCATION

B.A., Boston University, 1988
Dun & Bradstreet: Credit Risk Assessment, Credit Management, Finance Management

JEFFREY M. CULLEN

001 Potrero Street, San Francisco, CA 12345   Home: 415-123-2345, Work: 415-123-1234

OBJECTIVE: Position in International Human Resources

SUMMARY OF QUALIFICATIONS
- Intercultural sensitivity, having lived abroad (Europe and Asia) for over ten years.
- Ability to represent a company with professionalism and confidence.
- Highly developed communication skills: written, verbal and presentational.

INTERNATIONAL EXPERIENCE
- As official translator, facilitated communications between Americans living in Switzerland and local government and community officials.
- Developed curriculum on "survival" techniques for Americans living abroad, which was incorporated into teaching program at the U.S. Embassy School.
- Taught English Conversation to Chinese businessmen, spouses and children, while living in Hong Kong, China for six months.
- Recognized by International Academy of Business for outstanding research project and written report on the European Economic Community, involving multiple markets and business issues.
- Traveled extensively throughout Europe as a citizen abroad, age 12-21. Fluent in German and French.

PROJECT MANAGEMENT
- Assisted Manpower clients in career transition regarding educational steps needed to achieve professional goals.
- Recruited and interviewed Asian high school students for University of San Francisco.
- Trained new Gap administrative and sales employees from diverse cultural backgrounds.
- Ranked one of the top recruiters for the Salvation Army's "Shelter for All" event.
- Organized international and national projects for senior stock broker at MBNA.
- Maximized operations in University of San Francisco French department, as sole office administrator for six professors and their students.

WORK HISTORY
Manpower Placement Center, San Francisco, CA, Client Services Associate, 1999-present
Omega Corporation, Hong Kong, China, Teacher of English Conversation to Chinese, 1999
Salvation Army, San Francisco, CA, Intern/Events Coordinator, 1998-99

Mostly Concurrent with Education
The Gap, Inc., San Francisco, CA, Sales Representative, 1995-98
International Academy of Business, Berkeley, CA, Research Associate, 1994
MBNA, San Francisco, California, Assistant to Senior Stockbroker, 1993
University of San Francisco, San Francisco, CA, French Department Resource Assistant, 1992
U.S. Embassy School, Geneva, Switzerland, Interpreter/Instructor, 1992

EDUCATION
University of San Francisco, San Francisco, CA
Bachelor of Arts, International Relations/Business, 1997

SUSAN BAKER
2222 Main Street
San Francisco, CA 12345
(415) 123-1234
suebaker@domain.com

OBJECTIVE: An Administrative/Management position in Human Resources focusing on Project/Database Management

SUMMARY OF QUALIFICATIONS

- Eight years' experience in management and administration, with a reputation for high quality service to both internal and external clients.

- Exceptional organizational skills; able to integrate details and coordinate tasks to accomplish overall project goals.

- An excellent manager, able to match candidates with specific positions and encourage development of career and company objectives.

- Experience in database management, administration and coordination.

PROFESSIONAL EXPERIENCE

HUMAN RESOURCES MANAGEMENT & ADMINISTRATION
PeopleSoft

- Assessed organizational needs and guided staff in the development of skills and core competencies to further individual and organizational growth.

- Recruited, hired and trained top candidates for customer service positions.

- Created new-hire orientation and training procedures. Facilitated trainings of all new hires.

- Directed departmental changes resulting in a self-supporting and cohesive work group structure.

- Consistently inspired excellent staff performance and respectful relations in a pressurized, multi-tasking environment.

- Oversaw the delivery, registration and administration of 100 programs per year.

— Continued —

Human Resources

349

SUSAN BAKER
Page Two

PRODUCT DEVELOPMENT & PROJECT MANAGEMENT

PeopleSoft

- Co-leader in the design and development of custom software to automate administrative, tracking and financial management/reporting processes.

- Project director of membership program: Analyzed market research, developed strategies to attract and retain clients, initiated and implemented innovative programs for members and prospects.

- Assisted in creation of online registration form to enhance client accessibility to services via the Internet.

- Managed database to ensure integrity and quality of data, and timeliness of targeted mailings.

EMPLOYMENT HISTORY

1990-present	PeopleSoft, Pleasanton, CA	
	Human Resources Director	*1997-present*
	Education Manager	*1994-97*
	Customer Service Coordinator	*1993-94*
	Customer Service Representative	*1990-93*
1988-1990	Clear Concepts, Santa Fe, NM	
	Retail Management & Sales	

EDUCATION & TRAINING

B.S. Business Administration - University of Massachusetts, Amherst, MA
Computer skills include: MS Word, Excel, FoxPro, FileMaker Pro, and Internet

JASON MICHAEL WHARTON

123 Real Street • San Francisco, CA 12345 • (123) 123-1234

OBJECTIVE: A Project Management position focusing on Program Development and Training

PROFILE

- Highly organized, diligent and responsible, able to create and execute complex projects and programs to meet organizational needs.
- An enthusiastic and thorough trainer and team member, able to convey information with clarity, patience and the terminology appropriate to specific audiences.
- A quick learner, able to absorb new material with ease.

SELECTED ACCOMPLISHMENTS

Project Management / Program Development

- Conceived, planned and directed a summer music camp for children, reaching participation of up to 150 within three years. Designed curriculum, recruited staff, and developed all creative, advertising and promotional materials.
- Developed an extensive choir program for adults and children, including weekly rehearsal scheduling, event and performance planning, promotion and budgeting for seven distinct choirs.
- Set up and grew an alternative educational program, utilizing crafts, dramatic arts and music to spark interest and increase member participation.
- Utilized creative and methodical research techniques to explore and analyze innovative educational topics and presented findings to experts at the University of Colorado.

Training

- Designed and delivered illuminating and enjoyable classes as part of educational program; presented new material and developed testing for student evaluation.
- Trained individual vocal students in technique, production and performance readiness. Taught choirs of 8-50 members ranging in age from 5-95.
- Selected to train all new restaurant hires, based on thoroughness and the ability to communicate effectively with diverse individuals and groups.

Team Building & Client Relations

- As professional scorer, discussed grading criteria and interpretations for student projects in English, Science and Music in order to reach consensus with scoring team members, consistently maintaining productivity and cohesiveness.
- Provided leadership and counseling to church members to resolve concerns and maintain smooth relations between staff and membership.
- Regularly complimented on quality of service and client satisfaction at restaurant and church positions.

(continued)

Project Management

JASON MICHAEL WHARTON
123 Real Street • San Francisco, CA 12345 • (123) 123-1234

WORK HISTORY

1997-98	**Professional Scorer**	
	AMERICA SCORING, INC., Princeton, NJ	
1995-97	**Full-time Ph.D. candidate**	
	UNIVERSITY OF COLORADO, Boulder, CO	
1993-95	**Restaurant Associate**	
	BERTUCCI ORGANICS, Boulder, CO	
1987-93	**Music Director / Educational Program Development**	
	East End and St. Anne's Churches, Mayberry, NC	

EDUCATION

Ph.D. candidate, Music Literature, University of Colorado, Boulder, CO, 1995-97
M.M., Carlyle University, Asheville, NC, 1992
B.A., Central State College, Mulhill, NC, 1987

RAE LONDON

111 Halloran Street, #3 • San Francisco, CA 11111 • (123) 123-1234

OBJECTIVE: A position in Project Management

PROFILE

- Nine years experience developing, implementing, and managing complex projects within time and budgetary constraints.

- An organized, detail-oriented, and conscientious self-starter, able to strategize and prioritize effectively to accomplish multiple tasks and stay calm under pressure.

- A highly skilled listener and communicator, able to assess client needs and convey necessary information with clarity and enthusiasm.

- Computer skills include: MS Word, Excel, and Internet.

PROJECT MANAGEMENT ACCOMPLISHMENTS

- As Investigator, researched local businesses for state licensing purposes:
  - Interviewed clients to assess needs and establish rapport.
  - Inspected sites for compliance with state regulations.
  - Consulted with clients to explain procedures and respond to questions.
  - Mediated between client, community members, city and county planning departments, and law enforcement agencies to ensure communication flow and resolve concerns.
  - Prioritized and coordinated tasks to complete projects within deadlines.

- As Deputy Probation Officer, developed, marketed, and implemented a new job placement program for at-risk youth:
  - Created a manual of job skills for use by program educators.
  - Networked with local business and organizations to match youth with appropriate skills training or employment locations.
  - Achieved a strong record of success in a dynamic environment.

- Initiated, developed, and managed the creation and implementation of a "New Hire Manual" for SF County Probation Department employees:
  - Researched and organized materials for training curriculum.
  - Designed and delivered thorough and well-organized quarterly trainings to new hires.

- Supervised daily activities of 12 staff and 40 participants at Department of Licensing.

- Wrote comprehensive reports for supervisor's review throughout work history.

WORK HISTORY

1996-pres.	Investigator, State of California DEPT. OF LICENSING, San Francisco, CA
1990-96	Deputy Probation Officer SAN FRANCISCO COUNTY PROBATION DEPARTMENT, San Francisco, CA

EDUCATION: B.S., California State University, Sacramento, CA, 1990

Project Management

353

ROXY JEAN KENNEDY

123 Jones Street, #1 • Miami, FL 12345 • (123) 123-1234 • roxy1@thenet.net

CAREER GOAL

A position in Marketing & Promotions with an emphasis on Sales

SUMMARY OF QUALIFICATIONS

- Five years experience in marketing, promotions, and sales, with a flair for communicating effectively with people from diverse cultures.
- A highly organized and creative events coordinator.
- Flexible and energetic; skilled in multitasking to accomplish overall goals.

PROFESSIONAL EXPERIENCE

TECH TRAINING INTERNATIONAL, Palm Beach, FL   Sales & Marketing Consultant   1997-present
- Collaborated with promotional teams to coordinate grand opening events at new training facilities in Tampa, FL and Atlanta, GA.
- Built strong relationships with software vendors and negotiated agreements for customized trainings.
- Worked with marketing consultants to create incentives, generate leads, and attract new clients.
- Researched local trends and competition to identify opportunities for nationwide advertising spots and secure optimal market positioning.

BIG 5 INTERNATIONAL, LLP, New York, NY   Human Relations Specialist   1996-97
- Acted as primary liaison for international employees from Europe, Africa, and Asia Pacific: Secured visas, coordinated logistics, and guided the transition into U.S. culture and employment at the firm.
- Devised strategies and implemented both team-building and corporate-sponsored events, including Bay to Liberty, Home Chef, and Friday massage.
- Created and maintained an Intranet Web site for use by all employees.

KHAKIS R US, Hong Kong, China   Sales Representative / Merchandiser   1995-96
- Analyzed daily sales reports to identify market trends. Selected point-of-service marketing materials and created eye-catching displays for top-selling locations.
- Coached sales associates on key selling points of seasonal merchandise, and prepared products for presentation at national sales meetings.

ENTERTAIN U, Vienna, VA   Talent and Production Coordinator / Event Planner   1994-95
- Coordinated travel and performance logistics for national circus events, including an 18-elephant salute for the "Salute to Congress."
- Supported four Vice Presidents simultaneously in accomplishing multiple tasks within a high intensity, deadline-driven environment.

EDUCATION

B.A., Merchandising, Marymount University, Arlington, VA
Marketing emphasis, Digby Stewart College, London, England
Computer: MS Word, Excel, PowerPoint, Access, PeopleSoft, Lotus Notes

SANDRA O'MALLEY

123 Stonebridge, #2 • San Francisco, CA 94112 • (123) 123-1234 • somalley@ibm.net

OBJECTIVE: A Marketing Communications position within the high-tech industry

PROFILE

- A highly creative team member, able to brainstorm new ideas and deliver marketing concepts and presentations with clarity, enthusiasm and humor.

- A skilled listener, able to assess needs and develop programs and products that achieve results for a diverse clientele.

- An organized and detail-oriented professional with solid software skills and familiarity with dynamic high-tech environments.

SELECTED ACCOMPLISHMENTS

Marketing Communications & Sales

- Pitched creative ideas and "outside the box" projects to experts at San Francisco Design Group; discussed methods for realization and project improvements.

- Created an entirely new product line for UC students based on thorough research and perceived need, and completed all regulatory requirements and copyright procedures to ensure successful product launch.

- Quickly responded to in-person and telephone inquiries at Barnes & Noble, assisting customers with product selection and maintaining excellent relations within a fast-paced environment.

Technical

- Taught Adobe Photoshop, PageMaker, PowerPoint and MS Office Suite to diverse customers at Multimedia Graphics, Inc.

- Utilized 3D Studio MAX to develop innovative urban park in San Francisco and created animation for UC's School of Automated Design project.

- continued –

Sales/Marketing

355

SANDRA O'MALLEY
Page Two

Project Management

- Managed design, development and production of new product for College of Architecture students, which raised 40% of yearly funds.

- Completed project entitled *Digital Dynamics: A Live/Work Environment for a Software Designer:*
    - Conducted research and established priorities, tasks and work flow to meet strict deadlines.
    - Created an integrated high technology environment designed for optimal space utilization and productivity.
    - Designed and delivered impressive multimedia presentation to UC faculty, students and invited experts, utilizing 3D Studio MAX and AutoCAD 13.

WORK HISTORY

1997-pres.	**Sales Associate**	
	BARNES & NOBLE, San Francisco, CA	
1992-97	**Full-time Student**	
	UNIVERSITY OF CALIFORNIA (UC), Berkeley, CA	
1992	**Architectural Intern**	
	SAN FRANCISCO DESIGN GROUP, San Francisco, CA	

Additional experience includes: **Lab Assistant** for MULTIMEDIA GRAPHICS, INC. and **Research Team Member** at STANFORD UNIVERSITY and UNIVERSITY OF CALIFORNIA, BERKELEY.

EDUCATION

Bachelor of Architecture, cum laude, **University of California,** Berkeley, CA, 1997

FRANK GETTY

123 Fifth Street • San Jose, CA 12345 • (123) 123-1234 • fgetty1@thenet.net

Sales / Marketing Professional

QUALIFICATIONS

- An experienced high-tech professional with a broad base of industry knowledge, including OEMs, channels, end users and competitors.

- Skilled at product positioning and developing strategies for successful market penetration.

- Able to deliver dynamic sales and marketing presentations to diverse audiences.

PROFESSIONAL EXPERIENCE

1996-pres. **IBM,** San Jose, CA *Disk Drive Marketing Executive*

- Developed strategic plans based on customer needs, and trained business partners to penetrate target markets and increase market share.

- Delivered informative and convincing presentations on IBM storage strategy and business initiatives to business partners and end users.

- Coordinated and communicated daily marketing messages, promotions and incentives to business partners and end users.

1995-96 **AMDAHL,** San Jose, CA *Storage Systems Sales*

- Collaborated with mainframe client representatives to increase mid-range storage and server revenue within targeted accounts.

- Used knowledge of competitive products to determine successful sales and marketing strategies.

1993-95 **OPTI, INC.,** San Jose, CA *Regional Sales Manager*

- Designed and implemented the Optimum Value Partner Program, which included lead generation, direct marketing and co-marketing tools, for VARs and distributors throughout the United States and Asia Pacific.

- Coordinated business development projects, product positioning, incentives and motivational tools for channel sales team. Built Asia Pacific sales by 50%.

1991-93 **PREMIUM MICRO,** Palo Alto, CA *District Sales Manager*

- Generated $3.2M in sales of optical storage solutions within one year.

1990-91 **SYMBOL TECHNOLOGY,** San Mateo, CA *District Sales Manager*

- Planned and coordinated bi-weekly marketing seminars to educate end users at Fortune 500 companies on aspects of the data capturing industry. Followed through to cultivate strong business relationships and to close sales.

1989-90 **MICRO AGE,** Santa Clara, CA *Account Executive*

- Increased sales for over 100 VARs and resellers, averaging 115% of quota for two years.

EDUCATION & TRAINING

B.S., Marketing Communications, Yale University, New Haven, CT, 1989
Additional studies at Heidelberg University, Germany, and Imperial College, London, England
Certificate, Top Gun Storage Training, IBM

Sales/Marketing

SARAH H. BAKER, M.D.

123 Francisco Street #12 • Berkeley, CA 12345 • (123) 123-1234 • sarahb@the net.net

OBJECTIVE: A position in Medical/Pharmaceutical Sales

PROFILE

- Energetic sales professional with a knack for matching customers with optimal products and services to meet their specific needs. Consistently received excellent feedback from customers.
- More than two years as a medical doctor in hospitals and clinics in the U.S. and Europe.
- Lived and traveled abroad, developing a keen sensitivity to people from diverse cultural backgrounds. Fluent in Spanish and Italian; presently studying French.
- Computer skills include MS Word, Excel and Internet applications.

SELECTED ACCOMPLISHMENTS

Sales & Customer Relations

At Marshall's:

- Generated the highest sales volume in department within the first two months of hire, resulting in an unprecedented salary promotion.
- Transferred to highest paid commission area in the store after only four months.
- Cultivated excellent relations with customers and significant repeat business.
- Consistently maintained professional demeanor, treating customers and co-workers with friendliness, patience and respect. Particularly known for success with "challenging" customers.

Medical Expertise

- Collaborated with research team at Evanston Hospital in the study of Pre-Arrest Scoring & Outcome of CPR Cardiac Markers in Rapid Evaluation of Acute Myocardial Infarction.
- As the only physician at Madrid Hospital clinic, provided emergency medical care to onsite and homebound patients, including stroke and cardiac cases.
- Treated immigrants from the Middle East, Africa and Eastern Europe with medical and social needs at Plaza Del Toros Medical Center.

WORK HISTORY

1998-pres.	**Retail Sales Associate,** MARSHALL'S, San Jose, CA
1997-98	**Cardiovascular Research,** EVANSTON HOSPITAL, Evanston, IL
1994-96	**Emergency Physician,** MADRID HOSPITAL, Madrid, Spain
	General Practitioner, PLAZA DEL TOROS MEDICAL CENTER, Madrid, Spain

EDUCATION & TRAINING

Doctor of Medicine, Graduate with High Honors, 1994, University of Madrid, Spain
CPR and EKG Training for ER, 1993-94
Emergency Room Externship, University of Madrid Medical Center, 1992-93

ELIZABETH BURLINGAME

1234 Turnley Avenue • Palo Alto, CA 11111 • (123) 123-1234

OBJECTIVE: An Administrative position focusing on Client Relations/Customer Service

PROFILE

- More than 10 years administrative experience in diverse business settings.

- A highly organized and friendly professional, able to establish long-term, positive and fun relationships with clients, co-workers and outside resources.

- Skilled in working independently and as an enthusiastic team player.

SELECTED ACCOMPLISHMENTS

Organization & Administration

For George Johnson

- Prepared office for daily appointments, including office opening, chart setup, financial arrangements and adequate supplies for staff and clients.

- Balanced daily revenue and expense sheets; issued monthly invoices to clients.

For Abigail Court

- Coordinated master calendar of personal and professional engagements, acting as liaison between author, publicist and booking agent for national appearances.

- Oversaw coordination of national book and television tours, performing troubleshooting, research and follow-through to ensure smooth scheduling.

- Maintained office systems for AR/AP, file organization and time-sensitive project management.

Communication & Client Relations

For George Johnson

- Greeted up to 20 clients per day, cultivating rapport and smooth communication with each one.

- Created and maintained a cohesive and productive work environment, ensuring timeliness and efficiency of five-person staff.

For Abigail Court

- Responded to a high volume of telephone inquiries with friendliness and professionalism, referring callers to information-packed Web site and other appropriate resources.

- Worked with The Home Shopping Channel, Rosie O'Donnell Show and PBS to ensure on-time delivery of press releases and promotional materials for Abigail's guest appearances.

PROFESSIONAL EXPERIENCE

| 1995-pres. | **Administrative Assistant** | ABIGAIL COURT - AUTHOR, Palo Alto, CA |
| 1989-95 | **Office Manager** | GEORGE JOHNSON, DDS, Palo Alto, CA |

GINGA BARNES

123 Alhambra Street, #2 • San Francisco, CA 12345 • (123) 123-1234 • gingab@thenet.net

JOB OBJECTIVE

An Administrative position within a university setting

HIGHLIGHTS OF QUALIFICATIONS

- 10 years of administrative experience in educational settings; particular skill in establishing rapport with people from diverse backgrounds.
- Highly organized and efficient in fast-paced multitasking environments; able to prioritize effectively to accomplish objectives with creativity, enthusiasm and humor.
- Computer skills include: MS Word, Excel, Raiser's Edge and Internet applications.
- Working knowledge of French, Spanish and Portuguese.

PROFESSIONAL EXPERIENCE

1995-pres.   **Educational Resources, Inc.,** Oakland, CA
SENIOR CLIENT ASSOCIATE

- Supported Director in the design, development and implementation of services to maintain client satisfaction and organizational efficiency.
- Answered queries regarding course registration, membership and general information, and resolved client concerns in a dynamic environment.
- Developed innovative coding system to simplify tracking of financial transactions. Performed monthly financial reconciliations and submitted reports to senior management.
- Utilized Raiser's Edge database program to manage both membership and financial information for over 6,000 clients.
- Trained and supervised both permanent and temporary staff. Created and coordinated work schedule to ensure coverage and smooth office operations.

1993-95   **Oakland Unified School District,** Oakland, CA
PARAPROFESSIONAL / RESOURCE SPECIALIST

- Taught mathematics and physics to special needs students of diverse backgrounds. Developed creative and interactive curriculum to foster fun in learning.

1989-93   **Emerson College,** Boston, MA
COORDINATOR, STUDENT OF COLOR RECRUITMENT

- Designed and implemented programs which encouraged high school girls of color to apply and matriculate into college.
- Established and maintained collaborative efforts with other universities, high schools, churches, agencies and parents to recruit students.

EDUCATION

Ph.D. Candidate, Ethnic Studies, University of California, Berkeley, CA
B.A., Mathematics, Radcliffe College, Cambridge, MA

Edgar Ramirez

001 San Carlos Avenue • Los Angeles, CA 12345 • (123) 123-1234

JOB OBJECTIVE

Process or Device Engineer

EDUCATION

1996 - 1999   University of La Verne, La Verne, CA
　　　　　　　　B.S., Electrical Engineering and Computer Science, August 1996
　　　　　　　　B.S., Materials Science and Engineering, August 1996

1994 - 1996   Monterey Peninsula College, Monterey, CA
　　　　　　　　Engineering Major

PROFESSIONAL EXPERIENCE

1980 - 1994:   Maxim Incorporated, Salinas, CA
　　　　　　　　Line Maintenance Supervisor, 1993 - 1994
　　　　　　　　Senior-Level Electronics Technician, 1989 - 1993
　　　　　　　　Wafer Fab Engineering Technician, 1983 - 1989
　　　　　　　　Test Operator / Assistant Supervisor, 1980 - 1983

WAFER FABRICATION

- Conducted process characterizations to improve product yield and process repeatability.
- Performed failure analysis and dispositioned lots.
- Gained skill in working with the following equipment while monitoring product manufacturing.
  Ion implanters
  EPI reactors
  Diffusion furnaces
  Scanning electron microscope (SEM)

TESTING

- Received formal factory training in:
  Trillium VLSI testers
  LTX analog systems
  Teradyne systems
  Various automated test handlers
- Supported, maintained, and calibrated test equipment; updated maintenance documentation.
- Performed troubleshooting to component level.
- Developed and implemented circuit designs to increase reliability and compatibility between test equipment and tester interface hardware.

— Continued —

TEAM LEADERSHIP

- Supervised a technical team of 22, responsible for supporting Test / Burn-in manufacturing operations.
- Ensured technicians were involved in problem ownership, definition, and resolution to enhance their job satisfaction and personal growth.
- Led five task forces that achieved reliability, standardization, and cost-effectiveness of test systems and handlers.
- Interfaced extensively with the vendors and field service engineers to implement factory modifications.
- Served as an active member of the Quality Improvement Forum, a forum for discussing manufacturing / engineering ideas and strategies.
- Trained technicians and provided technical support on related manufacturing test systems.

Ken C. Hartsock
3-D Modeler and Animator

123 Elmo Avenue
St. Paul, MN 12345
(123) 123-12345
ken@hartsock.com

HIGHLIGHTS OF QUALIFICATIONS

- Skilled at generating organic models and character animation.

- Creative interest in surreal productions.

- Proficient in: SGI:
  Alias Power Animator with all advanced modules
  Macintosh: MacroModel, StradaVision, Sketch, Illustrator, and FreeHand

- Lifelong pursuit of drawing, painting, modeling, music, and acting.

RELEVANT ACCOMPLISHMENTS

3-D MODELING, RENDERING, AND ANIMATION

- Contracted by Crux Corporation as 3-D animator for Virtual Space Chase video game for the new 32-bit Morris by Glenco (to be released this December):
  - Generated all animation.
  - Created human and object models.
  - Produced a realistic feel despite restricted resolution.
  - Completed project prior to deadline.

- Modeled and animated pyrotechnical effects for Blast Off's new CD-ROM game.

- Applications engineer for Flashtech, one of the largest Alias retailers in the U.S.

- Generated models and flying logos for Channel 5 in Montreal.

FINE ARTS AND MUSIC

- Achieved scholarship to attend Frazer College of the Arts.

- Contracted by the Museum of Native American History to construct a model of a pueblo from the first millenium.

- Won the Granby Society Scholarship for gifted painters.

WORK HISTORY (Concurrent with education)

1995-pres.   Marketing Associate, Sleep Safe, Inc., St. Paul, MN

EDUCATION AND TRAINING

BS, Multimedia, University of Minnesota, 2000

Computer: SGI System Administration Course
              Advanced Animation Course by Alias

Fine Arts: Watercolor Classes, Frazer College of the Arts
              Architectural Modeling Workshop
              Portrait Painting with Bridget Snyder
              Landscape Painting with Lynette Long (renowned landscape painter)

Technical

363

Enrique Murillo

123 45th Avenue • New York, NY 12345
(123) 123-1234 • quique@hotmail.com

Business Trainer

International Business • Cross-cultural Relationships • Management • Marketing

SUMMARY OF QUALIFICATIONS

- More than 15 years experience in business training. Skills include:

Curriculum development	Presentations	Theater
Train-the-trainer	Negotiations	Writing
Race and gender relations	Team-building	

- Proven ability to "think on my feet" and adapt curriculum to meet individual and company goals.
- Outstanding command of language: written, oral and non-verbal.
- Quickly build rapport with individuals from diverse backgrounds and experience at all organizational levels.

PROFESSIONAL EXPERIENCE

1993-pres.   BUSINESS TRAINER
Business English Teacher, Center for U.S. Studies, New York, NY (1998–pres.)
Business Trainer, FYCSA, Madrid, Spain (1994–1998)
English Professor, University of Spain, Malaga, Spain (1993–1994)

- Trained executive, technical and administrative staff from all over the world in:
  - Building cross-cultural business relationships
  - The language and culture of U.S. business
  - Achieving personal and business goals
  - Negotiations and presentations
- Bridged intercultural prejudices by focusing on cultural similarities, maintaining an open demeanor and communicating with honesty and respect.
- Created a flexible, innovative curriculum—tailored on-the-spot to individual and group needs—which challenged clients to interact through role-plays and multi-media.
- Guaranteed repeat business for FYCSA in a highly competitive market when curriculum and improvisational style generated consistent enthusiastic client response.
- Taught practical communication skills which:
  - Improved the negotiation abilities of executives and government officials.
  - Increased sales.
  - Reduced communication errors and technical staff time by transforming technical language into "plain English".
  - Strengthened company reputations in foreign markets.

- continued -

Enrique Murillo
Page Two

PROFESSIONAL EXPERIENCE, continued

1992   Independent Study–Cross-cultural teaching methods

1974–1991   SUPERVISOR, Retail sales and customer service divisions
Barney's of New York, New York, NY

- Managed up to 30 sales and customer service staff.
- Sought out by manufacturers to provide expert consultation on intra-cultural marketing strategies.

EDUCATION & TRAINING

Teaching Accreditation, University of Cambridge, New York, NY

BA (degree pending) in International Relations and Broadcast Communications, University of New York, New York, NY

LANGUAGES

Fluent Spanish; basic Finnish

COMMUNITY SERVICE

Broadcast Journalist, Radio Free Europe, Munich, Germany
Chair, Iberian Council of New York, New York, NY
President, Spanish Society, New York, NY

Training

Arnold Granger

123 Fourth Street, Apt. 10 • Baltimore, MD 12345 • (123) 123-1234 • granger_a@thenet.net

Public Policy and Economic Analyst

- Communicate complex material in a clear and simplified manner.
- Analyze and develop options expediently.
- Understand the functionality of technical systems, including telecommunications.
- Facilitate interdisciplinary team endeavors.

EXPERIENCE

1991-pres. **Public Utilities Regulatory Analyst**
MARYLAND PUBLIC UTILITIES COMMISSION, Baltimore, MD
- Provide economic and technical expertise to commissioners and judges, and ensure compliance with the commission's decisions.
- One of four analysts currently developing policies and rules for local exchange competition in telecommunications.
- Developed options for restructuring the local switch transport market and analyzed their economic impacts.
- One of two analysts who calculated rates for Bell Telephone in Phase III of NRF, IRD.
- Lead technical analyst in the restructuring of Maryland gas industry through a capacity brokering program.

1990-1991 **Associate/Economic Consultant**
ICF RESOURCES, Fairfax, VA
- Served as economic consultant to corporations, utilities, and government agencies in the energy industry.
- Analyzed railroad behavior and investment patterns to develop an index of railrates for coal transportation.
- Provided analysis in fuel procurement negotiations for several major utilities.

Concurrent with Education:
Fall '94 **Teaching Assistant, Mathematics**
UNIVERSITY OF MARYLAND, Greenbelt, MD

Fall '93 **Project Consultant**
ECONOMIC DEVELOPMENT COMMISSION OF BALTIMORE, Baltimore, MD

Summer '93 **Research Assistant**
ARGONNE NATIONAL LABORATORIES, Bethesda, MD

EDUCATION

MA, Public Policy, 1995, University of Maryland, Greenbelt, MD

BA, Economics, minor in Mathematics, 1993, University of Maryland, Greenbelt, MD

Henry Blue

123 Columbus Avenue • Lucas, Kansas 12345 • (123) 123-1234 • hblue@thenet.net

JOB OBJECTIVE: Government Affairs Director

SUMMARY OF QUALIFICATIONS

- Six years as a professional consultant providing corporate clients with research and analysis necessary to comply with governmental regulations.
- Comprehensive knowledge of state and local governmental affairs.
- Ability to advocate positions before diverse audiences.
- French: speaking, reading, and writing competence.

EDUCATION

Ph.D., Political Science, 1997, University of Kansas, Lucas

M.A., Political Science, 1987, University of Kansas, Lucas

B.A, Politics, 1982, Midwest University, St. Louis, MO

PROFESSIONAL ACCOMPLISHMENTS

RESEARCH AND ANALYSIS

University of Kansas

- Researched and wrote dissertation on political responsibility, using case studies (North Korean Comfort Women and Reparation to Holocaust Survivors) to justify national apologies.
- As university lecturer, crafted and presented analyses of contemporary political, legal, and ethical issues, addressing up to 100 students from diverse socioeconomic and cultural backgrounds.

Infoex, Inc.

- Gathered and analyzed information using qualitative and quantitative research techniques such as interviews and primary and secondary source studies.

PUBLIC POLICY

Infoex, Inc.

- Contributed to the development of the World Bank's energy policy by presenting research and analysis of governmental strategies to encourage energy efficiency.
- Served as research/public policy consultant to corporate clients regarding their relationship to governmental agencies such as state public utility commissions.
- Rewrote marketing and implementation strategies to increase customer participation in a recycling program for the Kansas City Department of Waste Management.

WORK HISTORY

1994-present	Energy Consultant	Infoex, Inc., Lucas, KS
1993-1994	Visiting Professor	Political Science Dept., University of Kansas, Lucas,
1990-1993	Instructor	Political Science Dept., University of Kansas, Lucas
1986-1990	Teacher	The Athens School, St. Louis, MO

Potpourri

367

Carla F. Gent

123 Yale Street, #1 • Miami, FL 12345 • (123) 123-1234

JOB OBJECTIVE: A position in fraud investigation

SUMMARY OF QUALIFICATIONS

- Top security clearance position in a U.S. Secret Service fraud investigation unit.
- Adept at uncovering fraudulent activity through item inspection and pattern identification.
- Skilled at working with credit bureaus, retailers, and consumers.

EDUCATION

B.S.   Criminal Justice, emphasis: Private Investigation, 1996
           Northern Arizona University, Flagstaff, AZ

Diploma   Teller Training Institute, Miami, FL, 1991

EXPERIENCE

1999-present U.S. SECRET SERVICE, Miami, FL
Counterfeit Squad Clerk

- Assist agents in case investigations by flagging suspicious patterns in counterfeiting.
- Examine bills to determine authenticity.
- Open new counterfeit cases using Master Crime Index and First Choice Database (national databases of criminal information).
- Prepare statistical reports for review by headquarters in Washington, D.C.
- Educate bank and retail personnel on how to identify and prevent fraud.

1998-1999 BARCELON MANAGEMENT & ASSOCIATES, Miami, FL
Administrative Assistant

- Provided administrative organization for this private firm contracted by HUD to manage low-income housing for the elderly and the handicapped.
- Interviewed residents for funding re-qualification, using a diplomatic approach to elicit financial information.

1996-1997 LORRIE'S DEPARTMENT STORE, Miami, FL
Customer Service Representative, Credit Department

- Worked with TRW and CBI credit bureaus to clear customers' derogatory information.
- Investigated credit card problems: credit limits, lost and stolen cards, and collections.

1994-1996 **Full-time Student**, Criminal Justice Program, Northern Arizona University

1993-1994 SOUTHERN HYPERBARIC SERVICES, St. Petersburg, FL
Research Assistant

- Maintained medical records used in insurance claims and litigation.

1992-1993 CREDIT BUREAU REPORTS, INC., Tampa, FL
Credit Analyst

LAURA J. THOMAS

123 Brandywine Avenue • San Francisco, CA 12345 • (123) 123-1234

OBJECTIVE:　　　A position in the holistic health and beauty field,
with an emphasis on client relations, sales, and office management

PROFILE

- 10 years experience offering outstanding service to diverse clients, with a lifelong passion for holistic healing and a keen interest in beauty products and services that enhance a balanced lifestyle.

- Excellent telephone and in-person skills; able to quickly establish rapport with clients, identify needs, and match them with appropriate resources.

- Skilled in persuasive sales techniques; able to convey information with creativity and sincerity, consistently winning new business.

- Highly organized, efficient, and energetic; able to create office systems that improve workflow and enhance the overall environment.

SELECTED ACCOMPLISHMENTS

Communication & Client Relations

- Welcomed clients at The Tea Garden Spa and scheduled appointments for massage, facials, salt scrub, herbal wraps, hot tub and sauna.

- Performed additional daily front desk operations at The Tea Garden Spa, including office organization, payment processing, and consultation with health practitioners.

- Acted as primary contact for Wilderness Adventures clients, responding to a high volume of calls, scheduling travel packages, and invoicing.

- Maintained daily contact with outside contractors to discuss sales and marketing strategies, improve quality, and generate additional business for Wilderness Adventures and The Tea Garden Spa.

Sales & Marketing

- Top sales producer for Pacific trips at Wilderness Adventures, consistently increasing sales revenue each year.

- Conducted competitor studies and analyzed market pricing structures. Consulted with Wilderness Adventures president and presented findings to marketing team, recommending improvements to annual catalogue.

- Generated new business through incentive programs, mass mailings, cold calling, and referrals from previous Tea Garden Spa clients.

(Continued)

Potpourri

369

Laura J. Thomas
Page Two

Management & Administration

- Supervised and trained The Tea Garden Spa support staff, oversaw departmental operations, and delegated tasks to ensure timeliness and accuracy.

- Checked chemicals and pH balance at The Tea Garden Spa facilities to ensure proper levels for client safety and comfort.

- Coordinated complex logistics for hundreds of international adventure travel packages, servicing up to 12 Wilderness Adventures clients per trip.

WORK HISTORY

1992-pres.   **Pacific Operations Manager**
             WILDERNESS ADVENTURES, Seattle, WA

1989-92   **Front Desk Manager**
             THE TEA GARDEN SPA, Tiburon, CA

EDUCATION & TRAINING

C.M.T. (Certified Massage Therapist), McKinnon Institute, Oakland, CA, 1996
B.A., Theater Arts, San Francisco State University, San Francisco, CA, 1992
Computer skills include: WordPerfect 5.0 & 6.1, Quattro Pro, Excel, and Internet.

Ian Sanders, M.A., M.F.C.C.

001 Christopher St. • New York, NY 12345 • (123) 123-1234

EDUCATION

M.A., Counseling Psychology, Lindenwood Institute, Hastings-on-Hudson, NY, 1993
B.A., Psychology, Cornell University, Ithaca, NY, 1975

CERTIFICATION

M.F.C.C. License # MFC 123456
Certification, Imagery-In-Movement Expressive Art Therapy

PROFESSIONAL EXPERIENCE

1992-pres. THERAPIST INTERN
Group Therapy Intern, 1998-present
Village Drop-In Center, New York, NY

- As co-therapist, facilitate sessions for 13 men from diverse cultural backgrounds, working on intrapsychic and interpersonal relationship issues.

National Expressive Art Therapy Intern, 1997-present
Harris Sylvan, C.E.A.T., Brooklyn, NY

- Built a private client base of individuals, couples, and groups.
- Focus on the Imagery-In-Movement method, which integrates artistic expression, psychodrama, journaling, and dream work.

Marriage & Family Child Counselor Intern, 1996-1997
Centrum, New York, NY

- Provided therapy for a client base of individuals, couples, and groups.
- Designed and delivered public lectures and workshops, introducing expressive art as a means of addressing:

Depression	Illness	Adoption
Eating disorders	Death	Job transition
Sexual abuse	Trauma	Personal growth
Substance abuse	Divorce	Spiritual emergence

M.F.C.C. Intern, 1992-1996
Lindenwood Counseling Center, Yonkers, NY

- Worked with individuals and couples, drawing upon:

Psychodynamic theory (Heller)	Process psychology (Conley)
Family systems theory	Hypnotherapy
Imagery-In-Movement psychology	

— Continued —

Potpourri

371

Ian Sanders, M.A., M.F.C.C.

Page Two

1991-pres.   ADMINISTRATOR
Body Right, Inc., New York, NY
- Manage the administrative operations of this firm that grew from a start-up to a $10M business in eight years.
- Resolve personnel issues (interpersonal and performance); handled customer relations.

1983-1990   CUSTOMER SERVICE REPRESENTATIVE, Food and Beverage
Buffalohead Hotel, Buffalo, NY, 1988-1990
The Chasman Inn Hotel, Buffalo, NY, 1983-1988

PROFESSIONAL AFFILIATIONS

New York Association of Marriage and Family Therapists (NYAMFT)
National Expressive Art Therapy Association

Other Cool Resources

Books to Buy or Borrow

You want to read more? Here are some books I recommend for various aspects of your job search.

Life/Career Counseling

The Complete Idiot's Guide to Changing Your Career, by William A. Charland. ISBN:0028619773, Macmillan USA, Incorporated, 1997.

Composing a Life, by Mary Catherine Bateson. ISBN:0452265053, NAL/Dutton, 1990.

Do What You Are: Discover the Perfect Career for You Through the Secrets of Personality Type, by Paul D. Tieger and Barbara Barron-Tieger. ISBN:0316845221, Little, Brown & Company, 1995.

Do What You Love, the Money Will Follow: Discovering Your Right Livelihood, by Marsha Sinetar. ISBN:0440501601, Dell Publishing Company, Incorporated, 1989.

Feel the Fear and Do It Anyway, by Susan J. Jeffers. ISBN:0449902927, Fawcett Book Group, 1996.

I Could Do Anything if I Only Knew What It Was: How to Discover What You Really Want and How to Get It, by Barbara Sher and Barbara Smith. ISBN:0440505003, Dell Publishing Company, Incorporated, 1995.

Transitions, by William P. Bridges. ISBN:0201000822, Addison Wesley Longman, Incorporated, 1980.

Wishcraft: How to Get What You Really Want, by Barbara Sher. ISBN:0345340892, Ballantine Books, Incorporated, 1983.

Job Search Techniques

Complete Job-Search Handbook: All the Skills You Need to Get Any Job and Have a Good Time Doing It, by Howard E. Figler. ISBN:0805005374, Henry Holt & Company, Incorporated, 1988.

Get a Better Job The Lazy Way, by Susan Ireland. ISBN: 0028633997, Macmillan USA, Incorporated, 1999.

How to Get Your Dream Job Using the Web, by Shannon Karl and Arthur Karl. ISBN:1576101258, Coriolis Group, 1997.

Job Searching Online for Dummies, by Pam Dixon, Dummies Technology Press, and Pam Dison. ISBN:0764503766, IDG Books Worldwide, 1998.

The Vault Reports Guide to Schmoozing, by Marcy Lerner, Mark Oldman, Samer Hamadeh, H. S. Hamadeh, and Ed Shen. ISBN:0395861691, Houghton Mifflin Company, 1998.

Jobs and Companies

The 100 Best Nonprofits to Work For, by Leslie Hamilton and Robert Tragert. ISBN:0028618408, Macmillan USA, Incorporated, 1998.

The American Almanac of Jobs and Salaries: 1997-1998 Edition, by John W. Wright. ISBN:0380783614, Avon Books, 1996.

Cool Careers for Dummies, by Marty Nemko, Paul Edwards, and Sarah Edwards. ISBN:0764550950, IDG Books Worldwide, 1998.

Good Works: A Guide to Careers in Social Change, by Donna Colvin, Ralph Nader (editor). ISBN:0962303283, Barricade Books, Incorporated, 1993.

Hoover's, series by industry and region, Hoover's TX (publisher).

JobBank, series by industry, region, and year, Adams Publishing.

Occupational Outlook Handbook 1998-99, by the U.S. Department of Labor. ISBN:1563704641, JIST Works Incorporated, 1998.

The Vault Reports, series by the Vault Reports Incorporated Staff, Vault Reports, Incorporated.

Using an Executive Recruiter

The Directory of Executive Recruiters 1999, by LLC Kennedy Information (Compiler). ISBN: 1885922302, Kennedy Information, 1998.

Executive Recruiters Almanac, by Steven Graber (editor). ISBN:1580620299, Adams Media Corporation, 1998.

Selling to Vito: The Very Important Top Officer, by Anthony Parinello. ISBN: 1558503862, Adams Media Corporation, 1994.

Resume Writing

Electronic Resumes & Online Networking, by Rebecca Smith. ISBN: 1564143775, Career Press, 1999.

The Damn Good Resume Guide: A Crash Course in Resume Writing, by Yana Parker. ISBN:0898156726, Ten Speed Press, 1996.

Ready-to-Go Resumes (resume templates on disk), by Yana Parker. ISBN:0898157331, Ten Speed Press, 1995.

Resume Catalog: 200 Damn Good Examples, by Yana Parker. ISBN:0898158915, Ten Speed Press, 1996.

Resumes That Work Deluxe, (CD-ROM) by Susan Ireland. ISBN: 1575951436, Macmillan Digital, 1998.

Cover-Letter Writing

Cover Letters That Will Get You the Job You Want by, Stanley Wynett. ISBN:155870275X, F & W Publications, Incorporated, 1993.

The Complete Idiot's Guide to the Perfect Cover Letter, by Susan Ireland. ISBN:0028619609, Macmillan USA, Incorporated, 1997.

Interviewing

Sweaty Palms: The Neglected Art of Being Interviewed, by Anthony Medley. ISBN:0898154030, Ten Speed Press, 1991.

The Unofficial Guide to Acing the Interview, by Michelle Tullier and the Unofficial Panel (editor). ISBN:0028629248, IDG Books Worldwide, Incorporated, 1998.

Negotiations

Are You Paid What You're Worth?: The Complete Guide to Calculating and Negotiating the Salary, Benefits, Bonus, and Raise You Deserve, by Michael F. O'Malley and Suzanne Oaks. ISBN:0767901312, Broadway Books, 1998.

Dynamite Salary Negotiations: Know What You're Worth and Get It! by Ronald L. Krannich, Ph.D. and Caryl Rae Krannich, Ph.D. ISBN:157023079XP, Impact Publications, 1997.

Get More Money on Your Next Job: 25 Proven Strategies for Getting More Money, Better Benefits, and Greater Job Security, by Lee E. Miller. ISBN:0070431469, McGraw-Hill Companies, 1997.

Getting to Yes: Negotiating Agreement Without Giving In, by Roger Fisher, William Ury, and Bruce Patton (editor). ISBN:0140157352, Viking Penguin, 1998.

Negotiating Your Salary: How to Make $1,000 a Minute, by Jack Chapman. ISBN:0898158907, Ten Speed Press, 1997.

The Unofficial Guide to Earning What You Deserve, by Jason Rich. ISBN:0028627164, IDG Books Worldwide, Incorporated, 1999.

More Words of Wisdom

Dictionary of Occupational Terms : A Guide to the Special Language and Jargon of Hundreds of Careers, by Nancy E. Shields. ISBN:1563700549, JIST Works Incorporated, 1994.

John T. Molloy's New Dress for Success, by John T. Molloy. ISBN:0446385522, Warner Books, Incorporated, 1987.

Microsoft Press Computer Dictionary with CD-ROM. ISBN:157231446X, Microsoft Press, 1997.

New Women's Dress for Success, by John T. Molloy. ISBN:0446672238, Warner Books, Incorporated, 1996.

What I Learned on the Way to the Top, by Zig Ziglar. ISBN:1562925423, Honor Books, 1998.

The Employer's Perspective

The Employer's Guide to Recruiting on the Internet, by Ray Schreyer and John McCarter. ISBN:157023096X, Impact Publications, 1998.

The Employer's Legal Handbook, by Fred S. Steingold and Barbara Kate Repa (editor). ISBN:0873373707, Nolo Press, 1997.

Caught in the Web

Wandering around on the Web without a guide can be daunting. Keep this list with you as you venture into cyberspace. If a Web address listed here is out of order, go to my Web site, http://www.susanireland.com where you'll find an updated link.

By the way, the sites with asterisks after them are ones I particularly like.

Links that Work

Career Resource Center* (http://www.careers.org)

Internet Sites for Job Seekers and Employers*
(http://www.hitbox.com/wc/world.100.Employment.html)

Resumes That Work (http://www.resumesthatwork.com)

Riley Guide* (http://www.dbm.com/jobguide)

Yahoo! Jobs* (http://www.yahoo.com/Business_and_Economy/Employment)

Self-Assessment Tests

Birkman Career Style Summary (http://www.review.com/birkman)

Career Search* (http://www.collegeboard.com/career/html/searchQues.html)

The Career Interests Game (http://www.missouri.edu/~cppcwww/holland.shtml)

The Career Key (http://www2.ncsu.edu/unity/lockers/users/l/lkj)

The Keirsey Character and Temperament (http://www.keirsey.com)

Research Tools

Hoover's Online* (http://www.hoovers.com)

Occupational Outlook Handbook* (http://stats.bls.gov/ocohome.htm)

Vault Reports* (http://www.vaultreports.com)

Wet Feet Press (http://www.wetfeet.com)

Resume Banks and Job Lists

America's Job Bank* (http://www.ajb.dni.us/index.html)

America's Employers* (http://www.americasemployers.com)

career.com (http://www.career.com)

CareerCity* (http://www.careercity.com)

CareerMosaic* (http://www.careermosaic.com)

CareerPath* (http://www.careerpath.com)

CareerSite.com (http://www.careersite.com)

Classifieds2000/Employment (http://www.classifieds2000.com)

Headhunter.Net* (http://www.headhunter.net)

HotJobs (http://www.hotjobs.com)

JobSafari (http://www.jobsafari.com)

Net-Temps (http://www.net-temps.com)

The Career Builder Network (http://www.careerbuilder.com)

The Monster Board* (http://www.monster.com)

Other Web Wonders

AOL WorkPlace* (a channel off of the AOL main page)

Damn Good Resumes (http://www.damngood.com)

Futurestep* (http://www.futurestep.com)

Geocities Career Planner (http://www.geocities.com/Avenues/Business_and_Money/Careers)

JobSmart* (http://www.jobsmart.org)

Go Hire Yourself a Pro

I personally recommend the following resources. If a professional listed here is not in your area, don't despair—each of them can work with you by phone or e-mail.

If you know of someone who is superb and who you think should be listed in the next edition of this book, please e-mail me through my Web site: http://www.susanireland.com.

Career Counseling/Coaching

Victoria Zenoff
Career Strategies of North America
Richmond, CA
510-526-5210

Sharon Stearns
Lafayette, CA
925-937-6582
stearnscdv@aol.com

Alumnae Resources (career center)
120 Montgomery, 6th Floor
San Francisco, CA 94104
(415) 274-4700
http://www.ar.org

Career Action Center
10420 Bubb Rd. #100
Palo Alto, CA 95014
(408) 253-3200
http://www.careeraction.org

Information Researchers

Avril Draudt, Owner
AMDR Consulting
437 High Street
Sebastopol, CA 95472
Phone/Fax: (707) 823-4207

E-Reference
Alumnae Resources (career center)
120 Montgomery, 6th Floor
San Francisco, CA 94104
(415) 274-4711
arlibrary@ar.org
http://www.ar.org

Know-It-All Research
Walnut Creek, CA
(925) 933-2488
knowitallresearch@mail.com

Resume and Cover Letter Writing

Susan Ireland's Resume Service
San Francisco, Oakland, Cleveland, and Missoula
(510) 558-0632
http://www.resumesthatwork.com

Employment Law Attorneys

Jeffrey Demain
Peter Nussbaum
Altshuler, Berzon, Nussbaum, Berzon & Rubin
177 Post St., Suite 300
San Francisco, CA 94108
(415) 421-7151

Employee Rights Attorney

Don D. Sessions
23456 Madero, Suite 170
Mission Viejo, CA 92691
(949) 380-0900
http://www.job-law.com

Salary Negotiation Coaches

PinPoint Salary Service
Wilmette, IL
(773) 4-SALARY
http://members.aol.com/payraises

Jack Chapman
Salary Negotiations Telecoach
511 Maple Ave.
Wilmette, IL 60091
(847) 251-4727
jkchapman@aol.com

Index

OTHER BOOKS BY SUSAN IRELAND...

The Complete Idiot's Guide® to the Perfect Cover Letter
alpha books, ISBN: 0028619609

When it comes to composing a fantastic cover letter, does your mind freeze? Do you start wondering if there's time to catch the next flight to the Bahamas, where you can escape the drudgery of this important step in your job search? Don't panic! With *The Complete Idiot's Guide® to the Perfect Cover Letter,* you'll find quick and easy ways to:

- Make your cover letter stand out from the competition.
- Start your letter with an attention-grabbing lead paragraph.
- Handle sticky cover-letter issues.
- Initiate action—land a job interview!
- Create other powerful letters: thank-you notes, broadcast letters, and requests for information.
- Develop a style of writing that delivers personality, professionalism, and punch.

Get a Better Job The Lazy Way
alpha books, ISBN: 0028633997

We know you're not lazy. In fact, you're actually very busy! Your job alone makes your life hectic, what with those countless crazy deadlines. With all you have to do at the office, you probably think you don't have time to job hunt. Don't resign yourself to the same rung on the company ladder just yet! *Get a Better Job The Lazy Way* gives you the tools you need to launch a quick and successful job search:

- Tips for creating a game plan that will get you your better job in the most efficient way possible, without a lot of work!
- Painless techniques for planning your life goals, changing careers, and finding your next job through the Internet.
- The simplest ways to assess the job market, get the lowdown on employers, market yourself in today's job jungle, and come out a winner in job interviews.

No sweat! *Get a Better Job The Lazy Way* will have you in the corner window office in no time!

LOOK FOR THESE BOOKS AT YOUR FAVORITE BOOKSTORE; ORDER THEM ONLINE AT HTTP://WWW.RESUMESTHATWORK.COM; or call 1-800-428-5331 for more information.

Susan Ireland's Resume Service

Resume-Writing Service

From anywhere in the world, get your resume written through Susan Ireland's Resume-Writing Service. A professional resume writer will compose and produce your resume, working with you by phone, fax, or e-mail. For those of you who live in the San Francisco area, get your resume written during an in-person session. *This service is charged by the hour.*

Resume-Critique Service

If you've already written your resume, use Susan Ireland's Resume-Critique Service to be sure you have the most effective job-search tool possible. A professional resume writer will examine your resume and give you a half-hour critique by phone. (Believe me, we pack a lot of information into our half-hour sessions!) *This service is charged by the half-hour.*

For information, please log on to

**www.susanireland.com
or call (510) 558-0632.**

This is an exclusive service of Susan Ireland and not connected with Macmillan Publishing.